THE SEA WINS

SHIPWRECKS OF THE BAY OF FUNDY

ERIC ALLABY

NIMBUS
PUBLISHING
— NIMBUS.CA —

Nimbus Publishing Limited
3660 Strawberry Hill Street, Halifax, NS, B3K 5A9
(902) 455-4286 nimbus.ca

Printed and bound in Canada

NB1606

Editor: Claire Bennet
Design: Jenn Embree

All photos, paintings, and graphics by Eric Allaby
except where otherwise indicated.

Library and Archives Canada Cataloguing in Publication

Title: The sea wins : shipwrecks of the Bay of Fundy / Eric Allaby.
Other titles: Shipwrecks of the Bay of Fundy
Names: Allaby, Eric, author.
Identifiers: Canadiana (print) 20220243379 | Canadiana (ebook) 20220243417 | ISBN 9781774711378 (softcover) | ISBN 9781774711835 (EPUB)
Subjects: LCSH: Shipwrecks—Fundy, Bay of.
Classification: LCC G525 .A45 2022 | DDC 910.9163/45—dc23

Nimbus Publishing acknowledges the financial support for its publishing activities from the Government of Canada, the Canada Council for the Arts, and from the Province of Nova Scotia. We are pleased to work in partnership with the Province of Nova Scotia to develop and promote our creative industries for the benefit of all Nova Scotians.

CONTENTS

INTRODUCTION

⤿

I stumbled into marine history research through the back door, with a case of dynamite under one arm and a diving tank under the other. While putting myself through university by working as a diver for the weir fishers of Grand Manan, I listened to all the lore and sailors' yarns of ships lost around our island coasts and reefs. When I settled on Grand Manan after university, I spent more and more time diving, and soon went out to the ledges and reefs to look for the shipwrecks myself and see what was there.

Caught up in the stories of valuable payloads, I hunted elusive ships and even more elusive cargoes. To help finance this work, I visited several sunken steamship wrecks and stripped off the brass and copper, which fetched a fair price as scrap metal in Saint John. It didn't take too long to learn that I could free up a lot more brass and copper using dynamite, which makes an effective hammer to break things up underwater.

Through all of this I eventually learned a key lesson: do your homework before setting out for underwater riches. Just because an old-timer on the wharf passed along a story he had heard from an old salt years before doesn't make it fact. I could have concluded that hunting for cargoes that were not what the stories said they were was a colossal waste of time, but I enjoyed the challenge of overcoming the undersea odds and I enjoyed finding things that had been hidden so long, even if they had little commercial value. And through it all, I discovered that the stories of the shipwrecks would come to be of as much interest and value to me as the cargoes they carried.

Pursuing the fascinating stories that old shipwrecks can tell us, I applied for and received a Ford Foundation fellowship to do marine history research for a year in the United States, Canada, and England in 1970 and 1971. From 1973 to 1976, I was supported for three years through a National Museums of Canada grant administered by the New Brunswick Museum to do some basic underwater archaeological work in our Bay of Fundy waters. With this limited funding, I had to work by myself underwater. This constraint, along with having to work in strong tidal currents, forced me to develop a new way of doing underwater shipwreck surveys (see Chapter Three). I had the privilege of sharing the method and the results of this work at successive international conferences on underwater archaeology. After these programs ended, my fascination with shipwrecks continued, and I read old newspaper accounts to discover more of this rich heritage. These accounts described the deeply tragic disasters that were at the same time an all-too-common occurrence.

~

We are all drawn to the sea. Many of us will pay a premium to build a house on land that looks out over the sea, where we can watch the waves and listen to the surf. We look at the sea and find it soothing. I lived by the sea for many years and I loved its changing moods. I relished a morning coffee looking out over the water, because every morning is different. Whether the tide is up or down, wind calm or gale force, blowing from northeast or southwest, all these factors make each morning's sea unique. As I watched the waves, mesmerized, my mind's eye glimpsed back for vignettes of experiences on the water and in the water. And sometimes these moments took me back well before my own time, to imagine an age when the frightening power of the sea was too much for human ingenuity.

The earliest civilizations looked at the sea and saw terrifying, yet fascinating, challenges. In spite of that, since prehistory, humans have sought to master the sea. But the sea is not where humans are intended to live. We are land creatures; the sea does not lightly welcome us. Indeed, the earliest Jewish traditions, upon which Christian traditions are based, have regarded the chaos and power of the sea as a portrayal of evil.[1] And yet, even facing the fearful odds, early mariners persistently ventured out to master the sea to open up opportunities for trade and commerce. But over and over again, the sea won.

About six hundred years ago, as Europe was coming out of the Late Middle Ages, the development of larger vessels capable of venturing across oceans, along with a better understanding of navigation, opened up new possibilities for exploring the globe. A combination of curiosity and greed brought Europe to North America and for the formative years of European civilization in North America, the sea provided a highway of commerce. The very fact that we live in "Maritime" provinces is an indication of the importance that is attached to the sea and our relationship with it.

Along our Atlantic coasts, the sea also gives us an abundance of fish for the taking. I can certainly say that the seasons I spent catching herring in weirs along the coast were exciting years; there isn't an occupation as addictive as weir fishing! In our little corner of the Atlantic, the sea provides resources, trade and commerce, employment, lore, ambitions, entrepreneurship, and a sense of identity: all of this has shaped the heritage and culture of our coastal communities.

The cost, on the other hand, is quite beyond simple appraisal. Shipwreck loss was such a fact of life that little was said and written of the thousands of ships and thousands of lives expended in pursuit of the sea's commercial potential. Fraught as it was with real, life-threatening hazards, mariners still spent their lives on the sea in hopeful pursuit of an honourable and rewarding livelihood in a bold new country that promised growth and opportunity. Others simply sought to support the families they loved ashore. And all people who chose to follow the sea knew in earlier times, and still know to this day, that there can never be complete mastery of the sea—only truces for a season.

There are thousands of these tragic stories, these life and death dramas. The biggest dilemma in writing this book has been deciding which stories to tell, and which stories to set aside for another time and place. In choosing the stories to keep, I have naturally been biased toward those shipwrecks on which I have personally spent some diving time. This book is my journey, as I pick my way among these stories. I hope you will join me as I try to convey the indelible events that formed inhabitants of the East Coast as a Maritime people, to convey a sense of the intensity and drama of the times, and to draw out the humour and humanity of real people who faced great odds in their sailing ships, only to discover that, inevitably, the sea wins.

~

The era of wooden ships, powered by canvas sails and challenging the tides of Fundy, brought with it words and phrases today's reader may find unfamiliar. A glossary is provided on page 263.

CHAPTER ONE

THE TIDES OF THE BAY OF FUNDY

Those of us who call the shores of Fundy home take the twice-daily flooding and ebbing of its massive tides as a matter of daily routine. But to visiting mariners, the Bay of Fundy posed particular challenges for their seaborne commerce. Fundy tides are the highest in the world. The average rise and fall of tides around the world is about one metre (three feet), but a large tide in Minas Basin, at the bay's inner reaches, will range in vertical height more than fifteen metres (fifty feet), whereas large tides at Yarmouth, at the mouth of the bay, range no more than five metres (sixteen and a half feet). Each part of the Bay of Fundy has its own very particular tidal circumstances.

Twice each day, the tide at the head of the Bay of Fundy swells to fill every cove and then drains out to sea again. A billion tonnes of water come into the bay for high tide and leave for low water, which is "more than the flow of all the world's freshwater rivers combined."[2] Since the bay is much longer than it is wide, with so much water moving inward for high tide and back out again for low, Fundy's tides create very powerful currents. In fact, entrepreneurs are now eyeing these same currents that tested early navigators to harness this power to generate electricity.

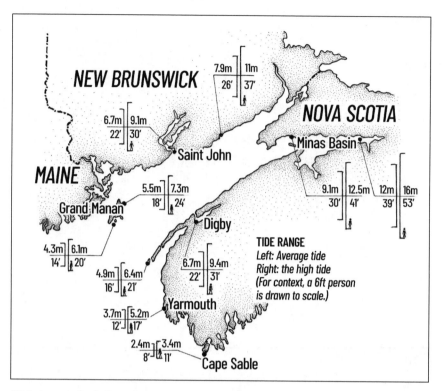

NEW BRUNSWICK

7.9m / 26'   11m / 37'

6.7m / 22'   9.1m / 30'

MAINE

NOVA SCOTIA

Minas Basin

Saint John

5.5m / 18'   7.3m / 24'

9.1m / 30'   12.5m / 41'   12m / 39'   16m / 53'

Grand Manan

Digby

4.3m / 14'   6.1m / 20'

4.9m / 16'   6.4m / 21'

6.7m / 22'   9.4m / 31'

TIDE RANGE
Left: Average tide
Right: the high tide
(For context, a 6ft person
is drawn to scale.)

3.7m / 12'   5.2m / 17'

Yarmouth

2.4m / 8'   3.4m / 11'

Cape Sable

Tide ranges in different parts of the Bay of Fundy.

Low tide occurs just over six hours after high tide, followed just over six hours later by another high tide. As the tide starts to crest at its peak height, the current in the bay slows down to become the "high water slack," remaining still for a short time before turning to flow back out of the bay. As the tide approaches its lowest level, the current slows until it becomes momentarily still at the "low water slack," after which it turns to run back into the Bay of Fundy. The current runs hardest at about half tide, halfway between high and low tides. Complicating the ever-changing current, the rocky features of the bay—headlands, coves, reefs, islands—all create eddies where the streaming water swirls and flows in differing directions from the prevailing current.

Added to these factors are the effects of the lunar cycle. The tides rise and fall as a result of the changing gravitational pull of the moon, as the earth rotates and moves our bay into and out of the moon's influence. Furthermore, the pull of the moon changes as the moon's location in its orbit changes. The moon's orbit around the earth is not circular, but elliptical: twice in its twenty-eight–day cycle it comes closer to the earth, twice it goes farther away. When the moon is closest to the earth, and when the sun and moon and earth line up, the moon's gravitational pull is the strongest, and the tidal rise and fall is at its greatest. These are called "spring tides." At points in the moon's orbit where the moon is farther away, and when the gravitational forces of the sun and moon are at right angles to the earth, the effect of the gravitational pull is weaker, and tidal rise and fall is less. These are known as "neap tides."

The main reason for the high tides, especially on spring tides, is the size and shape of the bay. Have you ever made water slosh back and forth in a bathtub? As you move your hand back and forth in the middle of the tub, the water will rise and fall much higher at the end of the tub. And if you time your hand to move with the water, the water will go higher and higher at the end of the tub. Your hand has set up a "resonance" in the tub. The length of the Bay of Fundy is just right to create a resonance with the ocean tides. Just as giving a child on a swing a little push at just the right time in the swing cycle will make the child go higher, the tidal pulse from the ocean gives the tide a push twice each day that is perfectly in sync with the shape of the bay to make the exceptional tides.

The large variance between spring and neap tides makes the complex tidal currents change radically from spring to neap and back to spring tides. Locally, the spring and neap tides are called "full" and "dead" tides. Even today, fishers plan their outings based on whether tides are full or dead. Spring, or full, tide currents combined with foggy conditions, storms, or general vessel distress, often proved to be the undoing of the best of nautical intentions and gave rise to a great many of Fundy's shipwrecks.

This spring tide factor was noted by long-time lighthouse keeper and my great-great-grandfather, Walter B. McLaughlin of Grand Manan, who—when he heard of the Allen Line steamer *Castillian* being wrecked on Gannet Rock off Yarmouth, Nova Scotia, on March 12, 1899—noted in his journal: "This is another case of the unknown currents setting in and across the mouth of the Bay of Fundy on the spring tides. About every wreck for the past sixty years that have taken place about the Murr Ledges and south Grand Manan have been on the spring tides, and the captains always thought they were on Briar [sic] island, N.S."[3]

So, the spring tides, or rather, the strong currents associated with these tides, are probably the greatest influence for shipwrecks in the Bay of Fundy. But a shipwreck is seldom attributable to one factor alone. Almost every shipping casualty is the result of a combination of problems working together to precipitate disaster. Cargo not loaded carefully on a vessel might shift in a breeze, causing the ship to list and become unmanageable, unable to respond to sails and rudder and at the mercy of winds and powerful currents. A drunken crew, perhaps able to cope with routine duties, might not be able to respond quickly and deftly to the immediate demands of a sudden squall, or initiate the precise procedures for tacking or wearing ship when winds and tides prove to be obstinate.

Wooden vessels, pounded by a succession of heavy gales, become strained, working the seams between the planks so they become leaky. A leaky vessel, half full of water, not only loses buoyancy, but also loses its tendency to remain on an even keel. A waterlogged vessel, therefore, is also much more likely to capsize. Shipwrecks rarely could be attributed to just one simple cause; almost always there were several compounding factors that together overwhelmed the ship and brought it to disaster.

When sailors are confronted with the whims of the Bay of Fundy's powerful tidal currents abetted by fog, stranding on rocky shores is an all-too-common occurrence.

SHIPWRECK LORE

From the first European settlement, through the heyday of wooden shipping until the invention of diesel and radar, shipwrecks occurred as a fact of life in our Fundy waters. Now, with engines and electronic navigation, a lost vessel is an exceptional catastrophe. One hundred and fifty years ago, the loss of lives was just as tragic, but the loss of ships was the cost of doing business.

Shipwrecks were usually very dramatic events, too often tragedies, but occasionally even touched with humour. There was also great local excitement about shipwrecks, as speculation mounted about the possibilities of sudden windfall profits. There was intense curiosity as to the cargoes aboard that could be salvaged or sold, and many impromptu celebrations materialized over shipwrecked cases of whisky.

In the early years of transatlantic travel, the only shipwrecks that offered fair prospects for salvage were those stranded above low tide. The world under the sea was still a forbidden world; nevertheless, it has always stirred human curiosity. We seek to mingle with the fish, to defy the barrier at the water's surface and to visit—living, breathing, seeing—the silent, unforgiving world below the surface of the sea. Primitive technology designed to take human beings underwater was not very effective and quite limited in application.

But early technology did lead to the first successful diving apparatus that we now call the hard-hat suit. This system relied on an air pump, hand-cranked by crewmen, to deliver air through a hose to a metal helmet that enclosed the diver's head. In the helmet were small glass windows that allowed the diver to look out at the underwater world around him. The helmet was sealed to a breastplate that was in turn sealed to the opening of a watertight, rubberized canvas suit. A weighted belt and heavy, lead-soled boots allowed the diver to walk slowly and ponderously about the ocean floor. One can imagine how hazardous it was to use of this kind of equipment, particularly before the invention of the telephone, which later allowed the diver to talk through a phone in the helmet to the boat.

Nineteenth-century salvagers accomplished some remarkable feats with hard-hat equipment in spite of the limitations and risks. Shipwrecks at this time were only visited by divers employed by contractors whose primary focus was salvage of machinery, reusable metal, and especially any valuable cargo, if not of the vessel itself. It was Jacques Cousteau's Aqua-Lung that really opened up the world of shipwrecks. With the mobility of self-contained underwater breathing apparatuses (scuba), people of all backgrounds and interests could visit shipwrecks; archaeologists could measure and record undersea sites; historians could drink in the visual mystique and write

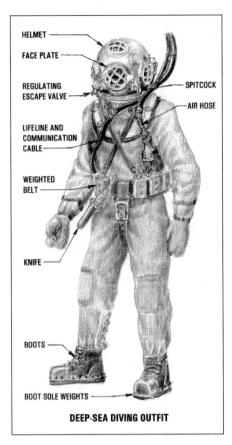

HELMET

FACE PLATE

REGULATING
ESCAPE VALVE

SPITCOCK

AIR HOSE

LIFELINE AND
COMMUNICATION
CABLE

WEIGHTED
BELT

KNIFE

BOOTS

BOOT SOLE WEIGHTS

DEEP-SEA DIVING OUTFIT

Walking across the bottom of the sea in heavily weighted boots, with air pumped down from the tending boat, the hard hat diver accomplished amazing feats under the sea for over a century.

of a time frozen in catastrophe; divers who were simply curious could poke around a shipwreck to see what fascinating souvenirs might be uncovered.

The shipwrecks themselves are time capsules of nautical commerce and technology, capsules to be unlocked by archaeologists through careful measurement and study. Stories of shipwrecks are snapshots of local history. Often well documented as major events in their time, these snapshots tell us a lot about the sailors and the people ashore, both the heroic and the ignoble of character. As we recount shipwreck stories, we learn more about how our ancestors coped, their values, what they thought, and what drove them. As we look at the shipwrecks themselves, we learn about the world these people inhabited, how they conducted their trade. All of this helps us understand who we were and where we came from as a people. It makes up an important part of the history and heritage of the Fundy region: shipwreck lore is Fundy lore.

CHAPTER TWO

THE EARLY YEARS: SINKING DETERMINED ROOTS

THE GRAND DESIGN

I n the early years of North America's colonization, with a lack of European settlement and little contact along our bleak coasts, a shipwreck might be months old before being discovered. And with few reference points, the tragedy's retelling often became confused as errors compounded one another.

For over a hundred years, a story set on the coast of Maine has been passed down from generation to generation: the story of the wreck of the *Grand Design* on Mount Desert Island, ME. Genealogists faithfully recorded this story with the annals of passengers who were on this ship. The story states that the *Grand Design*, bound from Londonderry, Ireland (now Northern Ireland), for Philadelphia, Pennsylvania, ran aground with two hundred people on board on Long

Ledge, off Seawall, Mount Desert Island. But no remains could be found of this, "the most famous shipwreck on the Island."[4]

The *Grand Design* first showed up in the genealogy of the Gamble family. Mrs. Isabel Galloway, widowed after being shipwrecked, married Archibald Gamble around 1743. The grandchildren of Mrs. (Galloway) Gamble appear to be the authors of the account of the shipwreck that killed Mrs. Gamble's first husband, which they referred to as the *Grand Design* shipwreck. With no settlement against which to reference the wreck's location, and passing decades blurring factual details, family lore became accepted as fact.

Historian Robert W. Tirrell, investigating this story in the 1950s, came to the conclusion that the Grand Design was not the name of the ship, but, in fact, the name of the undertaking to carry a shipload of emigrants from Ireland to Pennsylvania.[5] Contemporary documents that he discovered confirmed the name of the ship to be the *Martha and Eliza*, wrecked not on Mount Desert Island, but on Grand Manan Island. This location is quite clear in accounts in the *Boston News-Letter*, from November 26 to December 3, 1741.

The *Martha and Eliza* was a "snow," an early form of brigantine. Under the command of Captain Matthew Rowen, this modest vessel, probably about 27 metres in length, set sail from Londonderry, Ireland, on July 28, 1741. The *Martha and Eliza* was bound for Newcastle, PA, with 150 to 200 persons on board, many being immigrants who looked forward to joining family members who had gone on before and were successfully established there.

The Grand Design—the plan to immigrate to America—arose from the unusual deep freeze experienced in a normally temperate Ireland in 1740. The River Shannon froze to a depth of over 45 centimetres. Crops failed, including the Irish staple of potatoes. Starvation and disease spread across Ireland. People were desperate.

In 1741, piracy and privateering prevailed on the high seas of the North Atlantic. No safe passage could be guaranteed; indeed, it was frowned upon by the authorities as being entirely too risky.

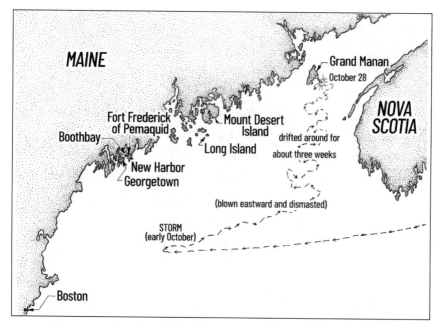

This map approximates the location of the Martha and Eliza's *journey along the coast of Maine.*

It was, therefore, a black-market business, and captains conveying immigrants did so outside the law. Captain Matthew Rowen (also spelled "Rowan"), therefore, accepted large sums of money to transport the passengers, and did so without maintaining a record of those who embarked with him. He was clearly a greedy and unscrupulous man, and the events of subsequent weeks would show just how wicked he really was.

From the detailed account written by nineteen-year-old Sarah,[6] one of the passengers, we are given a picture of the trip and its calamitous ending. About three weeks out, a "mortal fever" raged throughout the ship, claiming the lives of many of the passengers. Ten weeks out (early October), as the captain believed he was approaching the coast of America, a violent storm struck, during which the vessel was badly damaged and very nearly lost.

The storm drove them back eastward. The masts gave way, and the captain did not know where he was, having been unable to take celestial observations. Not knowing his location and with limited sail, the captain put all passengers on strict rations: one biscuit a day, a small portion of meat, and a quart of water. After ten days with no land in sight, this ration was halved, except for the water.

On October 28, they landed on a desolate island inhabited only by a few Indigenous people. From survivor accounts published in a Boston newspaper, it is clear that the ship was driven ashore on one of the islands of the Grand Manan group, probably one of the outer islands. From the descriptions provided, it was likely marooned on White Head Island. The passengers landed there and possibly on other nearby islands around Grand Manan (which accounts for their losing touch with other groups of passengers). The ship's officers and crew took the longboat and went in search of inhabitants.

Sarah's account of the landing shows the pathetic situation of the unfortunate passengers:

As my mother and sisters were landing, one of my sisters died. All being in confusion and trouble, there was no one to bury her but myself. I performed that service with great composure. I then had to take care of my mother and other sister, who were somewhat helpless…. When the boats were landing, as I stood on the beach, a child, about two years old, was put into my arms. I looked around to see who was to take it from me, but found that no one would own it. I inquired 'Who takes care of this child?' A little boy, about twelve years old, answered, 'Nobody, ma'am, but I.' How I felt, knowing that this child's parents had both died in the ship! I was obliged to lay down the child and leave it to the care of Him who had the care of us. The boy and child were soon after found dead, lying together. A most sorrowful sight![7]

The passengers became impatient and, fearing that the longboat may have been lost, about thirty of the "strongest and most healthy" of the young men (according to a subsequent petition) "went to ye woods designing to travel as fare as possible for inhabitants." [8] It is unclear whether they were aiming for the main island of Grand Manan or Maine, but whatever their intended destination, they were never seen again.

Again, the description of the young men going to "ye woods" would suggest White Head Island, for at very low tides the strong, young men would have been able to walk across the tidal passages to Cheney Island, Ross Island, and eventually reach the main island of Grand Manan (all densely wooded). But powerful currents flow through those passages, and as soon as the tide starts to rise, any person caught there would be swept away.

Eventually, the longboat with the ship's officers reached Fort Frederick at Pemaquid (now called Bristol), ME. The welfare of the hapless passengers was of little concern to the heartless captain. But he thought about the possessions of those he had conveyed. He reasoned that it would be worth the return to Grand Manan to plunder what was left on the ship.

Captain Rowen organized a rescue party, and in a little schooner and small sloop he and some crewmembers returned to Grand Manan. Around fifty of the passengers were rescued at this time. Just before the rescuers arrived, about eight or nine of the castaways had gone off along the shore that very morning searching for food, finding nothing but rockweed. The rescuers, having combed the remains of the ship and shore for the passengers' possessions, were unwilling to land and they returned to Fort Frederick without the remaining passengers, delivering the group of fifty survivors on November 14, 1741.

Sarah was among those who were left behind, as she described the two small vessels coming back "for the plunder of the ship" and taking with them a few of the servants and passengers. She continued:

"The rest of the passengers were left in the most melancholy of circumstances; but a kind Providence furnished us with something to support nature." They survived on mussels, sea kelp, and dulse for two months, but "[e]very day, more died… It was observed that the men failed sooner than the women, and that a greater proportion of them died."[9]

The situation looked very bleak for Sarah as she spoke of her darkest hour:

> The people began now to die very fast. There was no travelling anywhere, but dead bodies were found, as few were buried. All were so weak and helpless that they had enough to do to keep life in themselves. In this distressing situation we remained until every person of whom we had knowledge on the island was dead, except my mother, my sister and myself. At that time our fire went out and we had nothing to strike with. Several snows had fallen, but soon melted away. Another snow fell when we were in such distress for want of fire. This scene was of all the most hopeless; nothing to cover us but the heavens and nothing to eat but frozen mussels. In about one day after our fire went out my mother died, and there she lay, a lifeless corpse by our side. We were not able to bury her or do anything with her. My sister began to fail very fast and her spirits were very low. I laid me down beside a tree, to rest my head against it, but soon thought I must not lie there. I rose and went to the beach, got some frozen mussels and carried them to my sister, who ate them. We then both sat down beside a tree. Now my courage began to fail. I saw nothing to expect but death, yet did not wholly give up hope of deliverance. There we were, two distressed sisters, surrounded by dead bodies, without food or fire, and almost without clothing. I had no shoes to my feet, which were much frozen by reason of the cold.

The ground was covered with snow and the season was fast advancing, it being nearly the middle of December, so that we had every reason to expect that we should soon share the fate of our companions.[10]

At this darkest hour of discouragement, to their great surprise, the two sisters saw three men approaching. These men were no less surprised to find the sisters still alive. They were taken aboard the vessel where the captain gave each of them a spoonful of spirit and half a biscuit, the first bread they had tasted in two months. After plundering whatever they could find left from the shipwreck and stripping the dead, they sailed. Five days later, they arrived at New Harbor (a little east of Boothbay, ME). The rescuers intended to sell the two sisters as servants, but a man who came from the same part of Ireland as them came aboard and made arrangements for a friend to take them to his home to be protected from this fate. He wrote to Sarah's father in Pennsylvania informing him of their situation, and they stayed in this house until they were recovered. While her sister went to Boothbay to work, Sarah went to Georgetown. Her father came the following summer, but Sarah had had an offer of marriage to Mr. Porterfield, of Georgetown, and so settled there.

Meanwhile, back on the icy shores of the islands of Grand Manan, there were still survivors that had not yet been discovered. A third ship visited the island in April, nearly six months after the shipwreck, and found yet another group of survivors. This group of about ten included Mrs. Isabel Galloway and her one-year-old son Robert. Of the two hundred who sailed from Ireland, the three rescues account for sixty-three persons. It is possible that some of the thirty young men who went to "ye woods" survived, but no record of their arrival remains.

And what about the villainous Captain Matthew Rowen? In spite of complaints about his heartless treatment of the shipwreck victims, there was no effort to bring him to account before a court of justice—an indication of the low expectations of justice along our harsh coast nearly three centuries ago.

We know from various family histories that many of the survivors stayed on in Maine. It is quite probable that some eventually continued on to join relatives in Pennsylvania. That was, indeed, their "Grand Design." But for too many, their hopes for a new life were grimly dashed on the bleak shores of Grand Manan.

SAINT ANDREWS'S LOSS: THE *BRITANNIA*

During the time of the American Revolutionary War, loyalists to the British Crown streamed northward to escape a regime with which they had become enemies. This swelled to a massive migration of between thirty-five thousand and forty thousand persons. They left the relatively settled temperate lands of New England and headed to the wilds of Nova Scotia with its harsher climate.

Many families uprooted and moved in a major undertaking involving fleets of transport vessels. These ships banded together to travel in convoy, which gave them some protection from misfortune and a measure of comfort against uncertain navigation. As a result, the transport of these early refugees was remarkably free of mishap.

Indeed, so many people arrived along the stark northern shore of the Bay of Fundy that a new province was born to administer government to the flood of refugees: a province now known as New Brunswick. As people streamed northward, they considered every possibility for the establishment of new ports and centres for settlement and trade. Since the area was generally unknown to these settlers, they relied on the advice of traders and the local Indigenous Peoples. Even the border between the breakaway American colonies and those loyal to the British was undefined. One group of settlers, who established on the Penobscot River in Maine, discovered that they were still on American territory and knocked down their dwellings and moved northward once again, this time to the Passamaquoddy Bay.

On October 3, 1783, the settlers travelling in the convoy stepped ashore on the sands of a primeval peninsula. Courteous gentlemen in plum-coloured coats and powdered wigs assisted genteel ladies as they were lowered from wooden sailing vessels that reeked of tar and bilge into tippy little boats that carried them to the clam-flats and muddy sand of the tidal shore. There they were, facing a fall wilderness on an uninhabited Fundy coast, complete with priceless mahogany and silver plates, family paintings, expensive brass-studded storage trunks, attendant servants, and enslaved Black people. They also had with them boards, nails, and window glass, and most importantly, a vision of a town in which they could be at peace with their loyalty to the British crown. Thus was the beginning of Saint Andrews.[11]

Saint Andrews afforded an attractive location for settlement. It was a sheltered port, yet on a peninsula that could be easily defended against a land attack. Ice-free and temperate in winter and relatively fog-free in summer, the port of Saint Andrews was the New Brunswick mainland's port closest to the mouth of the Bay of Fundy, closest to the markets for seagoing trade and commerce; a port with the potential to become a great centre for trade and shipping in the new colony. There was, however, one drawback facing early shipping —a drawback that could not be overlooked: the powerful tidal currents of Head Harbour Passage. Passamaquoddy Bay is a large body of seawater that opens to the giant tides of Fundy through three narrow channels: Lubec Narrows, Head Harbour Passage, and Letete Passage. The deepest, widest, and clearly the best route from the Atlantic and the open Bay of Fundy into Saint Andrews is the S-shaped course through Head Harbour Passage.

Saint Andrews was built in the early days of trade. Little wooden ships set out for the West Indies laden with lumber and dried fish, and returned with puncheons of rum, molasses, fruit, indigo, and spices. Like all the other fledgling outposts of the British Empire, the port depended heavily on England for manufactured goods. Wooden ships with cargoes of furs, produce, and lumber were propelled by uncertain winds across the Atlantic, and manufactured goods—the trappings of refinement and culture—arrived in eagerly anticipated cargoes from England.

The English merchants, Hunter & Co., obtained the grand Dutch ship *Britannia*. Launched in 1793, the *Britannia* was registered at 932 tons, and was 3 decks deep in the hold. Indeed, it represented a major investment for its owners, and was a most important trade link between England and its new northern colony in New Brunswick. The *Britannia* (no lesser ship could have the audacity to call itself by a name so noble) was a proud showpiece for the English merchant marine.

In the spring of 1798, the *Britannia* sailed from Greenock, Scotland, bound for Saint Andrews with general cargoes, destined for the merchants of the colony. On the morning of June 15, almost within sight of its destination, the *Britannia* started in through Head Harbour Passage. It was flood tide, and powerful currents carried the ship along. As it entered the channel, the wind died out, and the ship lost steering. Normally when a sailing ship is becalmed, it simply slows to a natural drift and, if near shore, an anchor can be put out to hold it in place until a favourable wind breezes up. But the powerful currents of Head Harbour Passage carried it along too rapidly for an anchor to take hold. The current hurtled the noble ship along, totally out of control.

At ten o'clock in the morning, the *Britannia* struck Sandy Island Ledge, north of Campobello, and remained hard aground on the rocky shelf. It hit at high tide, firmly stranded, and would not move. As the tide ebbed, the crew worked hard at unloading cargo and shuttling it to Sandy Island via the ship's boats. The hull was badly damaged, however, and on the next flood tide it filled with water, rendering almost hopeless any chance at saving further cargo undamaged. The noble *Britannia* was a total wreck.

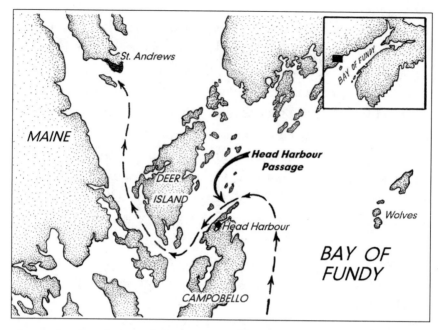

A map showing the intended journey of the Britannia *through Head Harbour Passage.*

Over the summer, the agents for the owners stripped everything salvageable. This ship, though a merchant ship, had been equipped with cannon for defending itself against marauders on the high seas. Among its ordnance were guns capable of firing nine-pound cannonballs. These guns were heavy, and those at work on the ship were unable to remove them. So, when the agents had felt they had stripped the vessel as much as they could, and there was no hope of floating the hull, the cannon were advertised for sale along with the wreck.

Apparently there were no bidders, for a newspaper advertisement the following spring suggested that John Black & Co., the agents for the ship's owners, still had a major interest in the wrecked ship. Indeed, it would appear from the advertisement that Black was not

A sketch of the Britannia *ashore on the ledge, with Sandy Island in the background.*

the only one interested in the wreck, for during the winter the wreck had been plundered and burned. Black was not at all happy about this and in the Royal Gazette of April 15, 1799, he offered a reward of forty dollars to anyone who could identify the culprits.

The once-mighty merchant ship had been reduced to a burned-out hulk. The ravages of time and storm took their toll, and all vestiges of the ship were completely swallowed up by the sea. Within a few years, memories of the *Britannia* faded into oblivion.

In early January 1964, Reginald Richardson Jr. of Lords Cove, Deer Island, NB, was diving for scallops off Sandy Island when he came across some items that were weather-worn and aged. On January 8, he arrived at the New Brunswick Museum with several pieces of china, a brass candlestick, pieces of grapeshot and bar shot, several cannon balls, half a small grist mill, and several wine bottles.

Over the next weeks and months, Reggie Richardson dived several more times to recover artifacts from the wreck. In May of that year, a special exhibit was assembled at the New Brunswick Museum, and opened by the province's lieutenant-governor. There was a great deal of excitement surrounding the mystery wreck off Deer Island. The artifacts predated 1800, but no one had any idea of the identity of the ship that was wrecked on Sandy Island Ledge.

China samples were sent to the Victoria and Albert Museum in London, and the ceramics department there verified the samples to be from 1790. Samples of rope recovered from the wreck were sent to the Smithsonian Institution in Washington, DC, and the noted marine historian Howard Chapelle stated that they had come from a "vessel of the eighteenth century."[12] Evidence on the sea floor suggested a sizable ship for the period, figured at the time to be forty-six metres long and ten feet wide.

In spite of all the material that had been recovered, the identity of the wreck continued to be a mystery. The New Brunswick Museum sent queries to Lloyd's of London, England; the Mariners' Museum in Newport News, Virginia; and the Smithsonian in Washington, DC. Ironically, while the world was being scoured for answers, the identity would be found right in the New Brunswick Museum Archives. In early 1970, the answer was found in the June 22, 1798, issue of the *Saint John Gazette and the Weekly Advertiser*. The story of the stranding of the *Britannia* came to light once again after being so long forgotten.

Shortly after I started the shipwreck survey program in the summer of 1973 for the New Brunswick Museum, I phoned Reggie Richardson, who was most cooperative in describing the wreck. On July 24, I sailed to Deer Island with Richard Green, whose boat had

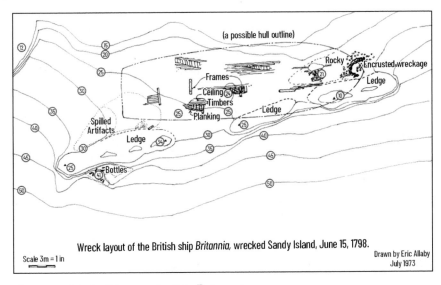

Within the figure:

(a possible hull outline)

Rocky
Encrusted wreckage
Ledge

Frames

Ceiling
Timbers
Planking
Ledge

Spilled
Artifacts

Ledge

Bottles

Wreck layout of the British ship *Britannia*, wrecked Sandy Island, June 15, 1798.

Scale 3m = 1 in

Drawn by Eric Allaby
July 1973

A survey sketch of the wreck of the Britannia.

been chartered for the summer for the shipwreck survey work. There, we met Art McKay, who had previously dived on the wreck and who would show us the wreck's location off the southern end of Sandy Island.

Based on the information I had, I dropped down to the bottom, east of the ledge. Looking around, I swam toward the ledge, went up the side of a steep slope, and found most of the wreckage on a shelf at a depth of about 25 feet. I explored around the general extent of the wreckage and then spent several hours photographing and surveying the wreck with the Polar Coordinate Survey Instrument (POCOSI), an instrument I designed myself and that I will describe in further detail in Chapter Three.

Returning home with the survey information, I drew up a basic plan of the wreckage of the *Britannia*, as it appeared at that time, with the basic layout showing the remnants of its hull. By plotting several prominent ledge peaks around the wreck, and with quite a number of depth observations, I developed approximate contour lines in the vicinity of the wreck to try to convey a sense of the bottom and how steep it is just off the shelf from the wreck. The steep slope accounts for the scattering of the materials and cargo down the side of the ledge.

The wreck of the *Britannia* has become a piece of Charlotte County heritage. To the seaside town of Saint Andrews, it serves as a reminder of its seaport roots and its role as a major gateway to the young colony for trade with England.

But the loss of the *Britannia* prompts an intriguing question: in these early times, one wonders just how much influence the stranding of the *Britannia* might have had in directing trade away from Saint Andrews and toward Saint John. History is shaped by the many separate successes and failures that influence what people decide to do and why they make their decisions as they do. We may never know how many merchants, when considering their choices for trade opportunities in Saint Andrews or Saint John, thought about the hapless *Britannia* and opted to have vessels sail the extra distance to facilitate a more direct harbour approach in Saint John.

THE WAR OF 1812: THE HMS *PLUMPER*

The people living along the Fundy coast of New Brunswick did not take the War of 1812 seriously as a national conflict. The primary effort in this region was to capitalize on the hostilities for economic gain for the provincial ports. This attitude played out before the backdrop of the American Embargo Act of 1807, which forbade the sailing of any American or foreign vessel from the United States to foreign ports for commercial purposes. This ill-conceived attempt to build domestic industry and markets by cutting the United States off commercially from the influence of foreign trade was quickly countered by the Free Port Act passed by the British government to open specific ports in the Maritime provinces to American shipping. Halifax, Shelburne, and Saint John were the first, with Saint Andrews added in 1811. Indeed, the many coastal indentations of Passamaquoddy Bay, next to the American border, made Saint Andrews a preferred port because of better opportunities for smuggling. The border ports of New Brunswick and Maine, therefore, became beehives of illicit trade.[13]

With the outbreak of the War of 1812, and hoping to deepen political divisions within the United States, Great Britain encouraged New Englanders to continue to exchange goods across the border, in spite of the American government's wishes. The result was an air of neutrality in the Bay of Fundy, where greed for trade took precedence over bellicose politics. Indeed, the citizens of Eastport, ME, unanimously voted to maintain good relations with the people of New Brunswick.[14]

Breaking the American embargo was a lucrative business opportunity, so New Brunswick's war effort was primarily directed at trade with the enemy. New Brunswickers welcomed American vessels that had broken the embargo and sailed into the Bay of Fundy. Below the border, there were allegations that some Yankee skippers deliberately surrendered vessels to the British Navy and were safely escorted to Saint John where their valuable American cargoes were unloaded at a good price, which enabled them to ransom their vessels and sail home with the proceeds of profitable trade.

To carry out this trade, American vessels had to elude their own country's warships, but were then hospitably received and escorted by the British Navy. Privateers, on the other hand, were given letters of marque to prey upon enemy vessels. Their motives were directed toward personal gain rather than national economic strategy. As a result, there was a delicate tension in effect, where privateers hunted for American vessels with lucrative cargoes, but these same vessels obtained escort by His Majesty's Navy, intent on assisting the trade that enriched New Brunswick ports. The busy shipping activity that took place during the War of 1812 would confuse any outside observers. Besides keeping privateers in check and escorting illicit American trade, naval vessels were also used to move soldiers and other citizens among the ports, as land transport was almost non-existent.

Because of the activity of privateers around the mouth of the Bay of Fundy, passengers wishing safe passage and citizens shipping valuables from either side of the border travelled aboard naval vessels, being afforded the authority and protection of powerful guns. Considering the threat of engagement from American naval ships and the clear dominance over privateer armament, His Majesty's naval vessels represented the most secure marine conveyance. One such naval vessel was the brig *Plumper*, belonging to the British Navy. A Saint John newspaper recorded the movement of vessels such as these. Their arrivals always sparked interest in the port, for this was how the most influential people of the day might arrive in the city.

After arriving in Halifax on November 30, 1812, with a convoy of six vessels, the *Plumper* set out from Halifax for Saint John with a full complement of seafarers and several passengers. But even the dominance of the Royal Navy could not prevail against the unforgiving elements. At 4:00 A.M. on Saturday, December 5, 1812, the *Plumper* ran ashore at Red Point, a little over 1 mile (1.6 km) down the shore from Dipper Harbour, which is in turn a little over 20 miles (32 km) down the shore from Saint John. The *Plumper* struck a shallow cove below a steep and rugged cliff in the mouth of the Bay of Fundy. In the darkness, confusion, and heavy seas, with the brig fast breaking up, those on board attempted to reach the shore—so near and yet beyond grasp for so many.

When daylight arrived and the survivors huddling on the bleak shore took stock of their situation, they found that their cold, wet, bedraggled group numbered only thirty. The only officer to make it ashore was midshipman Stephen Hall, who landed safely along with the pilot, Samuel Simpson; the rest were sailors and marines. Their commander, Lieutenant Bray, was lost along with the brig's master, Captain Marley. In total, forty-five people drowned: officers, crew, marines, and passengers.

Shortly after daylight, messengers were dispatched through the thick woods to Dipper Harbour, and thence the message was taken to Saint John, conveying the news of the catastrophe and a summary of the victims and survivors. The report also noted that the *Plumper* had been carrying nearly $30,000 in coin, but added that the money was expected to be saved. The authorities in Saint John wasted no time in responding. On Sunday, December 6, HMS *Bream* and government sloop *Brunswicker* set sail for Dipper Harbour to pick up the survivors at the wreck and assist in recovery. The following week, the newspaper published a list of those who died in the tragedy and those who survived, but no mention was made of the $30,000, whether recovered or lost.

The notion of treasure at this site persisted through the following century and a half; I recall hearing of it from a hard-hat diver in the 1960s. In the early 1970s, a Saint John diver, Gary Austin, thoroughly scoured the area of the lost *Plumper*, looking for clues as to the existence of the shipwreck and possible treasure. With all the speculation about the possibility of gold and silver coins, green-eyed divers took a keen interest in what he was doing. Austin explored the shipwreck in cooperation with the New Brunswick Museum, and this responsible approach was rewarded by a letter in September 1972 from a New Brunswick government official declaring "the site of an historic wreck considered that of HMS *Plumper* to be an historic site and also a protected site." Austin found enough evidence to suggest that this could indeed be the site of the *Plumper* wreck, including heavily encrusted cannon and pieces of old iron encased in a thick concretion.

I visited Gary Austin and, following his directions, dived on the wreck site in August 1973. The remains of the *Plumper* lie in fairly shallow water exposed to rough sea, under a cliff of red rock at Red Point.

The sea floor there is made up of rocks, boulders, and rubble, with these rocks moved about in every storm. Whatever might be left of the wrecked brig is badly beaten up, strewn about, and buried now.

When I first went down to the bottom, I could see no sign of wreckage anywhere. To be satisfied that this was actually a wreck site, I wanted to find at least some traces of shipwreck. Finally, I found some decomposed fragments of old iron, scattered and partly buried in rubble. Certainly, the divers working on this site faced a daunting task. Were it not for dreams of buried treasure, I doubt that anyone would have bothered with this site. Considering the unstable bottom, subject to heavy seas, the New Brunswick Museum should count itself fortunate to have acquired as many items from this site as it did.

The story and scant remnants of the *Plumper* are a direct link to the interesting naval activities of the War of 1812. While we cannot diminish the importance of this catastrophe, with forty-five lives being snuffed out that bleak December morning, it was the intrigue of sunken treasure—whether or not there actually was any there—that piqued such intense interest in this shipwreck.

THE NEW YEAR'S EVE GALE

The year 1819 closed with one of the most ferocious gales of wind ever to strike the Bay of Fundy. Shipping at the time was brisk, as merchants and traders tried to unload and re-load their vessels and get them on their way before the worst of winter settled upon them. The weather was pleasant as December came to a close. Some ships loaded and unloaded in harbours, some awaited fair winds and tides to leave, and still others approached port hoping for fair opportunity to dock.

Saint John awakened on Friday, December 31, 1819, to a gloomy, stormy day. A violent wind howled off the ocean. Blowing rain and ocean spray obscured Partridge Island from view at the entrance to the harbour. This was, of course, long before the stone breakwater joined Partridge Island to the mainland. Heavy surf thundered ashore, all but drowning out the sound of guns coming from the island at about eight o'clock in the morning. No one could see Partridge Island through the storm to know why the guns would be fired, but guns in these circumstances were a signal of dire distress. People lined the mainland shore, straining to peer through the storm, but seeing nothing, wondering…

The residents of Partridge Island, however, could see and knew all too well why the distress guns were fired. A brig was in deep trouble off their southeast point. People gathered along the shore to see if there might be something, anything, they could do to help.

Saint John pilot D. Walker, along with two of his boatmen, had gone aboard the brig a day or so earlier to guide it into port. Seeing the impending rocks before them—their stricken vessel reeling and thrashing about in the surging seas—pilot Walker was determined that all should leave the brig and get ashore as quickly as possible. The crew threw a buoy overboard with a line tied to it, which they reeled out as the buoy drifted toward the island. As the buoy rolled in on a big wave, a resident of Partridge Island deftly snatched it from the water. The people onshore then quickly gathered in some line, secured it, and used it to pull ashore the pilot and his boatmen, who, tying themselves to the line one at a time, jumped into the maelstrom of boiling surf and committed themselves to the people pulling them to land. The captain and his crew, tired from their voyage, elected not to attempt such folly, but decided to stay with the ship.

At about nine o'clock, the storm lifted a little, showing the people of Saint John the brig at the southeast end of Partridge Island, rolling uncontrollably with every sea. Even at that distance, the heaving of the brig was abundantly clear from the lurching of the masts still secure in the stalwart hull. This was not the measured roll of a ship in harmony with the cyclic rhythms of the sea; this was a hideous twisting, jerking, thumping, wrenching roll, the death throes of a ship being picked up, pounded, and pummelled on the rocks. Though it was clear to anyone along the shore that a serious disaster was unfolding before them, those on Partridge Island could do little to prevent the ship from breaking up before their eyes. They called to Saint John with their guns in the hope that someone there might be able to do something. Two Saint John pilots, Reed and Maybee, made a valiant attempt to row out of the harbour to offer assistance, but the storm was too powerful for them. They could not pull their little craft beside the shipwreck and they were forced back into harbour to save their own lives.

Saint John had not long to wait to discover the fate of the shipwrecked brig. Between ten and eleven o'clock, the entire shore along the lower part of town was covered with pieces of the wreck. There were bags of pimentos and oranges and other tropical cargo, and it was soon discovered from the markings on the bags and from part of the stern that washed ashore that the doomed vessel was the elegant brig *Mary*. Under the command of Captain George Bell, this fine vessel was owned by Messrs. Crookshank and Johnston of Saint John and was travelling from Savanna-la-Mar, Jamaica. Now knowing the identity of the brig, the people of Saint John became desperate to learn the fate of the crew—a crew of their own men. But the storm persisted all day and thwarted every effort to reach Partridge Island.

A heavy sea roared and crashed on the shores of Saint John all New Year's Eve and into the next morning. In spite of the frantic concern, there was no way of communicating between Saint John and Partridge Island to learn the fate of the crew of the brig. Finally, about noon the following day, boats were able to reach the island where they learned the sad truth: the captain and crew, thirteen in all, had stayed with the brig as it went to pieces and had all perished in the storm.

~

The day before, many miles to the south and well out into the Bay of Fundy, the same storm was tossing about the schooner *Perseverance*, which was heaving and wallowing in the mountainous seas, washed repeatedly by icy spray, and buffeted by a bone-chilling wind. The Saint John schooner, under the command of Captain McDonald, had set sail from Saint Andrews for Jamaica. Clearing Campobello on Wednesday, December 29, Captain McDonald sailed his schooner out into the Bay. The vessel idled along, experiencing light winds on Thursday and making little progress, but as the day closed, the calm gave way to a rising headwind, and through Thursday night a southerly gale buffeted the schooner, gaining strength as the hours of winter darkness deepened.

The seas whipped up by the gale pounded against the little wooden hull and caused a leak. The schooner was equipped with two bilge pumps, which were most vigorously manned by the crew. But the hull was leaking too badly to be kept clear, and the *Perseverance* settled deeper and deeper into the water as it filled. The deck-load of lumber was cut clear and jettisoned with each roll of the ship. In order to get rid of the load, however, the ship's boat also had to be cut clear, and before it could be secured again, it was unfortunately washed away. The water gaining in the hold rolled back and forth with the movement of the schooner, making the vessel less and less stable as more and more water poured in. The anchors and cables were cut away to lighten the deck and keep what little stability was still left in the heaving hull.

By early Friday morning, December 31, the gale was a full-blown storm. The schooner was completely waterlogged and helplessly battered by the seas, pushed along by the wind. Full of water, the hull rolled ponderously at the whim of each wave. All hands took to the mastheads for safety against being washed by the sea on deck. After being there about half an hour, the schooner lurched over and settled on its beam-ends, completely on its side, waterlogged hull-deep, dipping its masts down into the water and holding there.

Three of the crew were immediately washed off and drowned. The remaining crew quickly cut the rigging clear. Unsupported by rigging, the mainmast and fore-topmast broke away, and the hull slowly returned to an upright position. The schooner was now a little more stable, but with the masts gone, it had no possible source of power and the men on board faced grim alternatives: starvation, or death by exposure to the cold, relentless onslaught of the sea.

Captain McDonald's crew died one after the other from exposure to the cold wind in this awful winter storm. His mate was the last one to go, and then the captain was alone. The wind went around westward and abated somewhat, allowing the captain to make an effort to save himself. He found a topgallant sail wrapped around a timber, and in the sail he found a potato, his only food since the onset of the storm. He jury-rigged the sail on the stump of the foremast and, guessing his location to be off the Lurcher Shoal due west of Yarmouth, he steered as near as he could judge for Nova Scotia, his compasses all having been washed away.

> ❉ A ship's boat is kept on deck, much as a lifeboat would be–though it was not called a lifeboat then. A larger vessel would have had a longboat on deck to carry a larger crew.

Back in Saint John, the city was assessing the damages to shipping in the harbour. The ships *Lady Ridley* and *Bittern*, laden with cargo for London, had been driven ashore in the harbour. The *Bittern* was refloated but had to be taken to a shipyard to have broken planking replaced. The brigs *Mungo Park*, *Mary Ann*, *United Kingdom*, *William*, *Charles*, *Hope*, and a number of others were all damaged during the storm—virtually every vessel in the harbour was injured in some form. Soon the city received word that the schooner *Thomas Ritchie*, owned in Digby, NS, had gone ashore between Lorneville Head and Split Rock, a

Jury-rigging a topgallant sail to the stump of a foremast, Captain McDonald worked his waterlogged schooner, Perseverance, *toward the Nova Scotia coast.*

few miles down the coast. Only the master survived; the rest of the crew perished. In the city, the new barracks under construction and close to completion were completely levelled by the wind; roofs were blown off houses and, in general, the storm established itself indelibly in the minds and memories of the city of Saint John.

Out on the Bay of Fundy, the dismasted *Perseverance* drove all through the night, progressing eastward toward Nova Scotia. The wind had changed direction, clearing the air, but a heavy sea was still running, and all these circumstances sorely tested a cold and exhausted but determined Captain McDonald. When Saturday morning—New Year's Day—came, he could see the Nova Scotia coast and recognized the headlands of Yarmouth. He wanted to try to work the schooner into the shelter of Yarmouth Harbour, but his unmanageable vessel was all but derelict and would not respond; he was helpless before the wind and could not bring it about to shape the course into port.

Captain McDonald drifted into the breakers and heavy surf, and finally the *Perseverance* struck the rocks about seven miles up the coast from Yarmouth. People ashore saw what was happening and made every possible effort to render some assistance. One boat nearly reached the wreck but was driven back by the surf. The schooner soon started breaking apart, so Captain McDonald felt forced to take a desperate measure. He recounted the story once he had returned to Saint John: "At this time, the vessel going to pieces fast, I got on a plank and committed myself to the protection of Almighty God, who had preserved me so long; and when near the shore I was taken from the surf and through the kind attention of the humane inhabitants of Yarmouth, which will never be erased from my memory, was so sufficiently restored to health as to enable me again to return to this port."[15]

The captain had secured the bodies of John Whelpley—the mate and a native of Cornwallis (Port Williams area), NS—and Thomas Spencelay—a seaman who came from England— within the schooner, even as he fought for his own life. These bodies were removed from the wreck and given a respectful burial by the good people of Yarmouth—people who understood the awesome power of the sea and had a kinship with those unfortunate victims who paid the ultimate price for daring to make a life for themselves upon the ocean. And, somehow, they might have understood that the bodies they buried were in recognition and acknowledgement of the many other lives also lost upon the Bay of Fundy in the Great New Year's Eve Gale of 1819.

There are some events over the course of history that become larger than life in their later retelling. So it was with the loss of the brig *Charlotte*. As a typical merchant brig of the transatlantic trade in 1829, it took on board a valuable cargo of general merchandise in the Scottish port of Greenock over a two-week period in March. Saint John merchants had placed orders and, as the goods were stowed in the holds, agents noted quantities and descriptions to be sure that all goods shipped would be accounted for when received at their destination. The *Charlotte* set sail on March 24, 1829, bound for Saint John, NB. Captain Johnson, a native of east Scotland, had brought ships to and from Saint John on many occasions, though he was still in the prime of life.

Coming into the Bay of Fundy, the *Charlotte* sailed up the Grand Manan Channel. On the evening of April 30, the brig was observed bearing down for the southern head of Grand Manan. It then wore ship and stood out to sea as the wind went to the northeast and shut in with thick snow. The *Charlotte* was never seen again.

The following morning, about four miles north of Machias Seal Island, the schooner *Liberty* encountered a longboat and other fragments of wreckage.[16] The description of the longboat corresponded exactly with the *Charlotte*'s longboat. It was generally believed at that time that the brig struck the Western Murr Ledge during the night of April 30, came off the ledge, and, breaking up, filled and foundered immediately.

Meanwhile on Grand Manan Island, a strange dog coated with tar came out of the woods and approached the home of Dyer Wilcox, at Deep Cove near the southern end of the island. After taking in the dog, Wilcox and his sons tramped through the snow to Bradford Cove and on to Hay Point where they found evidence of a terrible tragedy: pieces of a wrecked ship. They picked up two compasses— both marked on the sides with the name *Charlotte*—a binnacle, three oars, part of a cabin berth, part of a cookhouse, the crosspiece of a

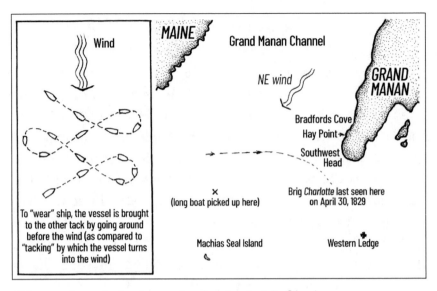

This map shows the last known location for the brig Charlotte.

gallows, a capstan, a stanchion, and part of a green bulwark.[17] Quite clearly, this was from the brig *Charlotte*. It would seem that the dog floated ashore on this wreckage and then made its way through the woods to civilization.

The circumstances around the loss of the *Charlotte* kept the tale alive, and so it grew in the lore and yarns swapped by sailors as they roamed the ports of the world. On an idle Sunday in Swansea, Wales, a Grand Manan seaman named Wooster was aboard a ship when sailors from other ships came aboard to swap sea yarns and pass the time.[18] Talk turned to the Bay of Fundy being called the "graveyard of the Atlantic." Wooster mentioned that he was from Grand Manan and that shortly before he had left home the brig *Charlotte* had been lost there. One of the sailors spoke up and said, "What do you know about the brig *Charlotte*?" Wooster didn't know much except that the vessel was lost with all hands apart from a dog with a patch of tar on it that made it ashore.

The other sailor was shocked to hear of the loss and added, "I know that dog and I was the means of him having that patch of tar on him." He explained how he was tarring down the rigging when the dog upset the tar pot on itself. He proceeded to describe loading the brig in port before it sailed (possibly embellishing the value and contents of the cargo as he recounted the story). He then told how he drew an advance on his wages and, as the ship was casting off, he jumped onto the dock and was not missed when it departed. He watched it sail away and knew nothing of its fate until he met Wooster that day.

Naturally, when Wooster returned to Grand Manan, he recounted the story of the sailor from Swansea, and the cargo grew more valuable with each retelling, as the authority of the last man to see the *Charlotte* was certainly beyond being questioned. By this time, it was readily accepted that this celebrated brig carried a general cargo that included $45,000 worth of bolt copper, silver plating, wine, and all kinds of liquor. There were also some who claimed that the vessel carried many thousands of dollars worth of payroll for the British soldiers quartered on this side of the Atlantic. But the payroll part of the story never quite crossed the line from rumour to accepted fact.

The story of the brig *Charlotte* became part of Grand Manan lore; it was a story to stir people to adventure, to imagine that they might find this wreck and recover its valuable cargo. The event was recounted in the *Saint Croix Courier* of June 27, 1889: "The brig Charlotte, laden with copper valued at £9,000 sterling, was wrecked on the southern side of Grand Manan, 60 years ago, and the crew all lost. A dog got ashore, was found, fed and cared for."

The story of the *Charlotte* simply would not go away. It was just too enticing for entrepreneurs to resist. The *Saint Croix Courier* reported two years later, on May 21, 1891:

Parties in Eastport, with Mr. Isaac Newton, Capt. Allen O. Guptill, and other prominent citizens are about to engage in a wrecking expedition to try to locate the wreck of the Charlotte, a vessel lost some 56 years ago near the Grand Cross at Southwest Head. Her cargo contained several thousand pounds of pure copper in bars and some silver plate. Divers have several times tried to find the wreck, but have never succeeded. Those who had a knowledge of the whereabouts of the wreck are long since dead. We hope our enterprising friends may be rewarded with a discovery of the wreck.

Grovesnor Newton was sent to Halifax to find a diver for the wrecking company. He returned on June 13, bringing with him diver John DuFrise. They scoured the shores around the southern head but found nothing of the wrecked brig. Wanting to try to recover some of their investment, the wreckers moved down to the Yellow Murr Ledge to work on the wreck of the barque *Victoria*. They did not find much, so returned to the back of Grand Manan to work up from the southwest head of the island to Dark Harbour, but found nothing.

Working throughout July proved fruitless. On July 30, 1891, the *Saint Croix Courier* reported that "the wrecking company [has] given up searching for sunken treasure and are satisfied that the treasure ship *Charlotte* cannot be found. The stories about [it] are classed as rather mythical."

~

I first became interested in the *Charlotte* when I heard the tales of valuable cargo and read old newspaper accounts based on the same old lore. When I was a university student, I spent my summers diving in the herring weirs for fishers around Grand Manan, doing repairs, tying the netting to the weir poles, sewing up holes, and carrying out general underwater maintenance. As a diver, I was particularly interested in shipwrecks, especially wrecks with valuable cargo.

So it was that in August 1963 I set out to search for the *Charlotte*. I was not alone in the lure of the Charlotte; fellow divers Carman Cook and James "Buddy" McLaughlin were also intrigued by the story. Realizing I couldn't cover much territory just by swimming along the ocean floor, I came up with a better solution: a sea sled. The first sled we built of pipe; it had a simple frame to surround a prone diver, with a footrest to support the diver's feet against the drag of the water. A joystick controlled large paddles on either side, which were angled to act as elevators to allow the diver to control the height at which they would be towed. The performance of the sled was less than spectacular: the controls were very sluggish. I returned to university shortly afterward and that ended our efforts for 1963.

Over several days in July 1964, the three of us resumed our search for the *Charlotte* at the back of Grand Manan Island, using an improved version of our sea sled. We scoured the back of Grand Manan Island, but found nothing. We continued searching from time to time, and in the course of looking for the *Charlotte* in 1966, I actually did find a shipwreck.

I was thrilled and hardly able to contain myself. Even though there was no sign of any cargo at all, we thought we had found the *Charlotte*. Over the next few days, we returned to the wreck and the more I looked it over, the more convinced I became that this was not the fabled treasure brig. About this time, I read an account of a visit to Grand Manan in 1867, in which the author described seeing the spars of a wrecked ship in Bradford Cove, which he identified as the barque *Mavourneen*, wrecked there on October 22, 1866. Our "treasure ship" turned out to be a Yarmouth barque, inward bound into the Bay of Fundy, carrying nothing but ballast rocks.

After discovering the identity of the shipwreck in Bradford Cove, our enthusiasm for the elusive *Charlotte* was sorely tested. Nevertheless, we continued our searches off the Southern Cross, at the lower end of Grand Manan. This is deep water with strong tidal currents, so we soon became discouraged with this effort. Furthermore, fishers who pepper the area with lobster traps and scour the bottom with scallop drags would certainly have encountered wreckage as significant as that of the *Charlotte*. Fishers working off the southern head did not have problems with gear catching on the bottom; it would be hard to imagine that they could consistently avoid catching on a large brig if there were one wrecked there.

However, I could not completely dismiss thoughts of the wreck of the *Charlotte*. In all of the work done hunting for this elusive shipwreck, one fundamental piece of research had been overlooked: what exactly was the celebrated brig carrying?

During the winter of 1971, while I was researching marine history in England, I pursued the *Charlotte* story. After I returned to Canada, with the help of the Scottish Records Office, I pored through the detailed record of exports loaded onto vessels at the port of Greenock the month before the *Charlotte* sailed for Saint John. Accordingly, I compiled a fairly detailed list of the cargo that was shipped from Greenock and that went to bottom somewhere off Grand Manan.

The *Charlotte* carried glass, iron, paint, and forty tons of coal. It also had a significant number of items presumably ordered by merchants for manufacturing or reselling, including cotton, linen, paper and books, silk and felt hats, sugar, and over two hundred gallons of brandy. Clearly all the tales of copper, silver, and the sundry exaggerations of history were unfounded. Nevertheless, when I read the list of the cargo, it is easy to see why the brig was of such value to the merchants of Saint John, and why its loss was of such commercial consequence. The cargo that went down with the brig would not have survived very long in a shipwreck, but it represented an important part of the retail trade of the day, and the loss of the brig meant short supply of these valuable stocks of merchandise, a demand that would have put severe strain on Saint John's economy.

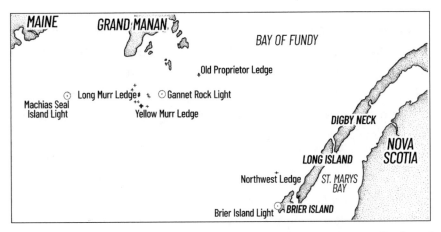

A map of the Bay of Fundy showing the location of the Gannet Rock and Machias Seal Island lighthouses in relation to the islands and ledges in the area.

No, the *Charlotte* was not a treasure ship in the conventional sense of the word, but this event has given us a rich heritage of sea lore.

THE BARQUE *JANE*

There is certainly no denying that the loss of the *Charlotte* was instrumental in bringing lighthouses to both Gannet Rock and Machias Seal Island, facilities that had been under consideration for a decade. Legend has it that the Commissioners of Lighthouses had, in the mid-1820s, built wooden test structures on both the Yellow Murr Ledge and Gannet Rock. The timbers washed away from the Yellow Murr Ledge, but stayed on Gannet Rock, confirming their decision to recommend that the light be placed on Gannet Rock. On the advice of the admiral stationed in Saint John, the lieutenant governor felt that the lighthouse should be built on Machias Seal Island, and in the end nothing was built. No doubt the Admiral was thinking more about the strategic value of a lighthouse and a British presence on Machias Seal Island, looking directly as it does at the coast of Maine. The loss of the brig *Charlotte* in April 1829 rekindled discussions on the issue and by 1832 there were lighthouses established on both Gannet Rock and Machias Seal Island.

The light built on Gannet Rock precipitated a new problem: confusion with the Brier Island light. Both lights at that time were fixed lights, appearing the same to a mariner. Powerful crosscurrents on the spring tides carried sailing ships off course from the south channel. Captains coming into the bay kept watch for Brier Island light, and sometimes they were carried off course by currents and mistakenly identified the Gannet Rock light as the Brier Island light. They would then adjust course to avoid Brier Island, unwittingly putting their vessels among the treacherous Murr Ledges.

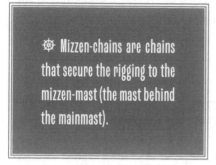

✿ Mizzen-chains are chains that secure the rigging to the mizzen-mast (the mast behind the mainmast).

The 404-ton barque *Jane* was one of these victims. Built in Saint John in 1824 by William Olive & Co., the *Jane* traded regularly with Europe over the following decade. On September 4, 1833, the *Jane* set sail from Liverpool, England, bound for Saint John with a cargo of coal and other goods under the command of Captain Britton, a young Englishman.

Coming into the Bay of Fundy on Sunday, October 13, during a strong southeast gale, Captain Britton mistook the Gannet Rock light for the Brier Island light, so he steered his barque to the northwest to give a wide berth to what he thought was Brier Island. However, this took him in among the Murr Ledges, and he did not discover his error until the *Jane* struck Long Murr Ledge. The captain, the mate, two seamen, and a lad of seventeen were all aft, and when the ship struck, the stern section broke away at the mizzen chains, and they all drowned. Within moments another section of the ship broke away at the mainmast. The rest of the crew (twelve in number), were on the bow on the rocks and were thus marooned on Long Murr Ledge for three days before they were discovered and rescued by Mr. Cheney of nearby Three Islands.

Saint John was shocked by the loss of life and the loss of one of its fine ships. Residents expressed outrage over the lights being similar in appearance, and one paper pronounced it "a great evil" that "should be speedily remedied."[19] As a result, the following February, the Commissioners of Lighthouses announced that in April 1834 a flashing light would be established on Gannet Rock, to make it readily distinguishable from Brier Island. The loss of the *Jane,* therefore, led to the light at Gannet Rock becoming a flashing light.

These lighthouses have been of great value to shipping in and out of the Bay of Fundy over the ensuing century and a half. Perhaps the great treasure of the *Charlotte* might best be counted in the many lives saved by the warnings provided to mariners by these outer Fundy lighthouses.

CHAPTER THREE

COMMERCE GROWS

∽

COMMERCE LOST: THE *WALLACE* AND THE *QUEEN*

As Saint John grew in importance in shipping and trade, so did the consumer demand for goods from England—this growth being especially strong in years of prosperity. The year 1840 ushered in a boom in the lumber trade accompanied by a similar spurt in shipbuilding. Ships carrying lumber eastward across the Atlantic brought manufactured goods west. With the surge in shipbuilding, there was, of course, a strong demand for iron and copper to make metal fastenings to tie together the frames and backbones of the wooden ships.

It was to satisfy this trade demand that the barque *Wallace* set sail from Liverpool, England, in April 1841, headed for Saint John. Before reaching its destination, however, it was wrecked on the Murr Ledges below Grand Manan, introducing a myth with just enough tantalizing fact to hook greedy would-be salvors.

For over a hundred years, the *Wallace* was the focus of some of the most intensive treasure-hunting salvage expeditions ever to be mounted on the basis of wishful thinking, misinformation, and speculation. The stories passed down with each retelling and successive generation became accepted as fact. Added to that, with the onset of scallop dragging in the Murr Ledges in the 1930s and '40s, it was common that a copper rod would come up in a scallop drag, intensely fanning the flames of interest. And so, dreams of quick wealth spawned a frenzy of expeditions.

When I first became involved with the quest for the *Wallace* in 1966, it was readily acknowledged by the speculators' expeditions that the ship carried six hundred tons of copper rods destined for the shipbuilding industry in the port city of Saint John. I was drawn into this race and spent many hours over the course of a year or so scouring the bottom of the ocean among the Murr Ledges. Apart from becoming familiar with that particular patch of ocean floor—finding a perplexing trail of traces of cargo across the sea floor east of the Wallace Rocks (named for the ship that struck them)—I finally came to the conclusion that I was not destined to gain riches from the wreck of the *Wallace*. Had I taken the time to do the proper background research, I could have saved myself a lot of cold, hard work deep on the floor of the Bay of Fundy.

~

George Thompson built the *Wallace* in Saint John. Launched in 1840, it was registered at 706 tons and was owned there by Thomas Wallace. It was, therefore, a relatively new ship in late March 1841, when it was loading cargo in Liverpool, England, bound for Saint John, NB. Having had more than a passing interest in this cargo, when I was working in England in 1971 I obtained the customs records that detailed each cargo item that went aboard the *Wallace* at its Liverpool dock. Certainly there was copper on board, but instead of 600 tons of copper, the ship carried 729 copper rods, 2 tons of bolt copper, and 896 pounds of braziers copper. Most of the cargo space was taken up with coal (545 tons). Along with that, the cargo contained about 150 tons of iron in rods, chains, spikes, and nails, and 90 tons of salt.

The *Wallace* set sail from Liverpool on April 5, 1841, under the command of Captain Toohig, with a crew of twenty-three men. After crossing the Atlantic and while coming up the Bay of Fundy on May 23, the *Wallace* struck a reef in the Murr Ledges that emerges at half tide and is completely covered at high water. This ledge has twin peaks rising out of the water and has since been known as the Wallace Rocks. Although no records tell us what happened, it would be reasonable to assume that as it headed up the bay, the *Wallace* was drawn off course by the tidal currents. If it was foggy, the captain would not be able to see the ledges or nearby islands. The Wallace Rocks rise up abruptly from 14 fathoms deep, so soundings would give no indication of danger until it was too late.

From the evidence strewn about the bottom, I would suggest that the *Wallace* struck a sunken breaker to the southwest of the ledge when the tide was down, then rode out over the submerged reef, tearing away its sternpost. As the tide flooded, the *Wallace* was lifted off the ledge and carried eastward by the current, leaking badly by the stern. With the hull settling away, the crew had plenty of time to launch the boats, gather their personal effects, and leave the sinking ship.

While the stern was sinking, the bow was still tight. As a result, the stern dropped deeper and deeper as the water deepened away from the rock, but the bow remained afloat. With the stern bumping along the bottom, the steeply inclined hull left a trail of materials and cargo as the wreck dragged eastward with the flood tide. The *Wallace* trail no longer deepened, but maintained the one-hundred-foot depth for quite a distance before stopping near a submerged ledge. At such a steep angle, an aft bulkhead could not withstand the weight of the cargo in the hold and gave way, allowing much of the

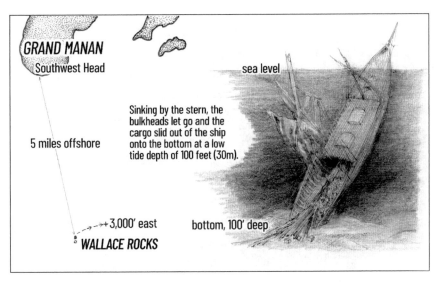

GRAND MANAN
Southwest Head

sea level

Sinking by the stern, the
bulkheads let go and the
cargo slid out of the ship
onto the bottom at a low
tide depth of 100 feet (30m).

5 miles offshore

3,000' east   bottom, 100' deep

WALLACE ROCKS

A sketch of the Wallace, *illustrating how there could be a pile of heavy cargo in deep water and no ship to be found on the bottom.*

cargo to slide out of the stern into a series of piles on the bottom of the bay. Considerably lightened, the wooden hull floated and drifted away on a more even trim and washed ashore near the southern end of Grand Manan. (This explains why piles of cargo were found near the Murr Ledges, but no ship.)

Saint John merchants were left short by the loss of the *Wallace*, so much of their merchandise was reordered from suppliers in England. On October 2, 1841, the 890-ton ship *Queen* set sail from Liverpool under the command of Captain Edward H. Huggins, bound for Saint John. It was also a Saint John ship, built there in 1840 by William and Isaac Olive, and owned by John Hammond. Coming into the Bay of Fundy, it struck North Rock, near Machias Seal Island (only about ten miles to the west of the rock that claimed the *Wallace*). Most of those on board were saved, with the exception of a passenger, but the ship was a total loss, sinking in deep water eastward of the rock.

The parallels between the two shipwrecks are quite striking: both were Saint John ships; both built in 1840; both sank in deep water to the east of their respective rocks; both were bound from Liverpool for Saint John with general cargoes. Indeed, even the dishes carried were strikingly similar. The *Queen* sank in deep water—over 200 feet deep—in an area known for scallops, and over the years scallop fishers have dragged up hundreds of dishes, bowls, and cups believed to be from the *Queen*. Many of these were donated to the museum on Grand Manan. I took some of the best dishes from the *Wallace* cargo to the museum, and we developed a display featuring both. The similarities are really quite remarkable. As the *Queen* sank about six months after the *Wallace*, it would be reasonable to speculate that some of the *Queen* cargo was intended to replace that which was lost in the wreck of the *Wallace*.

The *Wallace* cargo expeditions were at their height in the mid-1960s. A succession of greedy speculators arrived on Grand Manan Island with their teams of divers to look for the fabled piles of copper. Nobody trusted anybody else. The speculators, furtive in their comings and goings, not trusting the divers to tell them all that was down there, were quite suspicious of negative reports. One of the speculators hired a local fish dragger, Captain Garfield Wilson with the *Samella*, for his expedition. In the search area he would drop a heavy anchor on the end of the dragger's otter trawl cable, pay out extra cable, and do a large, loose, circle sweep. As and when the cable caught on something, he would send a diver down to investigate. Invariably the cable snagged an old anchor or a projection of submerged ledge. However, on one catch, the diver—Dusty Miller, an English salvage diver who had come to the expedition from salvage work in Newfoundland—reported a large pile of green rods, but being nearly out of air, he surfaced without being able to put a buoy line on the pile to return to later. Since copper takes on a green patina after extended time under the sea, this was certainly what the speculator wanted to hear.

Of course, the frenzy intensified, as everyone wanted to find "Dusty's pile." When the Saint John team went home one weekend, I went to the area with a local boat and crew. The weather was bad, with too much wind and heavy sea to tie the boat to the other party's buoy line. Nevertheless, as soon as we reached the buoy, I dropped over the side and went down the line and hunted around. With the rough seas, it was too dark to see anything in the deep water, and we had to give up for the day. The speculator quickly returned, but there was ongoing mistrust between divers and speculators; divers were sent back, more divers were brought in, and more searching exercises yielded negative results.

After the speculator sent a final batch of divers back, I offered to hire on, on the condition that I work underwater alone; I didn't trust the other divers either, but I did trust the local captain and boat crew. I spent a couple of weeks working with the expedition, doing their underwater searching, keeping careful notes of what areas we covered. I became familiar with the ocean floor in this search area: the large pile of iron rods, heavy chain extending across bottom, trails of other wreckage. But Dusty's fabled pile continued to elude us as our vessel groped about, dragging cables around the bottom, and I was sent down to check each snag. It struck me as a most haphazard way to try to find a target, but I wasn't hired to plan, just to dive.

Despite all sorts of promises, no paycheques came, so the captain, crew, and I made a trip to Saint John to visit the backers of the expedition. Our attempts to be paid for our work were as fruitless as the efforts to find the pile of copper. Returning to Grand Manan, we found that the speculator had skipped out. He had, however, left a few things aboard the boat, which we divided up and claimed. For some time after, I referred to an old work sweater as my "thousand-dollar sweater."

With the expedition dissolved, I took the information I had gained and, over the following winter, worked with Gordon MacDonald, a salvage diver from Prince Edward Island, to cover the area with underwater search patterns. We scoured the area and determined that "Dusty's pile" did not exist. Perhaps Dusty had seen the pile of iron rods and, in the greenish light of the hundred-foot depth, had thought the rods to be green in color. Whatever the explanation, great riches from the *Wallace* cargo were not to be.

During the course of these and later explorations of the *Wallace*, I did happen on several interesting discoveries. Cases of brass spikes of different sizes were quite a novelty. One of the most interesting concretions contained a wide variety of items: cutlery, handsaws, files, tortoise-shell combs, jackknives—to name but a few. Samples of these made an interesting display for the museum.

Later, I spent time surveying, photographing, and sketching the *Wallace* cargo. At this time, I limited my recovery of items to dishes, china, and bottles of different sorts—things that would not be as apt to disintegrate after being removed from the seawater. Although the *Wallace* has not yielded much material wealth, it has truly been one of the most interesting shipwrecks I have visited and worked, and it certainly has enriched the seafaring lore and tradition of Grand Manan Island and its Museum.

WINDSOR'S RAILROAD IRON: THE BRIG *GLIDE*

While the early settlers of our Maritime provinces relied on schooners to be the workhorses of coastal trade, they also envisioned building railways to tie together over land the new and growing settlements; to link communities and carry their people and goods of trade. In the early years, the iron for the railways came from England in sailing ships, delivered to the port nearest the railroad under construction. In the mid-1850s, when the Nova Scotia Railway was expanding its operations in Nova Scotia, the railway construction company ordered a shipment of iron from Great Britain. The brig *Glide*, under the command of Captain Ellis, sailed from the River Clyde in Scotland with a cargo of 195 tons of railroad iron: rails, chairs, and spikes. It stopped at Halifax and then continued on its voyage, headed for Windsor at the head of the Bay of Fundy. The cargo was intended for the Windsor Branch of the Nova Scotia Railway which opened in 1858. And, of course, to carry railroad iron from Halifax to Windsor required an ocean voyage all the way around the southern tip of Nova Scotia.

As the *Glide* was coming up the Bay of Fundy in the early afternoon of Saturday, September 1, 1855, the weather worsened and wind strengthened to a sou'-sou'west gale. By six o'clock, it had started to rain and the whole evening was dismal weather, with flashes of vivid lightning. During the night, thick fog shut in, and the *Glide* was completely dependent on the dead reckoning of Captain Ellis, all on board relying on his confidence in his estimation of the brig's position. But Captain Ellis had not realized how much his brig had been carried off course by the strong crosscurrents in the bay, nor had he made sufficient allowance for the heavy winds blowing his vessel to the north. He had committed a fatal error in reckoning.

At noon on Sunday, September 2, the fog lifted, and the light-keeper at Gannet Rock light, Walter B. McLaughlin, discovered a full-rigged brig sunk on the breaker to the southeast of Yellow Murr Ledge—"with her round tops out of water at high water," he noted in his journal.[20] From his light station some five miles away, all he could see clearly were the sails, and he carefully noted which sails were set and which were stowed. He could see no sign of life on the brig and assumed that the wreck had been abandoned. Using the signal guns at the light station, he made the proper signal for a wreck on the Murr Ledges, to advise the people of Grand Manan of the shipwreck.

Over the next couple of days, several vessels visited the wreck, but no word of the crew was ever discovered. Indeed, for quite some time no one even knew the name of the brig wrecked on the breaker

Walter B. McLaughlin, my great-great-grandfather, was head lightkeeper on Gannet Rock from 1853 to 1880, when he transferred to the Southwest Head light on Grand Manan, where he remained until 1900. (GRAND MANAN ARCHIVES)

(which is now called Glide Rock). On Tuesday, September 4, McLaughlin himself went over to the wreck in his small boat from Gannet Rock. He noted in his journal: "She is a Clipper Brig of about 300 tons Burthen and quite new. She is built of this country wood. Her spars and mast heads are painted black. Her cargo seems to consist of Railroad irons."[21]

It is likely that when the brig struck the ledge, it immediately started filling and settled away on the top of the breaker. It was likely flood tide, and the captain probably knew that with a heavy cargo of railroad iron he had no chance of floating his vessel off the rock, and if he did manage to free the brig from the ledge, it would probably sink immediately in deep water.

In the thick fog, Captain Ellis believed that he had struck a ledge off the coast of Nova Scotia, not realizing the effects of Fundy's strong crosscurrents. No doubt he gathered up the ship's papers, ordered all hands into the boat, and they left the wreck and almost certainly headed east, thinking they would soon land on the Nova Scotia shore. They likely pulled on their oars past Gannet Rock, to the south of the light station, not knowing in the fog that they were headed further out into the bay. This was, of course, long before fog alarms were put in place at light stations, and lighthouses were completely useless as navigation aids in thick fog. Once out in the open bay, their small boat swamped and all were drowned, for no sign of any of the crew was ever seen again.

Within two weeks, the vessel was well broken up. Lightkeeper McLaughlin noted in his journals of September 13 that he "saw the topsides of the wreck with mainmast drift past the Rock."[22] As the wreck broke up and disappeared with still no trace of the crew, the event soon faded from local memory.

~

The Glide Rock is a sunken breaker about a quarter mile southeast of the Yellow Murr Ledge (a channel of deep water lies between them). The rock steeply rises up from a depth of 66 feet to its crest just under the surface at low tide. In 1973, I visited the wreck over a period of several days, surveying the site, and drew up plans of the wreckage. As the brig's wooden hull broke up, some of the iron cargo spilled down over the steep ledge, though much of it simply remained where it was, lodged on top of the rock.

With the wreck being in such an exposed location, I really didn't expect to find much of the wooden hull. Only the heavy iron cargo could remain unmoved by the breakers crashing incessantly over the reef. Almost everything seen, measured, and plotted was iron from the cargo. Several rails spilled down over the side, completely clear of the other wreckage on top.

With the loss of all on board, little is known of what happened to cause the casualty, but what has been left on the bottom quietly guards materials that help to describe an early Maritime railway of the 1850s.

SHIPWRECK EXCITEMENT: THE BARQUE *PARKFIELD*

In the early 1860s, the demand for consumer goods in the Maritime provinces was growing. The economies of Canada West (formerly Upper Canada) and Canada East (formerly Lower Canada) had not become sufficiently industrialized to address this market demand, and the United States was preoccupied with the internal struggles of a civil war. Great Britain had important market opportunities in the Atlantic colonies: transatlantic shipping was strong and growing.

The 495-ton barque *Parkfield* was built in 1854 and was registered in London, England. In March of 1863, the *Parkfield* was in London loading a general cargo for Saint John, NB. It was a valuable general cargo to satisfy the necessities and fineries of colonial households in the city; a cargo that included brandy, wine, cutlery, paints, oils, dry goods, and carpets. The barque sailed for Saint John under the command of Robert Williams, a thirty-three-year-old Scot.

The Crews List noted the names of all the crew on board, their position, age, place of birth, last ship, last port of discharge, and wages. (An able seaman earned two pounds and fifteen shillings a month). I am struck by how young the crew was. Of the seventeen members of crew, thirteen were twenty-five or younger, and at thirty-three, the captain was the second-oldest man aboard. Certainly the way of the windjammer was a young person's life.

After an uneventful trip across the Atlantic, the *Parkfield* headed up the Bay of Fundy. On Wednesday, May 13, it tacked up by the Gannet Rock light in a light easterly breeze. With all sails set, it was a pretty picture. Gannet Rock's lightkeeper, Walter B. McLaughlin, described the vessel as he watched it sail by, its white clouds of canvas standing out against a backdrop of mist and drizzle. As it continued up the bay on it's starboard tack, McLaughlin became concerned and said to his assistant, "If she does not tack before long, she will hit the Old Ledge."[23]

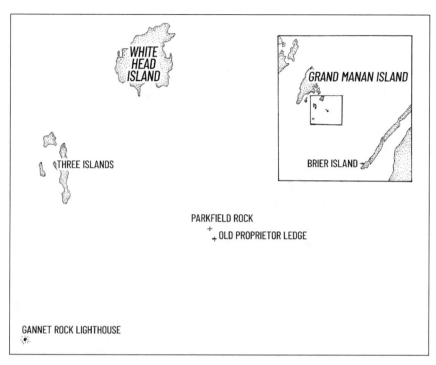

This map shows the proximity of Parkfield Rock to Old Proprietor Ledge.

At 11:30 A.M., the *Parkfield* struck a sunken breaker about a quarter of a mile inshore from Old Proprietor Ledge on what was later to be called the Parkfield Rock. The sea was calm and the crew did all they could to try to free it from the ledge, but it held hard and fast on the rock and would not be moved. A boat went out from nearby Kent Island in the afternoon, but then thick fog and mist shut in, deterring other small boats from attempting to reach the barque. The following morning the fog rose with the sun, and McLaughlin noted in his journal: "At 5 [A.M.], saw the barque still on the rock, also saw some wreck stuff floating near the [light]Station. At 7 A.M. saw two boats and one vessel go to the wreck." [24]

The wind that day breezed up to become a strong gale, preventing further salvage and battering the wreck mercilessly. Throughout the night and early morning hours of Friday, May 15, a strong easterly gale raged, pummelling the barque on the rock. Late in the afternoon the weather cleared, and from Gannet Rock McLaughlin noted that the wreck had disappeared, "but the water is covered with boxes, bales and casks as far as the eye can extend."[25] The following day, in the light breezes of Saturday afternoon, the lightkeeper "saw a number of vessels and Boats picking up wreck stuff among the rest, two Pilot Boats. They all seem to have loaded."[26]

A boat from Seal Cove was at the wreck picking up goods that had floated out of the ship, and had been quite successful in gathering up wooden casks of brandy, wine, and other liquors. Of course, all hands had to sample the goods frequently to ensure that the saltwater hadn't damaged anything. As they sailed about checking out the flotsam on the water, they came upon a large crate drifting with the tide. Bringing it aboard, they opened the crate to discover just the accessory as would befit such gentlemen adventurers: the finest silk top hats to be found in any London shop. Nothing else would serve the moment as appropriate head covering. Dressed like bankers in rubber boots, they put in the grandest day of their lives, picking up wreck stuff in their top hats, sampling fine brandy, and altogether having a rather jolly time.

The venerable nineteenth century evangelist, Reverend Joshua N. Barnes, spoke of the loss of the *Parkfield* in less than glowing terms in his autobiography, *Lights and Shadows of Eighty Years*:

> *In May, 1863, I made my first visit to White Head Island.... The people were a hard-working class, poor but honest, and were much neglected in religious things by the Christian Church.... Just as things began to look bright and hopeful, an untoward thing happened. An old ship called "The Parkfield" was wrecked on a rock just off Gannet Rock. The vessel was loaded with general cargo, such as liquors, cutlery, paints, oils, dry goods, carpets, etc. Every available*

boat was manned and put out to pick up the wreckage. As
we had only a few women at the afternoon service the fol-
lowing day, we decided to leave the Island and go home.
Very much of the liquor picked up was in casks, and was
scattered all over this Island, and the Main Island.[27]

The evangelist, his religious revival, and his classes all played a distant second fiddle to the excitement of a shipwreck cargo at Old Proprietor Ledge.

The next day, McLaughlin noted he "saw a few vessels and boats picking up wreck stuff"[28] but, by this time, just about all that would float up from the wreck had drifted off. Over the next couple of days, the vessels and boats sailed back and forth across the area around Old Proprietor Ledge looking for flotsam from the *Parkfield* cargo. A week after it had struck, little was left, and activity around the rock was waning.

Captain Judson Guptill of Grand Manan chartered his schooner *Guide* to the underwriters for some of the salvage work in the days following the stranding. As the *Parkfield* had broken up so quickly, the hull and cargo were sold at auction on Monday, May 18, for $328. Mr. Cline, the pilot, was the successful bidder. It was surmised in a contemporary newspaper, that it "will doubtless make a good speculation."[29]

One would speculate that the customs officers and ship's agents only located a portion of the cargo brought ashore. Lloyd's of London reported "200 to 300 packages, principally wines, spirits and oil"[30] were brought to Saint John and sold. But stories continued to be handed down over the years, of hidden caches of liquor, stashed here and there on the outer islands of Grand Manan. The customs officer from Saint John, visiting Grand Manan to seek Queen Victoria's share of the *Parkfield* booty, had expected to find half of the people of Grand Manan drunk. But to his surprise, he saw very little evidence of the vast quantity of liquor salvaged from the wreck and waters near Old Proprietor Ledge. Locals were not about to open up their indulgences to official-looking strangers. For years and years afterwards, tales persisted about casks of brandy buried on Wood Island. Many a futile shovel has turned over suspicious sods in a vain search for these elusive prizes.

Little remains of the *Parkfield*. The rock named after the ship is located about a quarter of a mile inshore from Old Proprietor Ledge. During the late 1960s, I swam around the area, but found nothing to suggest the wreck of the lost barque. The bottom there is strafed by powerful tidal currents and battered by seas from every direction, so I did not expect to find much. Nevertheless, the loss of this barque certainly provided a lot of excitement and windfall salvage to brighten the spring and summer of 1863.

THE INTACT SUNKEN SHIPWRECK: THE BARQUE *MAVOURNEEN*

Yarmouth, NS, was a Maritime shipping port significant far beyond its size. Supported by a modest population and economy, Yarmouth ships were seen in ports and on the seas all over the world. From the shipyards in little coves along southwest Nova Scotia came a steady stream of wooden shipping to be registered in Yarmouth, and to carry the Yarmouth hail with them to every imaginable port on the globe. The barque *Mavourneen* was launched at Tusket River on Friday evening, June 17, 1864, from the shipyard of Nathaniel Churchill. It was registered in Yarmouth at 618 tons. It was well-built, being braced internally with iron knees. Owned by a consortium of Yarmouth businessmen, the *Mavourneen* set out optimistically to take its part in world trade.

In the fall of 1866, under the command of Captain Cornelius Murphy, the *Mavourneen* sailed in ballast from Portland, ME, bound for New River, NB, to load lumber. On October 22, in dense fog, it went ashore at Gooseberry Point, in Bradford Cove, on the west side of Grand Manan Island. It floated off at high tide the following day, but its hull was so badly strained that it filled with water almost immediately and sank just off the shore at a low-tide depth of 85 feet. It settled upright on the bottom with a slight list inshore, its topmasts breaking up through the surface of the water where they remained visible throughout the following year. After the masts broke off, the wreck at the bottom of the sea was soon forgotten.

In the early days of purse seining inshore around Grand Manan in the 1950s, fishers set their seines—large nets hung vertically—for herring in many of the coves around the island. Fishers quickly learned to avoid that particular spot after tearing their seines badly on an especially rough piece of bottom just off Bradford Cove. When I started looking for shipwrecks in the mid-1960s, I took special note of what fishers had encountered, for they, more than any others, really know the bottom of the sea. Sailing very slowly back and forth off Bradford Cove in the *Moon Dust*, with my fellow diver Buddy McLaughlin, to investigate this purse seiner nemesis, we noted a very interesting target on the depth recorder—a target that gave the appearance of overhang. After crossing the target two or three times, we dropped the anchor as close to it as possible.

I was all suited in diving gear and chased the anchor line down to the bottom where I discovered a shipwreck only about ten feet away. Swimming the length of the wreck, I was elated. The ship was relatively intact, undisturbed. Just about everything was there in its proper position, although wrapped up with torn remnants of purse seine. I was particularly elated as I thought we had found the *Charlotte*, the fabulous shipwreck of local tradition (described in Chapter Two). However, in more dives over the next two weeks, I was bothered by the lack of any evidence of cargo, and the wreck was too large for a brig. To clinch the argument, I came across a

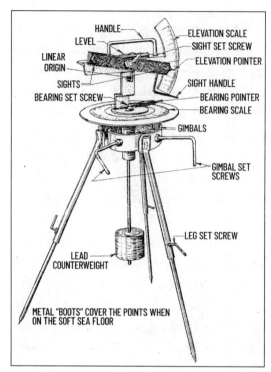

HANDLE
LEVEL
LINEAR ORIGIN
SIGHTS
BEARING SET SCREW
ELEVATION SCALE
SIGHT SET SCREW
ELEVATION POINTER
SIGHT HANDLE
BEARING POINTER
BEARING SCALE
GIMBALS
GIMBAL SET SCREWS
LEG SET SCREW
LEAD COUNTERWEIGHT
METAL "BOOTS" COVER THE POINTS WHEN ON THE SOFT SEA FLOOR

The Polar Coordinate Survey Instrument (POCOSI)—designed and built for underwater survey of shipwrecks.

reference to the loss of the *Mavourneen,* and everything I had found fit the description of the Yarmouth barque.

I soon lost interest in the wreck and didn't visit it often until I started the underwater archaeology project with the National Museums of Canada and the New Brunswick Museum. The shipwreck was in such good condition that it seemed worthwhile to attempt to study it comprehensively. I took several rolls of photographs around the shipwreck as there was so much of interest. But as I looked at the photos and thought about the large expanse of the shipwreck and how one could only see a small part at one time, I felt I had to survey the wreck and convey the appearance of the whole shipwreck rather than snippets in photographs.

Since I was working alone, I had to develop a survey method I could do myself. So I designed a survey instrument: the POCOSI, or Polar Coordinate Survey Instrument. With this instrument, and a tape measure, I could relate all points within visibility range (usually six to seven metres, or twenty to twenty-five feet) to a central origin. Then I would move the POCOSI across the bottom and set up with

Barque *Mavourneen,* wrecked in 1866
Drawn by Eric Allaby, March 1974
2m Scale: ━━

A drawing, developed with the help of POCOSI, of the Mavourneen *shipwreck.*

a new visibility range, relating the new range to the previous origin. As I surveyed, I plotted the relationships of the surveyed points and also took more photographs to give details.

Returning home after each dive, I plotted the survey and developed a fairly accurate map of a portion of the shipwreck. I transformed this map into a pictorial rendering and plotted several scales around the drawing to allow viewers to get a sense of the size of objects in different parts of the wreck. The result was, I felt, something of a breakthrough in representing shipwrecks pictorially. Others agreed, and I presented papers on the technique at international conferences on underwater archaeology. POCOSI was a sort of primitive underwater precursor to Google Earth.

The *Mavourneen* was a good testing ground for this survey technique that could provide people with an accurate rendering of a shipwreck. Indeed, it is a rendering that even divers cannot see, for limited visibility will not allow such a complete view to be taken. While this shipwreck provided no commercial gain from salvage, it did yield this new tool for the field of underwater archaeology.

THE STRANDED TUG: THE *GYPSUM KING*

The gypsum in the ground in the Windsor area of Nova Scotia, at the head of the Minas Basin, provided not only a livelihood for the local people, but also the basic raw material for plastering the interior walls in the homes of New England. This led to a very particular kind of seagoing trade in the Bay of Fundy. Gypsum is a bulky, heavy commodity of low value for its weight. As a result, small schooners found it increasingly uneconomical to carry gypsum. Schooners were built larger and larger to maximize payload. Still, shippers continued to search for cheaper ways to carry it from the mines near Windsor to the manufacturing plants in the United States.

As steam-powered shipping took over the major trade routes of the world, a new opportunity presented itself to bulk shippers in the coastal trade, and the gypsum trade in particular. The great wooden hulls of square-riggers had tremendous carrying capacity. With sail deferring to steam, such hulls could be obtained cheaply. These hulls could be turned into barges, so the vessels did not have to rely on their own power but could use the great carrying capacity of the old ship, with the steam power of a newer vessel to tow it. Powerful tugs were built to tow barges of gypsum from Minas Basin to the great market of the eastern United States. The J. B. King Transportation Company of New York was expressly interested in this trade opportunity.

At Port Richmond, NY, in 1899, a large oceangoing tug of 233 tons was launched. It was built of steel, with masts fore and aft, and was 154 feet long, 29 feet wide, and 16 feet deep. Named the *Gypsum King*, its express purpose was to tow barges back and forth between Nova Scotia and the eastern United States. Over the next few years, the *Gypsum King* became a familiar sight in the Bay of Fundy. Indeed, its master was a Saint John man: Captain Fred Blizzard.

There are times in winter when ice can cause problems in Minas Basin, so Halifax was sometimes used as the Nova Scotia terminus for gypsum cargoes. On January 15, 1906, the *Gypsum King* left New York with the empty barge *Daniel M. Munroe* in tow. The tug called at Eastport on Friday, January 19, for orders; should they proceed to Windsor or Halifax? The answer was Halifax, so the tug set out the next day, anchoring in the lower harbour until the following afternoon, on account of thick weather.

Even though the fog remained thick, the tug set out again. At about 4:00 A.M. on Monday, January 22, the *Gypsum King* struck on the St. Mary Ledge, the outermost of the Murr Ledges off Grand Manan. The fog was still dense, but the wind was calm at the time. Nevertheless, a heavy swell was rolling in from the open sea, and the St. Mary is an exposed ledge. The tug had struck so hard that it could not be backed off, and the heaving and pounding of the swell soon broke a hole in its bottom. Within an hour or two, the *Gypsum King* slid off the ledge until its stern wedged against a sunken breaker.

The crew of a dozen men took to the boat and, with only a compass to guide them, they rowed through the dark fog for Grand Manan, eventually reaching Seal Cove. With the tug ashore, the small crew of the barge had no alternative but to abandon it too, and they followed the tug's crew to Seal Cove. The barge drifted off into the night. A large barge was seen a few miles off Petite Passage on Wednesday, January 24, drifting up the bay on the flood tide with no lights and apparently no one on board. Observers thought it to be the same barge, but it was too rough for boats to check more closely to ascertain its identity.

When the tug crew arrived at Seal Cove, the weather cleared, and they engaged a boat to take them to Eastport so they could hire a tug to return to the *Gypsum King*. While they were gone, Seal Cove men Leavitt Benson and Lewis Brown went off to the wreck. Some years ago, when he was close to ninety years of age, I talked with Leavitt about his recollections of this visit to the wrecked tug. He told me:

The Gypsum King's *bow ran up on the ledge and the stern sank in deeper water beside the ledge.*

> *The captain said that he put her there on purpose because he wanted a bigger, better boat. He was a drinking man, you know. Lewis Brown got a phonograph and some records off it. She was a nice steel tug, well equipped. We got some medicine off it, and the searchlight, and the steering wheel, but we saw a tug coming, so we left. The captain and crew went to Lubec and got a tug to come back to her. We were the only ones to go on her, and it was starting to breeze up southerly, and she was working some when we left.*

The St. Mary Ledge is one of the outermost of the Murr Ledges and the seas and heavy swells pound it constantly. So the chances of a successful salvage operation were slim. Nevertheless,

Captain John Ingersoll, the master of the *Aurora*—the steamer that connected the Island of Grand Manan with mainland New Brunswick—purchased the wreck of the *Gypsum King*. The captain paid only $175 for the wreck, so it was generally acknowledged that the chances of recovering much of value were slim, as the tug lay on the offshore side of the ledge, stern submerged, with large holes in its bottom and only eight feet of its hull out at low tide.

The captain wished to save some valuable fittings from the wreck. But the following week, before the salvors had a chance to strip much off the wreck, a heavy wind hit the Murr Ledges, and the *Gypsum King* slid off the ledge, broke up, and disappeared under the waves.

~

The *Gypsym King* lay undisturbed for over sixty years. On Friday, June 7, 1968, Carman Cook and I visited the St. Mary Ledge with Deverne Green in his lobster boat, the *Judy N.*, to look for the remains of the tug. We sailed around on the offshore side of the ledge, getting a sense of the bottom profile from the depth recorder. I dropped to the bottom in the spot where I felt that I would be most likely to find the wreck. Drifting down to the bottom at a depth of 35 feet, I was pleasantly surprised to land right on the condenser. Looking around, I also found a generator, boilers, steam engine and shaft, and a great deal of copper pipe from the tug's engine room. Since we were there to try to locate and recover scrap brass and copper, this was an exciting discovery.

Over the course of the summer, we returned several times to the *Gypsum King* and, with the aid of several cases of dynamite, systematically took the engine room apart and recovered brass bearings, several pumps, copper pipes, and brass valves. All in all, it was a productive venture.

WRECKAGE OF THE OCEAN GOING TUG
GYPSUM KING

Before the creation of POCOSI, my early renderings of shipwrecks were purely subjective.

During the course of the work, we found the cast brass steering pedestal (it was brass so as not to influence the compass that had been mounted on top of it). Although this weighed about 250 pounds, it was too interesting to sell for scrap, so it ended up at the Grand Manan Museum. Another item that went to the museum was a small brass cannon, probably used for firing lines onto other vessels or barges, which could haul the towing hawser over from the tug to the vessel to be towed.

I recorded the wreckage area over the summer and, in the fall of 1968, I decided to convey the layout of the wreck in a pictorial way while the area was fresh in my memory. It was an interesting challenge to put these areas together to make up the whole site, while trying to be faithful to the actual relationship of the parts, one with another. This is even more difficult because underwater visibility is only about seven metres or so, much smaller than the scope of a shipwreck, so there is no way that I could see or photograph the whole ship at once. What I put together was a purely subjective impression; I made no attempt to measure or survey the site.

Nevertheless, developing a pictorial rendering of a shipwreck to share with the world above sea level, a world of people who have no chance to see the shipwreck for themselves, was an exciting challenge for me. It motivated me to look for more in shipwrecks than brass and copper. I decided to come up with a more accurate way to express to this world what a shipwreck looks like.

This started me on a path to a Ford Foundation fellowship to work in this field. That, in turn, led to a National Museums program in underwater archaeology, during which I developed POCOSI, the survey technique that would allow for the plotting of survey information into a perspective rendering, a technique that I was able to use on other shipwrecks with much greater accuracy than the subjective impression portrayed on the previous page.

Although the *Gypsum King* was generous in brass and copper, I most fondly remember the shipwreck as the project that sparked my interest in expressing what a shipwreck looks like to the world above the sea, leading to work in this field for several years.

CHAPTER FOUR

BROUGHT DOWN BY FUNDY'S CURRENTS

CUNARD LOSES THE STEAMER *COLUMBIA*

I n 1839, regular steam navigation across the Atlantic was first established. In the euphoria over the possibilities of this new technology, the imperial government of Great Britain advertised for tenders to carry mail to America on a regular schedule. Samuel Cunard of Halifax was the only party prepared to enter into such a contract. In company with George Burns of Glasgow and David MacIver of Liverpool, Cunard entered into an agreement with the British government to run a mail steamship service between Liverpool, Halifax, and Boston in return for an annual subsidy of £81,000. The service was to be fortnightly in the summer and monthly in the winter. This line was, at first, known as the British and North American Royal Mail Steam Packet Company, a cumbersome title that was soon dropped in favour of the simpler Cunard Steamship Company. The signing of this contract marked the actual

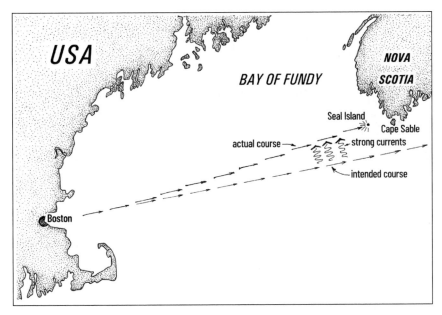

This map shows the last voyage of the Columbia, *compared to its intended course.*

beginning of regular transatlantic service. The pioneer ship of the new Cunard Line was the steamer *Britannia*. Joining it were the ships *Acadia*, *Columbia*, and *Caledonia*. The names are suggestive of the transatlantic venture, tying together interests in England, Nova Scotia, America, and Scotland.

The steamship *Columbia* was built, as most steamers were at the time, with masts and spars capable of carrying sufficient sail to power the ship with wind almost as effectively as with steam. Launched in 1840 by Robert Steele, the *Columbia* was rated at 1,138 tons and was 207 feet long, 34.2 feet wide, and 22.5 feet deep. Its side-lever steam engine was rated at 425 horsepower, which, powering the ship with paddles 28.5 feet in diameter, drove at a speed of 8.5 knots.

The *Columbia*, under the command of Captain Shannon, set sail from Boston on the afternoon of July 1, 1843, bound via Halifax for Liverpool. It carried eighty-five passengers, their baggage, and a general cargo. A pilot was on board as the ship set out in thick fog, and he took a prudent course that should have allowed the ship to clear the southern extremity of Nova Scotia by some twenty-five miles. The next morning, churning confidently through the fog at full speed, the *Columbia* suddenly piled up on a ledge, its momentum pushing itself far up on the reef, picking its bow up out of the water. The *Columbia* had hit Devils Limb, a reef just to the west of Seal Island, well out to sea west of Cape Sable.

Only two families lived on Seal Island at the time, that of the lightkeeper, Richard Hitchings, and the family of a Mr. Crowell. As soon as they heard the distress guns of the steamer, Hitchings's two sons and hired men went out in a small boat in the dense fog, at considerable personal peril, to provide aid to the stranded *Columbia*. Their skilled assistance allowed the passengers to be taken safely to Seal Island throughout the afternoon and following night. All landed without a mishap. This was a notable achievement, considering the conditions under which Hitchings's sons and hired men had to carry out this rescue. That they were successful stands as a tribute to their skill, seamanship, and courage on the water.

No one could imagine how this steamer, with a pilot on board, a good compass being faithfully followed, and a prudent course chosen, could end up so far off course. The *Columbia* had fallen victim to an unexpected and very powerful current at the mouth of the Bay of Fundy. Captains of other ships sailing from Boston at about the same time reported being carried as much as sixty miles off course by the powerful current. These others had near misses with Nova Scotia islands and reefs but avoided actual stranding.

One of these, the packet brig *Acadian*, also out of Boston, was similarly drawn into the Bay of Fundy by this current. After this error was discovered as the fog cleared, in heading out of the bay past Seal Island, the *Acadian* soon came within view of the stranded *Columbia*, perched high on the rocks of Devils Limb. Captain Jones, Master of the *Acadian*, stayed by the stranded steamship for several hours before proceeding for Halifax. When he left, he took along the third mate of the steamer who brought news of the catastrophe to the city, news which certainly caused a great stir.

All efforts made to try to float the steamer off the rocks failed; it was firmly held amidships, its bow high in the air. Working in the heavy seas, the hull was soon hogged and twisted, and the ship soon started breaking apart.

As this occurred, the heavy machinery soon settled away to be lost at the bottom of the sea. Meanwhile, the passengers, safely landed on Seal Island, were cared for there as well as circumstances would permit. The mail was also saved, landed on the island, and guarded there carefully.

⚙ "Hogged" means the ship is bent along the keel, the centrepiece along the bottom of the vessel, with the bow and stern sagging.

The steamer *Margaret*, the reserve ship of the Cunard Line, sailed for Seal Island early on the morning of July 5, with Samuel Cunard himself proceeding to the scene of the mishap. The *Margaret* picked up the passengers and mail, and took them to Halifax without delay. On July 9, only one week from the day of the disaster, the *Margaret* then sailed onward from Halifax for Liverpool, taking the mail and those passengers wishing to proceed immediately. Some passengers, however, decided to stay in Halifax and await the next regular packet.

Regular transatlantic steamer service was certainly still in its infancy, and Cunard was deeply aware of the need to maintain travellers' confidence in these new steamships and in his line in particular. He went out of his way to ensure that passengers were conveyed in safety, in as much comfort as possible, and with minimum delay. His efforts did not go unnoticed, as made evident by the remarks of a prominent Boston citizen, the Honorable Abbott Lawrence. Lawrence publicly thanked Samuel Cunard in Halifax on behalf of the shipwrecked passengers, before sailing on to Liverpool. Cunard's reply demonstrates his dedication to providing efficient, comfortable customer service in which all could have utmost confidence, qualities that would be closely identified with the Cunard Line as it grew to be the passenger shipping line that set the standards for others to imitate: "You may rest assured that I shall do everything in my power to send you on to England, with as much comfort as possible, and without delay. I shall not soon forget the kind disposition manifested by all of you in seconding my wishes. The duty I had to perform was made easy by your valuable assistance, and I beg to assure you that I shall always be happy to meet you again."[31]

OPULENCE AND OPTIMISM DASHED: THE STEAMSHIP *VICEROY*

A *Halifax Chronicle* article, reprinted in the *Yarmouth Herald* of June 17, 1850, lavished praise and expressed great hopes for transatlantic shipping with the arrival of the brand new steamer *Viceroy*, on its maiden voyage from Galway, Ireland, via Halifax, for New York.

> *The beautiful iron Steamship Viceroy, [with] Capt. Ewing, arrived in our harbour on Thursday last at 5 o'clock P.M. The Viceroy left Galway on the 1st of June, at about 10 o'clock A.M. She has thus accomplished the distance in little more than ten days.... It were needless to say that this pioneer of an entirely new era in Ocean Steam Navigation, was received with a hearty welcome. She came into port amid the cheers of a multitude, and the firing of cannon. Thousands of persons visited her on the evening of her arrival and during yesterday.[32]*

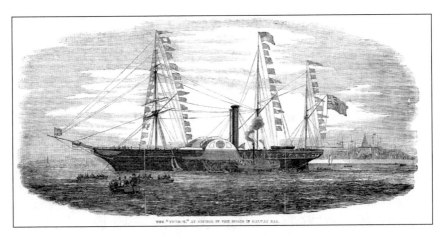

A print from the London Illustrated News *of June 8, 1850, showing the new steamship* Viceroy *leaving Galway, Ireland, with great fanfare on June 1 on its first voyage. On June 24 it was wrecked off Nova Scotia.*

The next article about this ship in the *Yarmouth Herald* just ten days later dashed all grand expectations: "The Irish Steamer *Viceroy*, on her return trip to Galway, is ashore on Shag Harbour Island— supposed to have struck on Monday night. It is feared that she will be a total wreck. H. M. Surveying Steamship *Columbia* is on the spot rendering assistance. In our next we shall probably be enabled to give full particulars of the deplorable disaster."[33]

The *Viceroy* had just been launched, was owned in Dublin, and was intended to establish a transatlantic service between Galway and New York, stopping each way at Halifax. A fine iron steamer of 800 tons, rated at 350 horsepower, its voyage to New York had been filled with great promise, as was noted in the first newspaper article quoted above. It unloaded in New York, stowed American cargo for Ireland, brought aboard passengers, and set out, under the command of Captain Ewing, to return to Galway with a stop at Halifax.

After leaving New York, fog enveloped the ship, and Captain Ewing set his course to go well out by Cape Sable. No doubt the *Viceroy* fell victim to the same currents that had drawn the steamer *Columbia* to its ignoble demise at Seal Island just a few years before. At half-past seven on Monday evening, June 24, 1850, in dense fog, the *Viceroy* ran ashore on rocks off Outer Island near Shag Harbour, not far from Cape Sable.

The passengers landed at Barrington in the surveying steamship *Columbia*'s boat (not the same steamer *Columbia* that wrecked a few years before) and were taken from there to Halifax. The crew remained at the ship to try to save the vessel. The *Viceroy* bilged (the lower part of the hull was broken and pierced) below the engine room. As the tide ebbed, the ship settled down on the rocks, worsening the damage, and flooding the engine room.

The *Columbia* returned with the steamer *Plumper* to assist in the recovery of the materials, furniture, stores, and cargo. The presence of these government vessels was helpful, not only to aid those doing the salvage work, but also to discourage looters. Over the week that followed, materials and furniture were brought ashore in Yarmouth. Six hundred empty barrels were secured in the hold of the *Viceroy* in an attempt to float the ship on the tide. Unfortunately, the weather interfered, and the hull broke up beyond repair. The ship was condemned as a total loss. All effort after that was directed to recovering whatever was salvageable.

There was a lot of interest in the auction of the ship, materials, and furnishings, which took place in Yarmouth at ten o'clock on Thursday morning, July 25. Along with a list of the ship's materials was a list of the furnishings that gave an indication of the opulence that had just been lost: "Rose wood Chairs, Settees, Tables, Mirrors, Paintings, Carpetings, Side Boards, with marble Slabs; Stools, Polished Steel Grates, marble cased; Brass Pipes for do., steel Fire Irons, silver plate, Glass & Earthenware, hair Mattresses, and Bedding, a large lot of linen Table Cloths, sheets and towels, and damask Curtains."[34]

Dennis Horton of Yarmouth purchased the wreck for £850. More of the heavier deck fixtures—such as davits, winches, and anchors—were offered at auction on July 30, and salvaging the machinery from the ship continued over the following months. Over the course of the following year, salvors recovered the engines and machinery, and brought them to Yarmouth. Agents arranged to sell these in New York, and in the fall of 1851, dockworkers loaded the engines, boilers, and machinery from the *Viceroy* on the Yarmouth brigantine *Gipsey* to be taken to New York.

The misfortune following the *Viceroy* was not yet fully dispensed. When it was three days out of Yarmouth, the crew abandoned the *Gipsey* at sea, and it sank with its heavy cargo of steam engine machinery from the new paddle steamer. The *Viceroy*, a new steamship that had held such great promise, brought down by the tidal currents of Fundy, broken up on Fundy rocks, had not even a reprieve for its new and valuable machinery.

HORRIFIC LOSS OF LIFE: THE STEAMER *HUNGARIAN*

The Allan Line steamship *Hungarian* sailed from Liverpool, England, on February 8, 1860, bound for Portland, ME. Along with the transatlantic mails and a general cargo, it carried 45 cabin passengers, 80 steerage passengers, and 80 crewmembers; a total of 205 people were on board. The *Hungarian* was a fine new 1,487-ton steamer, just built in 1859 by W. Denny & Bros. It was considered the finest ship of the Canadian Steam Company. Outfitted with a propeller instead of paddles, it was described as "a splendid iron screw steamer."[35]

Under the competent command of the experienced Captain Thomas Jones, all on board embarked on the trip with confidence. In fact, one of the passengers in a letter sent from England noted that he had delayed passage in order to travel on the *Hungarian* with Captain Jones. Nevertheless, the perils of such a voyage were well known, as indicated in an extract from a letter written by William Boultenhouse, a passenger from England, to his father on January 31, just before the *Hungarian* sailed. "I almost dread coming home in the month of February, but feel anxious to get home to my family…. It is awful work to cross the Atlantic in the winter season; with a new ship, as you do not know how she will work."[36]

The steamer successfully weathered the unpleasant winter passage across the North Atlantic. However, as it prepared to pass the southern tip of Nova Scotia on Sunday night, February 19, the *Hungarian* encountered a snowstorm. But snowstorms were common, and poor visibility was a fact of navigation, so it continued its westward course through the night.

At three o'clock on Monday morning, February 20, 1860, Thomas Nickerson, of Barrington, NS, saw lights of what he supposed to be a steamer off in the direction of the Horse Race (a treacherous shoal about a mile south of Cape Sable). There was a heavy sea running, with westerly wind and snow squalls. At daylight a large steamer was seen on the Great Rip (a tidal current rushing over a shoal), the mainmast and mizzen-mast standing, the rigging appearing to be crowded with people.

The heavy sea broke continuously over the ship and the westerly gale strengthened, buffeting the *Hungarian* with each crashing wave. There was no way to provide help from shore. By ten o'clock, the masts and smoke funnel had broken off and disappeared. The iron ship was falling apart fast, with no hope for those on board. Large numbers of buoyant packages from the wreck floated on the surface of the sea, drifting with the tide, but the ship itself went to pieces, and all 205 people on board drowned.

On Tuesday morning—the weather having moderated—hundreds of boats and small craft set out in search of the floating cargo and succeeded in saving much of it. Several of the mailbags were also picked up and sent on to Halifax to be forwarded to Portland. One of the steamer's boats drifted ashore at Port La Tour, bottom up, and bodies were discovered washed ashore all along the coast. With each discovery, every effort was made to try to learn the identity of the victim.

The loss of a fine new steamer and 205 lives was certainly a major catastrophe. With no survivors, the inquiry was forced to draw conclusions from all the evidence that could be obtained from shore. The inquiry established that there had been a grave dereliction of duty on the part of the lightkeeper at Barrington, on the mainland of Nova Scotia; on the night of the wreck, the light was not burning. If not the main cause of the tragedy, this was certainly a contributing factor.

The *Hungarian* broke up in about 25 feet of water, so the cargo was readily salvaged. Accordingly, the remains of the hull and cargo were sold at auction on March 15 for £4,070. Dennis Horton was the successful bidder. He was a principal in a Yarmouth consortium formed to realize a business opportunity in salvage from the wrecked steamer.

During the following spring and summer, divers working for the salvage company brought up large quantities of cargo, which were boated ashore and sold at auction. According to the advertisements in the newspapers of the day, the ship carried a wide variety of merchandise and manufactured goods. But the task was not a pleasant one for the divers.

Probably the best-known salvage diver of that day was Mr. Sheridan, of Halifax. He made several dives into the wrecked steamer and described what he saw in a Halifax newspaper in April 1860:

> *The scene that presented itself was appalling in the extreme:*
> *for although there were no corpses in the interior of the ship,*
> *there were nearly twenty bodies discovered entangled in the*
> *wreckage alongside and in the gullies close by.… These fright-*
> *ful remnants of poor humanity exhibited all the stages of dis-*
> *memberment, sans heads, arms, legs, &c., and all more or less*
> *in a state of decomposition. Those seen appear to have been up*
> *and dressed, or partly so, as some of them were evidently in*
> *the act of putting on their shoes, stockings, or other clothing*
> *when the king of terrors put a stop to their toilet for ever.*[37]

A newspaper correspondent for the *Yarmouth Herald* described a trip to Barrington in mid-July 1860. A highlight of that trip was a visit to the *Hungarian* to watch divers at work:

> *Four divers descended almost simultaneously. We got glimpses of them occasionally, moving at the bottom. Over their heads the escaped air rose in continuous bubbles to the surface. Fragments of cloths of all sizes and colors could be seen entangled at the bottom. The boilers and cylinders were plainly visible—the former 5 or 6 feet and the latter 3 feet below the surface.... It was an interesting, exciting scene. But our mind could not be diverted from melancholy reflections. We thought of the origin of these operations—of what had occurred on this spot on the morning of the 20th of February, 1860.[38]*

The shallow water allowed the cargo to be removed almost entirely and the ship to be stripped of most of the machinery before the summer was over. Little now remains of the mighty steamer *Hungarian*, but divers still visit the remnants on the bottom, off Cape Sable, from time to time.

THE QUESTION OF FAULT: THE STEAMER *WARWICK*

The Saint John Board of Trade was jealously thin-skinned about any perception that the Bay of Fundy approach to their port might hazardous for ships. Even back in Loyalist days, there was a vigorous rivalry between the ports of Saint John and Halifax, with newspaper editorials sniping back and forth between the cities. After the development of the railways, this competition intensified as each port vied to become the winter port of choice for Canada's Atlantic trade. Any time a ship bound for Saint John came to grief on a treacherous Bay of Fundy reef, the port promoters in Halifax could barely contain their exultation under a thinly-veiled cloak of nautical sympathy. The Saint John Board of Trade tried to affix blame on the ineptitude of ships' officers, rather than suggest that the approaches to their port were anything but perfectly failsafe and benign to incoming shipping. It was against this backdrop that the drama of the *Warwick* played out.

The Donaldson Line steamship *Warwick* left Glasgow on December 15, 1896, bound for Saint John with a general cargo of about 600 tons. The ship was an iron tramp steamer of 1,595 tons register, built in 1882, and sailing under the experienced command of Captain George Kemp. Most of the cargo consisted of coal for the Canadian Pacific Railway, along with iron and steel in sheets, bundles, and angle bar. The steamship also carried merchandise for Saint John stores. Of considerable added interest were fifteen hogsheads of beer and several hundred cases of Scotch whisky. Along with the thirty-three crewmembers were nineteen passengers—cattle ranchers returning home to Ontario.

The passage across the North Atlantic was typical for December: a succession of gales, cold winds, and rough seas. They had sufficient clear weather from time to time to take celestial observations to confirm the ship's latitude and longitude and trace their progress toward the Bay of Fundy port. Their reckoning was confirmed by the sighting of the Cape Sable light, which was passed eight miles away at 1:00 P.M. on Wednesday, December 30, 1896. Captain Kemp adjusted the course to clear Seal Island, which was passed four miles off, about 3:30 P.M.

First Mate Lauchlan McDonald took his watch at four o'clock in the afternoon. The weather was fine, with a little haze on the horizon, allowing those on the bridge to see nine or ten miles around them. The captain joined McDonald on the bridge frequently, and they maintained prudent observations, reckoning, and soundings.

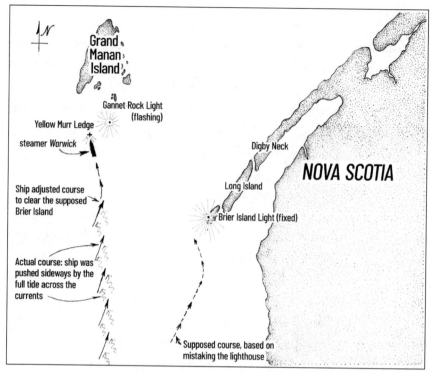

This map shows the Warwick's *intended course and its actual course after being pushed sideways by the currents.*

There was no cause for concern as the soundings continued to confirm their reckoning according to the chart. The ship was steaming along at full speed, which for the Warwick was eight or nine knots, and all seemed to be in order, other than a growing breeze building up a considerable sea.

Captain Kemp was cautious in his approach to Saint John. At eight o'clock, he decided to alter the ship's course to try to see the Brier Island light. Keeping an eye on the Brier Island light would ensure that the currents wouldn't carry them into the treacherous Murr Ledges off Grand Manan. McDonald concurred. They adjusted their course accordingly.

About 9:30 P.M., a bright fixed light was sighted almost directly ahead of them. Captain Kemp discussed this with Second Mate Bernard Webb, who noted that the Brier Island Light was reported on the chart to be a fixed light. The Gannet Rock light, off Grand Manan Island on the north side of the south channel, is a flashing light. The captain was puzzled. While he was looking for the Brier Island Light, he did not expect to see it almost directly in front of him. Both the captain and second mate trained their binoculars on the light and agreed that it was, indeed, fixed. Captain Kemp made up his mind that this must be Brier Island light. Shortly before ten o'clock, he changed course, and then again and again, all much more northerly courses. He was anxious to keep clear of Northwest Ledge, off Brier Island. The veteran navigator confidently maintained the ship's heading.

All of a sudden, Captain Kemp saw water breaking dead ahead. He ordered the engines reversed. The engineer responded immediately, but it was no use; within two or three minutes the *Warwick* struck the rocks with a crash that shook the vessel from stem to stern. It slid up on the massive, solid ledge and ground to a halt. Second Mate Webb looked at his watch: it was 10:40 P.M., about two hours after high tide. The ship was well aground and, with engines churning astern, steel plates groaned and cracked as the steamer rose up and pounded down on the ledge in the heavy sea.

The holds began to fill with water. Captain Kemp ordered the engines stopped and made no further attempt to try to back the ship off the rocks. With the holds filling, should he have been successful in powering the steamer off the rocks, there was a very real risk of the ship sinking, putting all on board at even greater risk.

Conceding the ship, the captain turned his attention to saving the lives of his crew and passengers. The ship had struck on the southeast corner of the ledge, so with more open water on the starboard side, the crew readied the two starboard boats within ten minutes of striking. With a strong wind and heavy seas, the captain considered it prudent for all to stay on the ship until daylight came, at least as long as the ship held together and there was no immediate danger of it breaking up. Furthermore, as the tide ebbed, the seas broke all around them. To launch a boat into such boiling surf would be foolhardy and was only to be considered in utter desperation.

Within an hour after striking by the bow, the steamer's stern had swung around westward, grounding out on the shallows that extended off from the ledge. The first mate tried to determine the ship's heading from the compass on the bridge, but the binnacle light was out, and he was unable to see the compass. Nevertheless, he judged that the bow was heading east-by-south. The fixed light was still visible, but it was now seen over the port bow, and appeared to be about five miles off. The mate and captain discussed this, still fully convinced that because the light was fixed it must be Brier Island. But this puzzled them, for they could not imagine what they could have struck, and furthermore, they felt they should have been able to see the Cape St. Marys Light from this position.

As the steamer filled with water and the tide ebbed, it lost all floatation and no longer rose with the sea, but lay on the hard ledge bottom, breaking successive swells into swirling torrents about the deck and driving spray over everything. The starboard side, now completely broadside to the sea, took the full brunt of the crashing combers. Indeed, the heavy seas washing over the ship carried away the two starboard boats that had been readied earlier. It was impossible to stay on deck, and all rooms below deck from midship aft were full of water. All hands that could fit huddled into the bridge, and the others were forced to shiver in what shelter they could find in the forecastle. Using the port boats to leave the ship was now out of the question; as the tide ebbed, the shallows between the ship and the ledge crashed and broke with surf and foam. There would be no choice but to wait for high tide the next morning to make an attempt to leave the ship.

Between three and four in the morning, Captain Kemp saw that the fixed light was now flashing. Consulting the chart, the captain and his mates came to the correct conclusion that the light they had seen was the Gannet Rock light, and that meant the steamer was ashore on the Yellow Murr Ledge. The question of why the light appeared to be fixed when it should be flashing would not be addressed until the inquiry into the wreck.

The westerly wind continued through the night with thick fog and cold, driving winter rain—a thoroughly awful night on the Yellow Murr Ledge, and a miserable night for all on board the doomed *Warwick*. Morning, however, brought a change in the wind. The fresh northwest breeze cleared the air, but also brought with it the icy breath of the Arctic. On Thursday morning, December 31, the weather had cleared sufficiently that the keeper at the Southwest Head Light Station, Walter B. McLaughlin (formerly of the Gannet Rock lighthouse), was able to discover the wrecked steamer. He sent a messenger to tell Mr. Harding, the inspector of marine and fisheries in Saint John, to send a vessel to help the crew. The messenger hurried the five miles from the light station to the village of Seal Cove, carrying with him the handwritten message for the telegraph office to send to Saint John, and a message for any Seal Cove seafarers who might be able to go out in a schooner to the Murr Ledges.

The Gloucester, Massachusetts, schooner *George S. Boutwell* had come into Seal Cove a few days earlier, looking for a freight of frozen herring. Built in 1869, it was old and feeble, and had been nursed up the coast from shelter to shelter. Nevertheless, it was at anchor in the harbour, with a full crew aboard, and ready for sea, so when the messenger arrived with the news of the wrecked steamer, the captain and crew were willing and eager to be of assistance. Some of the seafaring men of Seal Cove came along too, as they were more familiar with the waters, the hazardous reefs, and the treacherous currents.

The weather turned colder with the northwest wind. Icy spray drenched the hapless sailors and passengers on the steamer, and the arctic chill sapped what heat they tried to retain among them. The very survival of the men on the *Warwick* was sorely threatened. Fearing that the ship would break up, and with no shelter on the

Yellow Murr Ledge, the captain felt that the best possibility for survival would be to take to the boats and head for the light station at Gannet Rock, clearly beckoning only five miles away. By eleven o'clock in the morning, the high tide had turned, and the ship lay in the ebb tide eddy of the ledge, but there was still a good depth of water between the ship and the ledge on the port side. The conditions were as good as the captain could expect, and he launched the two remaining boats on the port side between the ship and the ledge.

The crew and passengers were ill prepared for this ordeal, having among them but a few overcoats and blankets, so they suffered terribly in the chill wind and biting ice spray. Loaded almost to the gunwales, and mustering all the sail the small boats could stand, the little crafts were taking in water at an alarming rate as it slopped in over the low sides, keeping all occupants busy bailing with whatever utensil could be found at hand. As they tried to work across the wind toward Gannet Rock, they found themselves being carried back by the ebb tide and being driven out to sea by the wind. Their efforts to reach Gannet Rock looked to be in vain as they were carried helplessly away, and the warmth and safety of the light station faded from their hopes.

The old *Boutwell* was a welcome sight, scudding and lurching toward them across the seas. Creaking along under all the sail the old masts would stand, the growing bone in its feeble teeth was a sure sign of help on the way, a new hope of survival over death from exposure to the bitter cold.

Captain Surette of the *Boutwell* lost no time in deftly bringing his schooner alongside the lifeboats, swamped with water and floating on air tanks, their occupants miserable, drenched, and cold. The many willing

❀ "Bone in its teeth" is a nautical phrase referring to the white foam churned up at the bow as a boat pushes through the water.

hands on the *Boutwell* quickly lifted each person out of the open lifeboats, pulling them up by ropes looped around them, and led them immediately to warm, dry shelter below deck on the schooner.

With all the cold, wet seafarers and passengers from the doomed *Warwick* aboard, the old schooner wheeled about and beat back into the shelter of Seal Cove Harbour. The shipwreck survivors were all kindly cared for by the people of the village as they recovered from their ordeal over the next couple of days, until they could be taken in the Grand Manan steam ferry to the city of Saint John. An appreciative British government later presented Captain Surette with a magnificent pair of marine binoculars for his role in saving the shipwreck survivors.

$\sim$

With the return of the *Boutwell* to Seal Cove, Mr. Nairn, a representative for the Donaldson Line, engaged the steam tug *Storm King* to go to Grand Manan to do whatever could be done to salvage the cargo. Nairn and the *Storm King* sailed from Saint John on Thursday night, arriving at Seal Cove by 7:30 A.M. on Friday, January 1. Nairn made arrangements in Seal Cove with local fishers and labourers to go to the wreck to recover cargo. Mustering its crew, and with the schooner *Emma T. Storey* and several fishing smacks in tow, the *Storm King* set out for the Murr Ledges.

However, the *Storm King* and its train were not the first salvors to reach the wrecked *Warwick*, for several Seal Cove fishers had gone out earlier to do some salvage of their own on the early morning low water. When the tug arrived, they discovered that the after cabin had been stripped of its furnishings and the delights of the hold discovered. Lloyd Cheney was involved with this undertaking, and wrote of the day in a letter several years later:

> *Well, I was there, and gentlemen there will never be another such New Year's day celebration on the Yellow Muir [sic] Ledge if the world should last a million years.... My uncle*

stood a cask of Guinness Stout on end, knocked in the Head and setting a large Chamber Mug on top, made it possible for everybody to indulge at will.... I saw men picking one bottle after another, breaking off the neck, sampling and throwing the rest away. I'll bet there were people there that never tasted Liquor before. But to cap the climax was when Frank Benson started for Home. Towing five or six bottles, towing astern on fishing lines and hauling in a different Brand every time. I have often wondered, which had the biggest load by the time they got to Seal Cove, the Boat or the Crew![39]

Nevertheless, the *Storm King* later returned to Seal Cove, towing the *Emma T. Storey* and several other smaller schooners containing a respectable recovery of salvage. The schooner *Higgins* and several smacks flocked around the wreck until dark and, on the evening low water, took all the cargo they could.

Back ashore later that evening in Seal Cove, there was considerable revelry (results of the earlier, unscheduled salvage expedition). During the official investigation into the stranding, a local witness offered the opinion that "some of the packages were broken open by the sea." He went on to state that when he got back ashore "there was considerable drinking. Everybody had a bottle, but [he] could not tell where it came from."[40]

Over the course of the next day, Nairn succeeded in securing seventy-five cases of whisky from fishers in Grand Harbour. The wreckers were reluctant to give up other goods, but finally consented to turn them over to the customs officer. All that was saved was gathered for further shipment to Saint John, where it would be sold at auction. The difficulties and frustrations he had encountered in gathering up cargo prompted Nairn to denounce the people of Grand Manan in the severest terms, characterizing them as "robbers of the hardest type."[41]

By Monday, the low tide had advanced to mid-morning, so this was the opportune day to carry out salvage at the wrecked *Warwick*.

From his vantage point at the Southwest Head Light Station, McLaughlin reported counting twenty-eight smacks and schooners at the wreck, along with two tugs. By the end of the tide, the *Storm King* had saved over four hundred cases of whisky, along with canned goods, carpeting, crockery, and other cargo, which the *Storm King* set out with for Saint John. Captain Kemp of the *Warwick* went along in the tug also and, by letter, left the wreck in the charge of the local wreck master, F. M. Gordon of Seal Cove. The agents for the Donaldson Line, aware of the condition of the wreck, turned it over to the underwriters.

On Monday, a report from Grand Manan to Lloyd's reported that the *Warwick* "lies in an exposed position, and it is expected she will go to pieces first southerly gale." The report continued: "Survey held yesterday reports that the vessel is strained and broken amidships, rudder gone, tide ebbing and flowing in her, masts and smokestack still standing. They consider it an impossibility to get the steamer off and recommend that she be sold and every effort made to save the remainder of the cargo."[42]

As he considered the rapidly deteriorating condition of the steamer, wreck master Gordon sent notice to the Saint John agents of his intention to sell the vessel and cargo on their behalf. However, the owners, Donaldson Bros. of Glasgow, had abandoned the steamer to the underwriters at Lloyd's. The agents in Saint John, therefore, advised Gordon that they could not authorize the sale and cautioned him to seek proper authority. Gordon sent further telegrams, advertised, and then conducted the sale on Tuesday, January 12, 1897. Claiming confusion over the legality of Gordon's authority on the matter, Saint John parties did not attend, so only local Grand Manan interests were at the sale. Isaac Newton of Grand Harbour purchased the vessel for seventy-five dollars and what remained of its cargo for fifty dollars.

The inquiry investigating the steamer's loss first convened a few days before the sale, on January 9. Captain Smith presided, with Captain William Thomas and James Hayes, of Saint John, as nautical assessors. The first witnesses to appear before the inquiry were

First Mate McDonald—who outlined the uneventful voyage across the Atlantic and into the bay and the condition of the ship's equipment—and Second Mate Webb, who added his recollection of the courses steered and the lights observed as the *Warwick* steamed up the Bay of Fundy.

This was all background information, duly recorded and reported, but the real question on everyone's mind pertained to the Gannet Rock light: was it fixed or was it revolving? Because Captain Kemp had seen it as fixed, he had thought that he was observing the Brier Island Light, not the Gannet Rock light, which was supposed to be a flashing light. Several of the ship's crew corroborated the captain's observation that the light was fixed. To add to the mystery, another witness was called, Captain Thompson of the ship *Treasurer*, who testified that he was in the bay on December 23 with a local pilot, Henry Spears. Sighting Gannet Rock after 8:00 P.M., Thompson noted that it looked more like a fixed light than a revolving light, and mentioned this to the pilot, who remarked that it was sometimes that way.

It certainly did not look good for the Lighthouse Service; all evidence pointed to a fault with the revolving mechanism at the Gannet Rock light. In preparation for the inquiry, John Kelly, inspector of lights for the marine department, went to Grand Manan to seek some testimony in support of the light station. On Thursday, January 7, he visited Walter McLaughlin at the Southwest Head light station to question him on the light at Gannet. McLaughlin was a highly respected veteran of the lighthouse service, having spent over thirty years at Gannet Rock and another sixteen years at Southwest Head. The Lighthouse Service desperately needed a favourable testimony from a witness of this stature. Kelly sent a triumphant telegram back to the inquiry committee saying McLaughlin would testify that, at nine o'clock. on December 30, the revolving light at Gannet Rock was indeed revolving!

As insurance to clinch his case, Kelly took affidavits from the cattle ranchers on the *Warwick* that, after December 24, the captain and crew of the steamer had drunk a considerable amount. Kelly hoped to blame the captain and crew for being too drunk to tell whether a light was fixed or revolving, and then seal his case by having McLaughlin testify that the light was working properly, and showing the correct flashing signal.

There was some question of the admissibility of these affidavits as evidence, as they were circumspect and suggestive. The officers and crew vehemently denied them, and witnesses on the rescuing schooner did not support them either. But the Board of Trade was desperate to lay blame on the ship's crew, stating that it "would use every possible effort to get the facts brought out as the subject matter of the [i]nquiry was of Vital Importance to the port of St. John."[43] But the case really rested on the evidence of their star witness, the venerable keeper of the Southwest Head light. He was the authoritative witness to answer once for all the question about the light at Gannet Rock: was the light revolving or was it fixed?

When Walter B. McLaughlin took the stand, he corroborated the Board of Trade's contention that the Gannet Rock light was revolving when he looked at it at nine o'clock on the evening of December 30. But before Inspector Kelly could breathe his long-awaited sigh of relief, McLaughlin dropped a bombshell that completely turned around the direction of the inquiry. He stated that, although he was fully satisfied that the revolving mechanism of the light was working, it would have appeared to be fixed to Captain Kemp and his crew. He explained that in cold weather, frost formed on the windows of the lighthouse, and this frost reflected the light beam when the signal was supposed to be in eclipse. McLaughlin went on to point out that the very short eclipse in the Gannet Rock sequence could easily be lost in the light reflection off frosted glass, and he could support the captain's contention that the light had appeared fixed.

Then, to exonerate Captain Kemp with even more finality, McLaughlin noted that where the *Warwick* was wrecked, six vessels had been lost during the past forty years and all had been looking for the Brier Island light. All the casualties had occurred on the spring tides, when unusually strong crosscurrents carry ships well off course. He stated that soundings off both lights would give similar information: if a ship cast a lead at a presumed bearing and distance from the Brier Island light, the depth would be similar at the same bearing and distance from the Gannet Rock light. So, McLaughlin could readily explain how the *Warwick* was carried so badly off course by the spring tides. The effect was made greater by the strong southerly wind, and this error would not be discovered because frost on the windows reflected light over the eclipse, making the revolving Gannet Rock light appear to be the fixed Brier Island light. The warming of the southerly wind through the night probably melted the frost, allowing the eclipse to be seen at three o'clock in the morning by the crew on the stranded steamer.

The Board of Trade and the Lighthouse Service's case did not look good. The keeper of the Gannet Rock light, A. O. Kent, was called to the stand. He explained how the revolving light worked, powered by a heavy weight that ran a clockwork mechanism. He had to crank up the weight every four hours using a hand winch. He further admitted that on cold nights the light was imperfect due to ice on the glass, and he would be not at all surprised at a stranger coming into the bay mistaking the Gannet Rock light for a fixed light. Kent stated that alcohol—which was typically provided to keepers to wash the windows—would remove white frost, but not ice; it became adulterated by the melting ice and refroze. Furthermore, the tower at Gannet Rock was cold, without any place for a stove and not so much as a hole for a stovepipe.

When McLaughlin was called back to the stand, he recalled his time as fisheries overseer on Grand Manan. In 1867, a dioptric light had been installed at Gannet Rock, and shortly after that, he discovered on frosty nights the eclipse could be seen with a telescope but not with the naked eye. Over the next few years, he tried using increasing amounts of alcohol to get rid of the ice, but with little success. He suggested that a heater be installed in the lantern, and the Department of Marine and Fisheries agreed to do this and made preparations to carry this out. In the meantime, however, McLaughlin received a transfer to the newly completed Southwest Head light station in 1880, and sixteen years later nothing had been done about installing a stove in the Gannet Rock lantern.

Captain Smith had heard all he needed to render a decision. Sifting through the evidence of several days' hearings, he exonerated the captain and crew of the *Warwick* and attributed the stranding to a combination of two factors: a strong surface current setting the *Warwick* off course and frost on the glass of the Gannet Rock light, which prevented the captain from discovering his error. The main part of the decision was presented as follows:

> *[The master] had two unfortunate circumstances to contend with, which can scarcely be said to have been under his control. As there is no proof in evidence that the casualty was caused by any wrongful act or default of the master of the ship or any of the certificated officers, and it has been shown that the said master was navigating his vessel with the utmost care, being at his post of duty on the bridge for a considerable time previous to and at the actual time of the disaster, and he has produced testimonials from his owners and agents speaking of him as a man of ability and a competent, careful official, being strictly sober and attentive to his duties, the court refrains from dealing with the said master's certificate.*[44]

This decision came down on April 8, and the matter should have been closed. But the Board of Trade viewed the findings of the court as being derogatory to the port and its approaches, and went to the Minister of Marine in Ottawa to have the court's findings overturned. For the minister even to consider doing such a thing was unprecedented and caused something of an uproar in the shipping world, with rather censorious editorials appearing in the newspapers of important shipping ports internationally. Things eventually quieted down; the master of the steamer maintained his certificate, and the Port of Saint John continued to attract shipping, in spite of the hazards in the Bay of Fundy. The Board of Trade was not anxious to speak of the *Warwick*, but looked ahead to try to find other ways to make the access to this Fundy port safer for navigation.

Back out at the Yellow Ledge, Newton Bros., the new owners of the wreck, wasted no time in getting to work at salvaging machinery and cargo from the remains of the *Warwick*. They engaged a schooner and boats to go out to the wreck, working from daylight to dark stripping and removing anything of value. A gale sprang up on Monday, January 18, and as McLaughlin observed from the Southwest Head Light Station, "the wrecked steamer *Warwick* has broken in pieces and not a vestige is to be seen from this station. She has dissolved and left not a wreck behind. The Yellow Ledge looks lonesome."[45]

$$\sim$$

This was the situation when I first visited the *Warwick* in 1966, almost seventy years after the stranding. At that time, on the very lowest of spring tides, the blades of its propeller emerged at the southwest point of the Yellow Ledge. On the ebb tide, this part of the ledge lies in an eddy, still water relatively free of current. I visited the wreck several times over the next few years, recovering brass and copper along with lead pipes, scouring the bottom for anything of value.

The scattered remnants of the *Warwick* lie quietly now, beat upon by the relentless swells of the Atlantic, strafed daily by powerful currents, but resting nevertheless, a solid reminder of the whims of the Fundy tides.

THE LOSS OF THE STEAMSHIP *HESTIA*

Thirty of her crew and four boy passengers drowned in the raging waters of the Bay of Fundy; her third mate, second engineer and four able seamen at Seal Cove recovering from their awful experience on the submerged wreck before being rescued yesterday afternoon by the Seal Cove life saving crew, the Donaldson liner Hestia lies a sunken wreck on the submerged ledges, five miles off the coast of Grand Manan.

On October 27, 1909, the opening lines of the *Saint John Daily Telegraph* relayed to the world the story of one of the worst Fundy shipwrecks of modern times: the loss of the steamship *Hestia*, which struck Old Proprietor Ledge early on Monday morning, October 25, 1909.

W. Doxford and Son built the *Hestia* in 1890 in Sunderland, England, for Donaldson Bros. of Glasgow. It was 364 feet long, 44 feet wide, weighing 3,790 tons and drawing 20 to 23 feet of water. The *Hestia* had plied for years back and forth across the Atlantic, calling regularly at the port of Saint John, and its visits heralded retail activity among city merchants.

On Sunday, October 10, 1909, the *Hestia* sailed from Glasgow, Scotland, under the command of forty-five-year-old Captain Harry M. Newman and with a valuable general cargo, bound for Saint John and then Newport News, VA. Much of the hold space was taken up by several hundred tons of Scottish hard coal, and, more importantly, hundreds of tons of iron and steel for the construction of an American naval ship in Virginia. Of considerable interest to Saint John consumers were the many cases of Scotch whisky in its holds. And retailers looked forward to the steamship's arrival for all sorts of manufactured goods, from sugar to firebrick, from pickles to linoleum, from plumbing sink traps to fabrics. It carried one of the most valuable cargoes to be destined for the port of Saint John that year.

The *Hestia* had a stormy crossing, meeting with the usual succession of gales on the autumnal North Atlantic, but there was no undue apprehension as the ship came into the Bay of Fundy to approach Saint John. The *Hestia* had a reputation for being difficult to steer, having a tendency to veer to port. But those responsible for the helm knew its idiosyncrasies and, faithfully watching the compass, felt no reason to doubt the courses they followed.

Coming into the Bay of Fundy on Sunday, October 24, 1909, Third Officer Samuel Stewart came on watch at 8:00 P.M. shortly after the steamer had passed the Lurcher Shoal. The night was misty with a southerly wind, and as the *Hestia* surged through the dark, rolling seas, its deep steam whistle was blown intermittently to warn any other ships that might be in the vicinity. The lead was cast every half hour, and Stewart was comfortable with a sounding in excess of 100 fathoms. About 11:30 P.M., the ship stopped for a few minutes, perhaps five, and as it drifted, its head dropped to port, in keeping with its eccentric steering. The captain took the bearings of a light seen off the port bow. He then reshaped his course and rang the engine room for a full headway. By midnight, the mist had cleared up some, but the wind was still blowing hard, and the *Hestia* ploughed ahead, pitching before its following seas.

Seaman William McCandless came on watch at midnight and was posted on the bow as lookout. It was dark, and the wind was accompanied by driving rain. An hour into the watch, McCandless saw something ahead that, in the pitch darkness, he took to be the form of an unlighted schooner. He immediately cried out to Seaman Archibald Murray, the steersman, who quickly spun the helm to try to bring the ship around. But before the steamer could respond, at 1:10 A.M. on Monday, October 25, the *Hestia* crashed on a submerged ledge, which proved to be the dreaded Old Proprietor Ledge.

The crash and subsequent groaning and grinding of the iron hull pinned firmly on the ledge, writhing in the heavy seas, quickly brought passengers and crew out of their sleep and up onto the deck.

Theodore Reid, the passenger who was looking after the horses in the cargo, immediately climbed into one of the port lifeboats, so as to be ready, waiting for it to be launched. This proved to be a fatal mistake, for in short order a big sea came along and, rolling heavily over the ship that already had a bad list to port, carried away both port lifeboats, and the others on the ship never saw Reid again.

Captain Newman attempted to maintain order on the *Hestia* as he considered the situation. He was still in disbelief that his ship could be on Old Proprietor Ledge. After passing the Gannet Rock light, he had been on the lookout for the light on the Old Proprietor buoy. Obviously the light was not working, as the path of the steamer would have been within feet of this buoy and no light was observed by the lookout nor by anyone on deck, nor could the buoy be seen by the stranded crewmembers clinging to the washing deck of the heaving steamer impaled on the ledge. But this was no time to worry about blame; the most immediate need was rescue. The captain had Third Officer Stewart fire off signal rockets at ten-minute intervals. This he continued to do throughout the night, but in the stormy, thick weather, the signals went unheeded. The captain ordered the ship's steam whistle to be continuously blown, but its sonorous tones were all but muted by the mighty roar of wind and waves.

The night was black, with a gale blowing and heavy seas washing against and over the ship. The captain felt it would be most prudent to stay aboard the ship and await daylight and, hopefully, better weather, before taking to the remaining lifeboats. However, as the night hours passed, the pounding on the ledge was taking its toll and the ship was settling away as it filled with water, straining and working its hull, and heeling over more and more to port.

Water covers Old Proprietor Ledge at about half tide, and the ship struck on a submerged outer part of the ledge. Sounding at the bow showed 18 feet of water, with 25 feet aft. The water was deeper amidships, so as the ship settled, the stern hit the ground on a southwest shelf off Old Proprietor. Impaled on the rock at the bow,

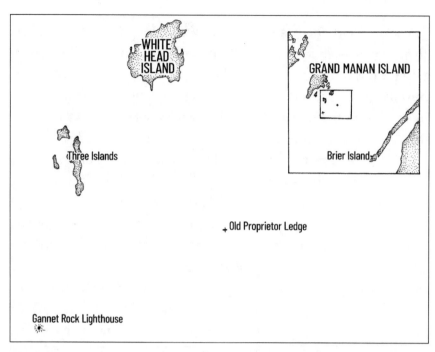

This map shows the proximity of Old Proprietor Ledge, where the Hestia *crashed, to the Gannet Rock lighthouse.*

pounding heavily at the stern, and with a heavy cargo of hundreds of tons of iron and coal, the steamer's hull strained and buckled amidships. By 4:00 A.M. the engine room was sufficiently flooded that the fires were put out and the big steam whistle was silenced.

At 5:30 A.M., while yet dark, the captain felt that the condition of the steamer was precarious and he dared not keep anyone aboard any longer, so he ordered everyone to take to the boats. Eleven people boarded the smaller of the two boats remaining on the starboard side, and the others started lowering the lifeboat into the heaving, mountainous seas. While it was still hanging from the tackle, a great sea came along and momentarily picked up the lifeboat. In that instant, the tackle holding the forward end of the boat came unhooked. As the wave swept by and dropped away, with the stern of the lifeboat still held by its tackle, the bow dropped away, throwing and spilling its occupants into the sea. One managed to hang on long enough to cut the after tackle, dropping the lifeboat among splashing, screaming, flailing bodies.

Immediately, whatever lines could be found were lowered into the darkness by those left on deck. Most of the ship's lanterns had been smashed; there were only a few small bull's-eye lanterns and they did not offer much light. Two men, Second Engineer Andrew Morgan and Seaman Colin McVicar, caught hold of the lines and were hauled on board. Another man, hanging onto a line, was hauled up almost to the rail, when he suddenly let go and dropped back into the sea. Out of the darkness and above the roar of the crashing breakers came the pathetic cry of a young Scottish lad: "Oh Mama save me!" These were awful minutes of indelible horror unfolding for those on deck, powerless to deal with the unforgiving sea. There was the sickening pounding and cracking of timbers as the lifeboat crashed and broke up against the cold steel hull. From the darkness below, the cries and screams, hauntingly audible above the roar of the storm, were quenched one by one. Within moments, nine of the eleven who boarded the first lifeboat were dead, drowned right beside the *Hestia*.

The captain ordered all hands to the larger lifeboat. He gathered up his ship's papers, stuck them inside his lifebelt, and supervised as men climbed into the boat, making sure that all were wearing lifebelts. But the two men who had just survived the loss of the other boat could not be persuaded to leave the security of the big steel ship. Four others also elected to take their chances on the stranded steamer rather than commit to a small boat on the windy, raw October sea in the cold and merciless Bay of Fundy. The captain tried to persuade them to come with him, but they would not be moved. Finally, the captain got into the boat himself, and the six who remained helped to ensure that the lifeboat was safely lowered. They stood by to assist as the tackle was deftly and safely unhooked and they watched as the lifeboat with twenty-five men aboard pulled away into the misty pre-dawn, heaving at the mercy of monster seas.

After the lifeboat left, the six remaining on the *Hestia* turned their attention to their own survival aboard the wave-washed ship. Gathering what they could find in scraps of wood, mattresses, and wooden straw-packed Scotch whisky cases, they took shelter in a lantern compartment on the starboard side of the forecastle, the heavy list submerging the port side. They whittled into the wood to get at the drier inside parts. Soaking down the wood and straw with whisky, they managed to build a fire to keep warm and hopefully to attract the attention of a passing vessel.

With the tide down, they got into the cook's galley and storeroom and hunted for something to eat. But all they could find was a large Spanish onion and a can of condensed milk, everything else having washed away. There was another small boat still aboard, and later in the morning they contemplated attempting to leave the ship in it. As they were deliberating, a big sea came along, tore it away, and smashed a side in, rendering it useless. They rigged a makeshift raft, should they be forced to leave, and lashed a cask of fresh water to it. Two men went up into the rigging and raised the Union Jack upside down as a signal of distress. They also hoisted blankets in the rigging, hoping these would attract attention. Several times throughout Monday they saw schooners passing at a distance, but the schooners did not see the remains of the *Hestia*, which was by then all but submerged.

The rising tide gradually encroached higher and higher toward the survivors' precarious forecastle shelter, and the flood tide waves rolled over the ship, dousing their bonfire. For their own protection, they were forced into the rigging. They lashed themselves there with bits of rope to prevent being swept away by the winds and blowing spray. They spent the night there, the chill wind biting through their wet clothes to make them numb with cold.

On Tuesday morning, they were raising another blanket on the foremast when they saw a schooner approaching, and although it signalled an answer to their distress, the vessel did not come by to pick them up, but bore away. This was the schooner *Mizpah*,

Seal Cove fishers and lifesavers rescued the six survivors of the Hestia *in dories.*

under the command of Captain Joseph Gaskill, of North Head, Grand Manan. Captain Gaskill soon returned to North Head and reported the wreck and the signals of distress, but it was too rough at the time for him to render any assistance.

The report was telegraphed to the life-saving station at Seal Cove, so help was on the way. Instead of using the lifeboat, however, Captain Frank L. Benson of Seal Cove set out in his own sloop *Dreadnought*. Accompanying him were Guy Benson, Joseph Hatt, James Dalzell, and George Russell. At the same time, Captain Loren Wilson set out from Seal Cove in his schooner *Ethel*, taking along with him his sons Arthur and John Wilson, Horace Schofield, Leonard Benson, Turner Ingalls, Ashton Guptill, Fletcher Harvey, Mayberry Russell, George Stewart, and Dr. B. F. Johnson.

The *Ethel* arrived at Old Proprietor Ledge about 1:00 P.M. and waited while two Seal Cove sailors took a dory alongside the *Hestia*, followed almost immediately by a dory from the *Dreadnought*. The seas were still running high and the people in the dory summoned all their skill and strength to stay in position alongside the wreck while holding lifelines to allow the shipwrecked men to come aboard. The first man taken off the wreck was the second engineer, almost completely exhausted from exposure; he was one of the two saved from the upset lifeboat in the early hours of Monday morning. With another man lowered aboard, the dory returned to the *Ethel*, then pulled back to the shipwreck for a third castaway. The *Dreadnought* dory went alongside the wreck and took off the other three men. The *Ethel* and the *Dreadnought* returned to Seal Cove as quickly as they could. Warren Wooster, who had a store in the middle of Seal Cove, housed the six shipwrecked men in his store, and fed and cared for them there.

Word quickly spread around the community and, with great enterprise, many fishers capitalized on the situation, reaping a rich harvest in the absence of underwriters who had not yet appeared to start the legitimate salvage operations. As the *Saint John Daily Telegraph* of October 29, 1909, reported:

> *The Grand Manan fishermen are displaying great daring in their work of salving the Hestia's cargo for their own benefit. Despite the rough weather on Tuesday afternoon, Wednesday and Thursday scores of fishing boats have hovered about the wreck picking up whatever cargo floated out of the hatches and in some cases even going aboard the steamer in the face of waves fifteen to twenty feet high to search for choice packages. The preference seems to run very strongly in favour of the cases of whiskey and many thrifty "herring catchers" have laid in a supply of "Black and White" that will keep them warm for many months. To illustrate the danger and the risks that these men run to secure these prize packages it is only necessary to state that on Wednesday four dories were smashed against the side of the big steel ship. The occupants of the boats, however, all being good swimmers, escaped with nothing worse than a cold bath and a battle with the waves.[46]*

Meanwhile, over on the Nova Scotia shore, some grisly discoveries had been made. A boat from the *Hestia* was found to have drifted ashore at Salmon River, containing the body of one man, identified from the papers in his pockets as Theodore Reid of Saint John. He was the one who had climbed into a lifeboat immediately after the stranding, only to be carried away when a big sea tore the lifeboat away from its tackle. Farther down the coast at Chegoggin Point, about eighteen miles from Yarmouth, another boat marked *Hestia* was found. Overturned by the surf crashing ashore, men arriving on the scene quickly righted it. They discovered three bodies entangled in the thwarts, one being that of chief engineer P. F. Munn. Over the next few days, more than a dozen other bodies came ashore, including that of Captain Newman. They were all taken to Yarmouth to be identified and were assembled there to be given a proper burial.

On Monday, November 1, the mournful task of burying the eighteen bodies was undertaken in Yarmouth. Sailor James Smyth was a Roman Catholic by faith, and his body was buried in the Catholic cemetery there. At the Yarmouth Mountain Cemetery, the caretaker prepared a large grave area suitable for thirteen bodies, and another smaller one for the four officers. Each grave was marked with a small, engraved stone. The casket containing the body of Captain Newman was taken to St. John's Presbyterian Church, where, at 2:00 P.M., pastor A. M. Hill conducted the service for the seventeen victims. The captain's remains represented those of all the victims. The church was filled to overflowing and large numbers lined the streets. The captain's casket was completely covered with floral tributes, and people brought bouquets of flowers for the rest of the caskets at the cemetery. All the bells of the Yarmouth churches tolled continuously as the solemn procession wended its way to the cemetery. Even though the dead men were strangers, the kinship of the sea pervaded—the special bond between seafaring folk to care for one another, especially in such times of ultimate sympathy.

Of the forty-one people aboard the *Hestia*, six survived the wreck and thirty-five perished, of whom eighteen bodies were recovered and seventeen were lost. The tug *Lord Kitchener* was engaged by the Donaldson Line to take their agent to the wreck. (This vessel had also taken two of the survivors to Yarmouth to identify the bodies collected there.) Captain Gillis, of the Donaldson Line, surveyed the *Hestia* and pronounced it a total loss, noting that with favourable weather conditions, some of the cargo might be saved. The government steamers *Lansdowne* and *Curlew* were also at the scene of the wreck, the *Curlew* searching for any of the missing bodies that might show up, and the *Lansdowne* carrying government officials to verify the buoy and light, which they quickly pronounced to be in good working order (even though the newspaper questioned how they might verify this in the middle of the day).

Third Officer Samuel F. Stewart, however, had a very different story to tell. He claimed that Old Proprietor Ledge's automatic gas and whistling buoy was not working. (Captain Ingersoll of the Grand Manan ferry steamer *Aurora* corroborated this report, stating that the buoy had been out of commission since the spring.) In a letter dated October 31, 1909, Stewart wrote:

> *My direct complaint is that the Old Proprietor Ledge buoy has neither light nor fog signal, whereas it is listed as having both. It is also well known locally that this buoy has been in this condition for months.... Can anyone imagine a worse trap laid for any man than a buoy listed as marking dangerous ledges and having a light working at stated intervals, also an automatic whistle signal, whilst neither whistle nor light exist? It is simply a trap worse than any ever thought of by even old time wreckers that are now but a winter's tale. It is impossible to describe one's feelings when he finds that what he thought was his great factor of safety has proved his ruin.*

He continued his letter with a scathing attack against the light-keeper at Gannet Rock:

Again, the keeper of the Gannet admits he did not fire a warning gun because he was afraid he might wake the doctor [of Grand Manan]. Can anyone imagine a man, keeper of an outlying lighthouse, seeing a vessel standing into a probable danger, and not warning her because he thought the doctor might mistake the signal as being intended for him. A few explosive signals from the lighthouse would have been quite sufficient to warn this ship and save her from destruction; still they were not given, although the keeper admits seeing the vessel and thinking her too close in, because they might call the doctor; and the vessel was allowed to go to her end. Is there any way of describing such stupidity or incompetence?

Against this backdrop, Captain W. R. Lugar of Halifax, the wreck commissioner of Nova Scotia, convened an inquiry into the wreck of the *Hestia* in Montréal. At the opening of the inquiry, the commissioner stated that after his inquiry had concluded and his report made, the government would investigate the allegations that the Old Proprietor gas and whistling buoy was not working. The later investigation would also consider what was done following the stranding. Lugar was very clear on this; he would only entertain questions dealing with the cause of the stranding.

The survivors were the key witnesses, particularly Third Officer Stewart, who had had the watch that ended less than two hours before the ship struck. Stewart stated that the captain had been on the lookout for the Old Proprietor buoy and, since the ship had to have passed within a few feet of the buoy had the buoy been lighted, the accident would not have happened. This opinion was corroborated by Captain Gillies, superintendent of the Donaldson Line, a veteran of many years navigating in the Bay of Fundy.

Captain Lugar did not want the buoy drawn into the investigation, adding in his remarks, "No navigator should rely on floating lights when a fixed light such as the Gannet was available."

"No one will ever, I am sure, again rely on floating lights in Canadian waters," retorted Captain Gillies.

Later in the exchange, Captain Lugar noted "the fact that the light was not burning was published in all the Halifax newspapers."

"Perhaps, but not in the official notification issued to mariners by the government," responded Captain Gillies. [47]

At the conclusion of the inquiry, Captain Lugar blamed the captain of the *Hestia* for the stranding. His reasoning was based on four points: one, the presence of 800 tons of iron in the cargo caused an error in the compass; two, the master neglected to take soundings in the sight of Gannet Rock; three, sufficient allowance was not made for the effects of tides and wind; and four, the captain should have taken a bearing on the Gannet light, which was only five and a half miles away. No mention was made of the Old Proprietor gas buoy or the fact that it was in darkness.

The newspapers received this ruling with great cynicism. The headline in the *Digby Weekly Courier* stated, "Dead Men Blamed for her Loss…"[48] In a terse comment on the *Hestia* investigation, the paper summed up a great deal of the bitter sentiment felt around the Bay of Fundy on the matter: "The verdict in the wreck of the steamship *Hestia* throws the whole blame on the captain and the officers. Nothing in the verdict mentions whether the gas buoy on Old Proprietor ledge was properly lighted. In other words, the government officials do not appear to find fault with the government. The dead men are unable to defend themselves."

This *Hestia* investigation found its way into question period in the House of Commons in Ottawa. The minister of marine was attacked for allowing the Old Proprietor buoy to have remained unlighted for almost ten months, with the shipping world not being properly notified that the buoy continued to be unlighted. Hon. Mr. Brodeur, minister of marine, defended his department, claiming that the buoy was not an essential aid to navigation and that there were ample lights in the vicinity to guide mariners.

This explanation did not impress many people around the Bay of Fundy. The *Saint Croix Courier* in southern New Brunswick commented on "the fine spun argument of Mr. Brodeur that the wreck was caused by 'Gasson's error' instead of being attributable to the negligence of the department of marine and fisheries.... It is hard to find why 'Gasson's error' is responsible for the light on the buoy in question being out for ten months."

Notwithstanding the official response from Ottawa, the *Courier* did not mince words: "The department was to be blamed for neglecting the repairs to the Old Proprietor light for ten months, and it is fair to assume that if this light had been burning the *Hestia* would today be above instead of below the waves."[49]

Meanwhile, back at Old Proprietor Ledge, fishers were removing coal and other cargo from the wreck under the watchful eye of a special officer from His Majesty's Customs. The Grand Manan people denied that whisky found its way ashore on their island, adding that some had been reported drifting over to Nova Scotia, but not to Grand Manan. The customs officer apparently believed them. As November wore on, the weather prevented much being done at the wreck, and the ship was breaking up rapidly. With only a portion of its cargo removed, the wreck broke up and disappeared in a storm in early December. But that did not deter completely interest in further salvage. Over the next few summer seasons, wrecking companies returned from time to time to glean what they could find of value from the remains. After that, the ebb tide eddy of Old Proprietor lay quiet for several decades.

~

I first visited the *Hestia* on March 9, 1968. I explored all around the wreckage, my interest being in copper pipes and brass fittings, and the effort was certainly rewarded in that regard. Over the next year and a half, I returned to the *Hestia* every so often to recover brass, copper, and lead, digging into the remains of the engine room with dynamite. However, as was reported in earlier newspapers, several salvors had been there ahead of me, and the pickings of salvageable metal were slim indeed.

The fore hold yielded several interesting discoveries: carpet, fabric, rope, a sizeable shipment of lead sink traps, and even a number of tombstones. One innocuous recovery led to an amusing occurrence some time later. While exploring the wreck in 1969, I happened across three unopened jars of pickles lying together, buried in a small pocket of gravel under a steel plate. Not a lucrative discovery, but novel nonetheless. I gave one of these jars to the New Brunswick Museum. Shortly after, there appeared in the *Saint John Telegraph-Journal* a feature article about this wreck with a large photo of the pickle jar beside the smiling face of Keith Ingersoll, noted historian and curator of Canadian history at the museum at the time. A few days later, an old gentleman—somewhat the worse for his liquid indulgence—accosted Ingersoll, looking for "Pickle Puss." So, the serious and lofty significance of this historical artifact from the sea was never quite the same again!

The *Hestia* was a logical wreck to visit and survey under the National Museums program of shipwreck survey. In spite of the fact that the wreck site is in an exposed location amid strong tidal currents, with no shelter from storms of any direction, the *Hestia* actually offers pleasant diving conditions. The water is generally shallow, and the visibility is good. Storms have beaten the steel steamship wreckage and thrown the pieces into hollows and crevices. Some heavier pieces, however, have moved very little. The engine, with its heavy crankshaft and thrust bearing, connected to the heavy iron propeller shaft, has probably moved very little since the wreck first broke up after the stranding. The holds before and abaft the engine room contained hundreds of tons of pig iron, which stubbornly resisted the efforts of the sea.

Old Proprietor Ledge breaks through the surface of the water a little after half ebb. From that time of tide until shortly before low water, when the tide turns, the wreckage lies in the eddy of the ledge, free from the powerful current that flows swiftly around the rock. Old Proprietor is an awesome place. One can moor a boat on the wreck, bobbing like a duck on a millpond, and a few metres away, the Bay of Fundy roars by. Even though the water surrounding the ledge is deep, the quantity of water being pulled past the rock is so immense that it actually roars, sounding almost like a big river flowing swiftly over cataracts, even on a perfectly calm day.

This wreck site is quite large, so I modified POCOSI. Since the storms had torn the ship apart to such an extent, I felt it would be a waste of time to try to relate the whole wreck in a series of polar coordinate stations. To cover the large distances quickly, I used triangulation, obtaining changes in elevation with a depth gauge (which I corrected from time to time to adjust for the ebbing tide). Using triangulation to relate the various areas of the wreck site and using POCOSI to survey these components, I was able to do up a general layout of the wreck site, sufficiently accurate to appreciate what was there.

During the course of surveying the wreck, I happened on a most interesting discovery: three cases of Scotch. The cases were constructed of wood, about a centimetre thick, with finely dovetailed corners. The bottles were packed in straw, neck to neck. The cases were stowed with the bottles on their sides. There were two cases of Black & White and one of Whyte & McKay. Some of the bottles were broken, and seawater had infiltrated the corks of others to turn the contents into a foul-smelling liquid. But a few remained sealed and whole. Some were given to the New Brunswick Museum, but a few were checked, and the contents carefully meted out to interested historians who wanted to get a sense of the authentic tastes of the century's first decade.

The *Hestia* stranding was one of the most tragic wrecks of recent times in Fundy. The loss of the ship raised controversial questions in government; it also raised the level of accountability of the ministry of marine to maintain safe, working navigational aids. The *Hestia* has become a part of local history and lore. Its remains will continue to be a delightful place to dive, to give divers a hint of this little part of our heritage under the sea.

CHAPTER FIVE

THE TREACHEROUS BLONDE ROCK: THE HMS *BLONDE*

≈

All shipping that travels from northern Europe to the New England states must pass by the southern tip of Nova Scotia, Cape Sable. Seventeen miles to the west of Cape Sable lies Seal Island, which is about two and a half miles long by half a mile wide. Located about three and a half miles to the south-southeast of the Seal Island light is one of the most treacherous reefs of the coast—Blonde Rock. Just awash at low tide, the rock is generally hidden from unsuspecting mariners. While it would be impossible to know for certain just how many vessels and lives have been lost here, the rock was named for one of the more notable early ships to strike this rock: HMS *Blonde*, wrecked here on January 21, 1782.

Originally built as the thirty-six-gun French frigate *La Blonde*, this warship was captured on February 28, 1760, near the Isle of Man

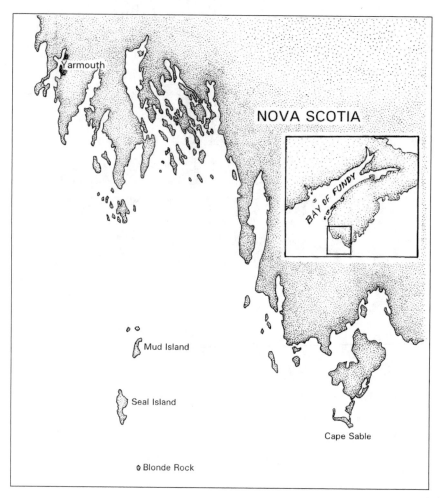

Blonde Rock—named for the HMS Blonde *—lies just off of Cape Sable, south of Seal Island.*

by HMS *Eolus*. It was recommissioned as the thirty-two-gun frigate HMS *Blonde*. Carrying twelve-pounder cannons, it saw considerable action in Nova Scotia waters during the American Revolution.

Early in 1782, under the command of Captain Thornborough, the *Blonde* captured the American privateer *Lyon* outside Salem Harbor. Heading back to Halifax with sixty-five prisoners on board, on January 21, the *Blonde* struck a sunken rock, which later became known as Blonde Rock. The crew and prisoners launched boats and reached Seal Island. Suffering terribly in this bleak, windswept island in the dead of winter, they were providentially discovered two days later when two American privateers, the *Scammell* and the *Lively*, visited Seal Island in search of water. When the landing party from the *Lively* discovered the castaways, a deal was struck: the prisoners would be released in exchange for the British sailors being set ashore in Nova Scotia. Both sides kept their word, and the crew of the *Blonde* were landed some thirty miles from Yarmouth.

The HMS *Blonde* disappeared, but Blonde Rock has continued to wreck vessels of all description, from the smallest smacks to large ships. Among the earliest recorded wrecks was the twenty-seven-ton Yarmouth schooner *Jane*. In 1810, owned and commanded by Captain Othniel Beal, while bound for Yarmouth from Boston with an assorted cargo, the little schooner was wrecked on Blonde Rock. Thankfully, all survived. Over the following years, newspaper articles reported other losses at Blonde Rock with alarming regularity.

THE CLIPPER SHIP *STAFFORDSHIRE*

The greatest loss of life claimed by Blonde Rock accompanied the wreck of one of the proudest and finest of sailing ships. The 1850s, in introducing the second half of the nineteenth century, also ushered in the zenith of square sail—the clipper ship. Without a doubt, clippers symbolized the very best the age of sail could build. Built for speed, with a profitable capacity, clippers carried more sail than had ever been imagined and were certainly most impressive to behold, with great clouds of canvas responding to a fair wind to propel the ship along even faster than the newfangled steamers. East Boston turned out the most magnificent of the clippers, built from the vision and design of Nova Scotian Donald McKay. Although the fastest sailing ship of its day was the *Marco Polo* of Saint John, NB, the Boston clippers were more widely known as representative of this ultimate sailing ship.

In 1851, McKay launched the clipper ship *Staffordshire*, at 1,817 tons, built for the Boston-based Train & Co., for their Liverpool and Boston Packet Line. It was a relatively new ship, therefore, that left Liverpool, England, on December 9, 1853, bound for Boston with 225 people on board, of whom 198 were passengers, mostly immigrants to America; two-thirds of the passengers were women.

For the next two weeks they experienced fair weather—as fair as could be expected on a winter crossing of the Atlantic. On December 24, however, the ship encountered a full gale that carried away its bowsprit, fore-topmast rigging, and rudder. Two days later, Captain Richardson went aloft to examine the damage to the fore-topmast and in doing so was caught by the wind and fell to the deck, breaking his ankle and injuring his spine. The captain was taken below to his cabin, and command of the ship then devolved on the first officer, Joseph Alden, who managed to work the ship towards its destination under jury-rigged steerage until the wind moderated on December 29. When the second officer took charge that evening in the mouth of the Bay of Fundy, he met with a snowstorm that cut the visibility to almost nothing. Dead reckoning in the bad weather was almost impossible without proper steerage, so they proceeded in the hope that the weather soon might clear enough for a celestial observation or, if not, they might at least make landfall on the coast of New England. They tried to work the ship westward as best they could, unaware of the effect of powerful currents on the ship.

At one o'clock in the morning on December 30, 1853, the *Staffordshire* struck Blonde Rock. The clipper ship came off, but had started a bad leak. In the darkness, wind, snow, and confusion, two of the boats broke adrift. The mate, second officer, and seventeen others took to a third boat and landed at Barrington at about ten o'clock the same morning. Other men took smaller boats ashore, and the schooner *Expert* picked up fourteen men from the wreck and landed them at Shelburne. However, the *Staffordshire* sank about three hours after striking, about five miles southeast of the Seal Island light. Captain Richardson declined a chance to escape. Staying in his cabin, he went down with his ship. In all, one hundred and seventy-five people drowned, mostly women. It was a rather sad commentary on the conduct of the officers that only one woman was saved.

THE STEAMER *ST. GEORGE*

In 1869, the first steamship was stranded on Blonde Rock. The eight-year-old Allen Line steamer *St. George*, registered in Montréal, sailed from Portland, ME, bound for Glasgow with a cargo of twenty thousand bushels of wheat in bags and two thousand barrels of flour. As it plied its way eastward, the steamer fell victim to the tremendous currents in the mouth of the Bay of Fundy. Badly off course during the night of April 29, the steamer was closer to the Seal Island light than the captain had thought, and at eleven o'clock, the *St. George* struck a sunken breaker off Blonde Rock, punched several compartments, and settled right there.

The steamer *Royalist* went to assist the stricken vessel the following morning and the crew, numbering fifty, were rescued and taken to Barrington. The ship broke up completely during a gale on May 2, and barrels of flour floated clear and drifted about, to be picked up by fishing boats and coasting schooners. The wrecked steamer *St. George* was sold at auction in Halifax on May 13. John Ryerson was the high bidder, paying $1,400 for the hull and $420 for the several hundred barrels of flour salvaged.

In 1891, the Furness Line steamer *Ottawa* struck Blonde Rock. The *Ottawa* was a new ship of 1,719 tons, launched earlier that same year from the shipyard of A. Stephen & Sons. On a voyage from London for Saint John, NB, carrying a general cargo, the *Ottawa* stopped in Halifax briefly on October 30, sailing from there at 1:00 P.M. the following day, down the Nova Scotia coast on its way to Saint John. All that afternoon and night, the *Ottawa* bucked a southwest gale and heavy head sea. The night was dark and rainy. The crew saw the Seal Island light in the early morning hours of Sunday, November 1, but even though they faithfully followed the compass course, the ship struck Blonde Rock at 5:00 A.M. They later blamed a faulty electric light thought to have created a magnetic field that affected the compass.

The *Ottawa* struck at about low tide, riding out on the rock on its port bow, giving it a starboard list. The rock pierced the engine room compartment, and the steamer filled with the flooding tide. As the water rose, the sea became rougher and, buffeting the bow, swung the ship broadside to the sea with an even heavier list to starboard. The rising seas swept over its deck, fore and aft.

Four men and the steward, Annie Lindsay, boarded the port lifeboat and pulled clear of the steamer. When only a couple of boat lengths away from the wreck, a tremendous sea broke over the lifeboat and turned it over. All but one man were underneath; he had managed to clamber onto the upturned keel. After a few minutes, the mate came out from under the lifeboat and also climbed up onto the keel. The lifeboat was blown by the wind and carried by the tide, upside down, toward Seal Island. The heavy seas turned to roaring breakers as the water became shallower near the Seal Island shore. The lifeboat was rolled upright again in the boiling surf. As it rolled, the two men on the keel scrambled over the gunwales into the swamped lifeboat, sluggishly wallowing in the breakers.

> ✦ A jolly boat is a type of ship's boat, usually carried at the stern, used predominantly in the eighteenth and nineteenth centuries.

Amazingly, the two other men who had been trapped inside were still alive, though just barely. They had clung to the inside of the boat—holding their heads above water and breathing the air trapped there—from the time the lifeboat had rolled over until it righted again in the surf of Seal Island. Lindsay failed to survive the ordeal, but her body was recovered as the lifeboat was assisted ashore by the people of Seal Island who had come out to help when they saw the craft being driven helplessly ashore in its piteous condition. The sailors were given shelter and simple, sincere hospitality by the kind folk, who also interred Lindsay's remains right there on Seal Island.

On board the steamer, after seeing what had happened to the lifeboat, the rest of the crew were apprehensive about taking similar chances. Awaiting the right lull in the seas, the pilot and four men launched the port jolly boat, and boarded as the tiny craft rose and fell beside the heaving, rolling steamer, groaning and grinding on the rocks. They pulled away successfully and landed on Seal Island.

The storm was worsening and the seas were rising as the tide flooded toward high water. The remaining crewmembers poured buckets of oil from the side of the steamer, windward of the final boat being launched, in an effort to smooth the seas. After the rest of the crew lowered themselves aboard, the captain was the last one to leave his steamer. By this time, the tide and wind had turned against the sailors, and they were drenched with spray as they rowed for seven hours into buffeting seas to reach Seal Island.

After the weather had abated, crewmembers went back out to the wrecked steamer to survey the situation. Leaning badly to starboard, the stern was submerged at high tide. The engine room was full of water. The rudder and rudderpost were gone. The hatches were off, and the cargo had washed out and was adrift all about the approaches to Fundy. Indeed, over a month later, candy boxes and other wreckage from the *Ottawa* drifted ashore on Long Pond Beach, Grand Manan, far across the Bay of Fundy.[50]

Blonde Rock is open and exposed to every sea and wind, so prospects for salvage were doubtful. The captain stayed by to take charge of the wreck, but the rest of the crew were discharged. On November 9, a Lloyd's agent sent a cable back to London: "Just returned from the wreck, broken in two, after part sunk, the only visible part of the wreck is 100 feet from stem at low water; has been surveyed, condemned, and will be sold."[51] Certainly prospects for salvage were very poor indeed; at the auction sale, the successful bidder was a junk dealer from Saint John, Mr. Lantalum, who bought the ship and cargo for just $55. It was an ignoble end for the newly launched steamship that had days before been the pride of the Furness Line and its English builders.

THE STEAMSHIP *ASSAYE*

The steel steamship *Assaye*, under the command of Captain Robert Carruthers, sailed from Liverpool, England, on March 23, 1897, bound for Saint John with two thousand tons of general cargo. It carried forty-four crewmembers, nineteen passengers, sixteen cattle ranchers, and three stowaways (three boys bound for Montréal to earn a living). It was a fine ship of 3,987 tons register, built in Belfast, Ireland, in 1891 by the famous shipbuilder Harland & Wolff. The *Assaye* was owned by the Elder Dempster Co. of Liverpool and had been chartered by the Beaver Line to make a number of voyages to Saint John.

After a rough passage across the North Atlantic, experiencing a succession of heavy gales, the *Assaye* arrived off Cape Sable, NS, at 8:30 A.M., April 5. The third officer was in charge of this watch, but the captain did not stray far from the bridge, returning frequently to check on the progress of the ship. He told the third officer to watch for a buoy to the south of Seal Island.

They saw Seal Island between 11:00 and 11:30 A.M., and in a short time he saw the buoy on the port bow, about a mile and a half away. The captain was alarmed: the buoy should have been visible from the starboard bow, for the ship should have gone around this buoy on the offshore side. So the captain immediately ordered "full speed astern," and "helm hard a-starboard." He wanted to stop the ship and aim the bow offshore to clear the buoy and the perilous rock it marked: Blonde Rock. Slowly, the heavy vessel came around. By the time Captain Carruthers had the *Assaye* stopped in the water, the buoy was off the starboard bow, as it should be, but it was due south of the ship. Clearly, very powerful currents were carrying the *Assaye*.

Blonde Rock is covered at high tide, making it a particularly treacherous hazard. The captain went into the chart room to check his chart to try to ascertain the ship's position in relation to the rock. Within two minutes, the ship bumped and grounded on a rock and remained, held fast there.

The captain tried to back the ship off with the engines, but to no avail; it held firm on the rock. The steel hull scraped on the ledge in the gently heaving sea and in a very short time had torn a hole in the bottom under the engine room. The *Assaye* began to leak quickly so the fires were extinguished, and the captain ordered the crew to prepare to abandon ship.

It was high tide and about noon when the ship struck. This would explain the unexpected strong currents; noontime high water occurs when the tides are higher than normal, which results in stronger currents.

The wind increased, making up a heavy sea, which made launching the boats and keeping them alongside difficult. Indeed, boats went adrift before all the men boarded and, despite their strenuous efforts at the oars, the strong current and gale carried them away. The life-saving crew from nearby Seal Island noted the stranding and in short order were alongside and taking off the remainder of the crew, the last one to leave being the captain. It was about four o'clock in the afternoon when the last boat finally pulled away from the wreck, and within about two hours, all sixty-three people had successfully landed on Seal Island. Although only a small number of people lived on the island, their warm hospitality was extended to all the castaways.

The next morning, Tuesday, April 6, dawned thick with fog. Nevertheless, Captain Carruthers was determined to return to the wrecked steamer. With a handful of officers and a boat's crew, he set out for Blonde Rock. After spending three hours groping about in the fog and carried by strong tidal currents, they eventually reached the steamer. The wreck was lying in a bad position on this lonely ledge, rolling heavily in the seas. The seas were breaking over its deck and it was filling with water. But the captain and some of his men were able to board the steamer and save some of the personal effects of the men. After the captain had fully assessed the condition of the wreck, they returned to Seal Island late in the afternoon.

The steamer *Wanda*, on its regular lobster trip, arrived at Seal Island on Wednesday morning. As soon as Captain Kinney learned of the wreck of the *Assaye*, he took aboard fifty-six of the ship's men and immediately returned to Yarmouth. The captain and some of the officers remained on Seal Island to look after the interests of the ship. Seeing that the wreck would break up in the next storm, the captain engaged fishers to salvage cargo for 50 percent of the value of the cargo successfully landed on Seal Island.

Over the next few days, fishers worked on the wreck, which lay grounded on the rock. The tide ebbed and flowed within the torn steel hull. The bow was firmly impaled on the ledge, with the stern afloat, rising and falling with the tide. Owing to the seas heaving and swirling around the wreck, steamers and schooners could not go directly alongside the wreck. This meant that all large bales and cases had to be broken open, and the goods passed by hand into small boats pulled alongside the wreck, to be carried off to larger crafts. Some of the smaller vessels shuttled goods to Seal Island and then returned to the wreck for more. Most of the salvage work was done at low tide. With a tremendous effort over the next few days, almost half of the cargo was saved, but in a damaged condition. However, islanders looted some of the cargo.

The wrecked steamer *Assaye* was sold as it lay at public auction on April 17, along with all its gear, anchors, etc., still on board. Edward Lantalum, a Saint John junk dealer, was the successful bidder, and purchased the hull and gear for $185. Fred Peterkin of Yarmouth purchased the cargo still on board for $56.

Over the next few weeks, as the hull was stripped of anything useful and removable and the remaining cargo on board was removed, the wreck settled deeper on the rock and started breaking apart amidships. Finally, in mid-November, the *Assaye* broke apart, slid off the rock, and sank into deeper water, disappearing from sight and gradually from memory.

THE STEAMSHIP *GERONA*

The steamship *Gerona* left Portland, ME, about 7:00 A.M. on December 31, 1897, bound for London. Owned in Dundee, Scotland, this 2,025-ton ship carried about 4,000 tons of general cargo, along with 300 cattle and 94 horses. Along with the thirty-eight crewmembers were eighteen cattle ranchers. The *Gerona* was ten years old, having been built by the Gourlay Bros. of Dundee in 1888.

After dropping off its Portland pilot, the *Gerona* set out on its transatlantic voyage. A celestial observation at noon established the ship's position, and the course was set to pass Seal Island and Blonde Rock at a safe berth. All seemed well with the ship as they headed out across the Gulf of Maine.

At 2:13 A.M. on January 1, the Seal Island light came into sight. On the bridge, as the light was identified, they were surprised that its bearing was only one point off the port bow. Looking at the ship's compass and course, the captain calculated that the currents had set him northward by about sixteen or seventeen miles. Estimating Seal Island to be eighteen miles off, he adjusted to his course only slightly to pass Seal Island and Blonde Rock. This was a serious error. There was a southeast wind blowing, and it was flood tide, and the ship continued to be set northward in spite of the captain's correction to the course.

At five minutes to four on New Year's morning, January 1, 1898, the *Gerona* struck something that so severely damaged the steamer that within half an hour it had to be abandoned. By the tidal currents and southeast wind, the ship had been carried to the north and had struck on the wreck of the steamer *Assaye*, wrecked on Blonde Rock less than a year before.

The ship came off immediately after striking, and the captain steamed full speed ahead toward Bon Portage Island. However, the water gained rapidly in the heavy iron hull and soon the fires in the engine room were flooded and put out. Half an hour after it struck, with 15 feet of water in its hold and the engines rendered helpless, the captain ordered all hands to abandon the steamer. Within a few minutes, all fifty-six people on board abandoned ship in three boats, saving nothing of their belongings.

News of the disaster spread quickly. Carcasses of cattle and horses washed ashore on the beaches of Seal Island, Bon Portage Island, and Cape Sable Island. Steamers set out in search of the wreck to see where it might have foundered. The tops of the *Gerona*'s masts were discovered emerging out of the water, by which the depth of the water where it lay was estimated at 20 fathoms (120 feet).

The Lloyd's agent in Yarmouth auctioned the ship on a "no cure, no pay" basis, but he received little interest from salvage operations. The only feasible operation would be to raise the ship using pontoons, but this would have been difficult in such an exposed location off southwest Nova Scotia, subject to such strong tidal currents. There wasn't the equipment in Nova Scotia to undertake such a job, so the bid was extended to Boston and New York where interest was expressed in working on a daily charter basis. However, this would have been financially risky for the underwriters.

With no bidders for salvage of the ship, the Lloyd's agent sought interest in salvaging cargo. The Boston Tow Boat Company offered to work for $600 per day, but with the ship lying in 120 feet of water in such an exposed location, little recovery could be assured each day, so the profitability of such an operation would be highly questionable for the underwriters. The general cargo was valued at $236,000 and the steamer at $150,000, so certainly if it were feasible, the rewards would be significant. But 120 feet of water reduces the amount of time a diver can spend on the bottom, and holding a diver in position with over 120 feet of hose being dragged by strong tidal currents would be very difficult, so work would be effectively confined to slack tides. In these conditions, working by the day would be profitable for the salvage company, but foolhardy for the underwriters.

Considering the difficult location of the *Gerona*, there was not much salvage to be done, even though two of the ship's four masts remained standing for a year after it sank. There it lay, with masts protruding from the water's surface to taunt salvors and tease the imagination, until the *Gerona* eventually disappeared completely from view.

~

With the arrival of radar and global positioning systems, Blonde Rock has lost much of its sting. Lurking just below the surface of the sea, the rock is still just as dangerous, but navigators are now better able to know their position and avoid the hazardous reef. No one knows how many ships have come to grief on this rock, perhaps some even predating the loss of HMS *Blonde* over two hundred and forty years ago. My records show at least fifteen vessels have struck Blonde Rock. It is hard to know the exact number of lives lost because of it, but it is certainly in the hundreds. Located near paths of shipping, exposed to the powerful Fundy currents, and hidden from view, Blonde Rock is arguably the most treacherous reef in the entire Bay of Fundy.

CHAPTER SIX

HEROIC EFFORTS

SCALING THE CLIFF: THE BARQUE *LORD ASHBURTON*

Ashburton Head is a bold cliff promontory at the northern end of Grand Manan Island. Extending into the sea from the base of the headland is a large, sail-shaped ledge that stands as a natural monument to one of the better known shipwrecks to have occurred at Grand Manan, a significant piece of the island's history.

The barque *Lord Ashburton* set sail from Toulon, France, on November 17, 1856, bound for Saint John in ballast. It sailed under the command of Captain Evan Clarke Crerar, a thirty-seven-year-old native of Pictou, NS. Crerar was a captain with an established reputation for skill and resourcefulness at sea. The crew was made up of twenty-eight men of various nationalities.

The *Lord Ashburton* had been built in 1843 by Briggs & Co. at Brandy Cove, near Saint Andrews, NB. The barque was registered at 1,009 tons, measured 155.6 feet in length, 30.1 feet in width, and 22.9 feet depth. Immediately after launching, it was transferred to Liverpool, England, where it was registered under the ownership of Robert Morrow, John Morrow, and Clarkson Garbutt, Liverpool merchants.

There was nothing unusual to suggest any sense of foreboding as the *Lord Ashburton* undertook its stormy December crossing of the Atlantic. The barque spent Christmas Day of 1856 rounding the southern tip of Nova Scotia. It continued up into the Bay of Fundy, and within a few days Grand Manan was spotted off in the distance. Fierce headwinds blew, and the captain withdrew to the safer deep waters of the open ocean to await more favourable breezes to take them up the bay. Three times Grand Manan was approached and as many times the barque withdrew.

Earlier in the voyage the *Lord Ashburton* had made contact with the barque *Mauritius*, which was coming across from Newcastle, England, and had kept company with it for a period of time out in the Atlantic. Coming up the Grand Manan Channel on Friday afternoon, January 16, the *Lord Ashburton* discovered the *Mauritius* ashore at the base of the tall cliffs along the western side of Grand Manan Island.

It was a bitterly cold -23°C as the barque continued past Grand Manan, heading farther up into the Bay of Fundy, beating against icy north-northwest winds. The *Lord Ashburton* approached Partridge Island off Saint John late on Saturday in a southwest gale. As the wind veered to the west in the evening, the captain felt it would be prudent to await daylight before attempting to enter Saint John Harbour across the wind. But the wind went northwest and blew a gale all the following day, and the barque was driven out into the Bay of Fundy and forced to try to weather the gale.

Without a lull in the winds, a northeast gale sprang up, accompanied by a snowstorm, and the barque was driven helplessly down the bay. It lay in the trough of the seas, all but unmanageable. Several times the crew tried to bring it about, but it would not respond to its helm. Twice they wore ship in an attempt to enter the more open Grand Manan Channel, but the barque would not maintain its heading, wallowing instead at the mercy of the wind and sea. Blown by the gale in blinding snow, in the black of a winter night, the doomed barque drove unwittingly and mercilessly toward Grand Manan.

At one o'clock in the morning on Monday, January 19, 1857, the *Lord Ashburton* struck a rugged headland at the northern end of Grand Manan Island. It struck the rocks abreast its fore-chains, and the cracking of the timbers of its breaking hull went unheard in the roar of the storm. As the wave that carried it onto the rocks dropped back, the barque—caught aground—listed badly offshore, and its three masts immediately snapped off. The crew rushed up on deck in time to discover one of the boats being washed away. It circled around the lee side in the swirling surf, between the stranded barque and shore. While someone went for oars, others tried to snag the boat with a line, but in the darkness, confusion, and heavy seas beating over the ship, the boat drifted ashore empty, cutting off their best chance for a safe escape.

In short order, the stern broke apart. As the breakers tore the ship open, water poured over the decks. Crewmembers scrambled to cling to whatever they could find. Very soon, the captain, his three officers, and many of the crew were swept overboard and drowned. Ten of the crew jumped over the side and, grasping pieces of flotsam adrift from the collapsing wooden hull, they paddled for their lives to reach shore. One fortunate young man, Tom Clare, scrambled on top of a big chunk of the cabin and was carried ashore right out of the water.

The wind wailed through the tattered remnants of rigging, the sea roared as waves pounded over the ship and crashed onto the beach. And yet, the more fortunate to reach the shore could hear above the noise of the storm the wild shrieks and terrified shouts of drowning men, beaten about by flotsam, smashed up onto the rocks by breakers, and hauled back off into the sea by the undertow, only to be pummelled again.

James Lawson, a native of Bornholm, Denmark, was one of the survivors. Amid the howling confusion, the blackness, the icy sea spray, and the driving snow, Lawson paddled, stumbled, and clawed his way ashore, swept back, struggled to shore again and again. He finally made it and fell exhausted to the beach. Before he could recover to struggle farther up the beach, another wave washed over him. His last desperate cry for help was answered. From the darkness came the firm hand of a shipmate on surer footing; he held him against the undertow and as the pull of the water subsided, the two managed to crawl to the safety of higher ground.

Lawson had lost both boots, and his feet were cut and bruised; later, in the snow and bitter cold, they also became partly frozen. In desperation, Lawson made his way over the rocks and up the cliff in the dark and blinding snowstorm. The wind howled over the crest of the cliff as he stumbled through the snowdrifts and into the woods searching for some sign, any sign, of civilization. He had walked unknowingly in the wrong direction, away from the village of North Head. At first grey light, he came upon a lone hay barn and limped, half crawling, into it, and lay down to die.

Meanwhile, a dog at James Tatton's home near Eel Brook, and closer to the scene of the wreck, howled all night with such urgency that Tatton left his house at daybreak to investigate. He found Lawson's tracks in the snowdrifts and followed the trail to the barn, discovered Lawson, and moved the exhausted sailor as quickly as possible to the nearby home of Elijah Bennett.

Word quickly spread, and early in the morning men gathered at the scene of the disaster to try to do whatever they could to help. As they approached, they encountered a sight that would etch itself indelibly in each mind's eye: the once-stalwart ship was a forlorn wreck, submerged aft, a gaping hole in its forward quarter, masts gone, tethered tatters of canvas heaving on the rolling seas. Strewn along the beach were remnants of the ship and its voyage: boxes and pieces of the ship tumbled and heaped, torn clothing limply clinging to rocks.

Of those who had managed to reach shore, four had made it up to the top of the cliff (including Lawson). Six men were found huddled against the base of the cliff, but of these two were dead. Bodies were strewn along the beach, the drowned having washed ashore by the tide. Residents of Eel Brook and North Head respectfully

After the sun rose, the scene was bleak: a wrecked barque, a few of the crew huddled below the ice- and snow-covered cliffs, bodies scattered along the shore.

gathered the cold and battered remains. Shocked shipmates identified their dead comrades, and all were accounted for: the bodies of the captain, three mates, and seventeen crewmen.

The survivors were warmed and cared for in nearby homes. The folk of the seafaring community, sympathetic to the final needs of these unfortunate victims, buried the twenty-one men in the North Head cemetery. The body of Captain Crerar, however, was later exhumed and reburied in his hometown of Pictou, where he was marked with a granite monument commemorating the life of the exemplary sea captain and the tragic shipwreck that ended it. The wooden plaque erected in North Head at the time of the burial was replaced in 1910 by a permanent monument, prominently located at the entrance to the cemetery behind the Anglican Church. A hundred years later, due to the ravages of time, a granite stone replaced the concrete monument and was unveiled in July 2011. Just across Whale Cove from the monument, Ashburton Head still looks out to sea, coldly austere, unchanging.

The survivors were taken to Saint John, some needing to be hospitalized as a result of their ordeal. James Lawson had to have part of both feet amputated as a result of frostbite and remained a patient at the marine hospital for over five years. Being Danish, his command of English was poor. He was physically disabled and had no trade. But during his stay in the hospital, he learned to work with leather and learned harness- and shoemaking.

After leaving the hospital, Lawson stayed in Saint John for three more years, but was not really content there. Though he had suffered greatly on Grand Manan Island, the kindness of its people had touched him deeply. And perhaps he was reminded of his own home, Bornholm, a similar island in the Baltic. James Lawson returned to Grand Manan and settled there. He set up shop and became the recognized boot- and shoemaker of the community. His cobbler's bench is now part of the collection of the Grand Manan Museum. He became a British subject, married an Island girl, and raised a family on Grand Manan. As years went by, wide-eyed schoolchildren listened, enthralled by the old man's story of the night of terror he suffered on bleak Ashburton Head. James Lawson died in February 1918, at the age of eighty-four.

The ship itself was a total wreck. Its remains—whatever might be stripped and gathered up—were sold for $2,000. The bell was recovered a century later and is now in the Grand Manan Museum. In short order, the seas broke up whatever was left of the wooden hull. Some pieces drifted off, other heavier pieces sank to become lodged among the undersea crevices in the rock bottom, and still others were tumbled by the sea, down over the rocks to rest on quieter, deeper sea floor. Some pieces of timbers held together with copper rods were recovered in 2018 and donated to the Grand Manan Museum.

James Lawson sits in his cobbler's shop in North Head, Grand Manan. Notice how small his feet look: they were partially amputated as a result of being frozen during his ordeal on the icy cliffs of Grand Manan. (GRAND MANAN ARCHIVES)

I visited the site on several occasions in the late 1960s and early 1970s, but nothing beyond isolated timbers and wreckage defines the remains of the ship itself. In terms of loss of life and property, there have been worse sea disasters about the island, but with a survivor settling there, and often retelling his personal ordeal, the loss of the *Lord Ashburton* is probably the best-known shipwreck of Grand Manan.

UNSUNG HERO: THE BARQUE *SARAH SLOAN*

The ongoing struggles of people living, working, surviving; the conflicts of competitive business, the merchants, the poor labourers; ambition over judgment, unsung heroism: these all come together to tell the daily story of humanity. But as each new day unfolds, yesterday's story fades. Only when a major catastrophe strikes are these elements frozen into place, permanently preserved in the written retelling.

The barque *Sarah Sloan* was a typical merchant ship of the day. Built in St. Martins, NB, in 1866, it was registered at 344 tons. It was not large, as barques go, so did not require as large a crew as many ships. Besides the captain were two mates and seven men before the mast. Documents of the day note that all deckhands, as well as the steward, were Black.

The *Sarah Sloan* was to sail from Saint John, NB, in early March 1872, destined for the Cuban port of Matanzas, carrying shooks and hay, a cargo of lesser consequence. The importance of its sailing was to be in the return; it was probably chartered to bring a cargo of sugar and molasses back to Saint John. Indeed, the presence on board of prominent businessman and shipbuilder Hugh McQuiston (who was also the builder and a part owner in the barque) suggested an importance to the voyage greater than shooks and hay.

The weather that March had been boisterous, and Captain William Sloan had delayed sailing, awaiting more favourable winds and seas. Indeed, the owners were getting very impatient, including McQuiston. They scoffed at his caution and urged that he get on with earning the charter. Finally, they prevailed, and against his best nautical instincts, Sloan set sail at noon on March 12, 1872, with a potent sixty-mile-per-hour northeast gale blowing, and the mariners ashore shaking their heads and muttering dire predictions. The pilots of Saint John told him the *Sarah Sloan* wouldn't stand the rough sea, and it would be a miracle if Captain Sloan got by all the rocks at the mouth of the Bay of Fundy in such weather.

Captain Sloan knew that his barque was sturdy and well-built. A northeast wind would blow them almost directly out of the bay, so he made the decision to sail. They passed the Wolves Lighthouse, and as the wind went out to the eastward, Captain Sloan then decided to sail down the Grand Manan Channel, on the north side of the island rather than the broader south side. Sailing before the wind, the captain set the course and turned the helm over to Seaman Charles Turner of Baltimore, who had just shipped aboard the barque that very day. Since it was early evening, the captain went below for supper, confident that in spite of the storm, the barque would soon be in the Grand Manan Channel, behind the tall cliffs of that island, and that they would have smoother sailing in the easterly.

All were below but for Turner and the crewmember on bow watch. The storm was wild, blinding snow blown by the gale. Nothing could be seen beyond the bow. The deck of the barque was the whole world, lurching on a following sea, with wind shrieking in the rigging and the roar of the breakers all around, engulfing the groans of the wooden hull straining under the mountainous waves. Since Turner had only joined the crew that very day and had little experience on the barque, no one will ever know how well he maintained its heading on the captain's course. But the crew felt no danger and had no warning of any problem until the moment the *Sarah Sloan* struck the rock headland at the northern end of Grand Manan, just north of Ashburton Head, at about eight o'clock in the evening. The moment it struck, Turner ran forward to the part of the ship that was impaled on the shore.

The surf was swirling all about the ship. The seas were washing in over the stern and buffeting the craft with awesome fury. Those below quickly came up on deck. Some took to the rigging, others were torn from the ship by the sea, tumbled about in the foam, their lifeless, battered bodies tossed upon the rocks. About ten o'clock, the *Sarah Sloan* broke apart amidships and went to pieces. Turner, clinging to the forward wreckage, drifted ashore. He found shelter from the wind behind a large rock at the base of the high cliff.

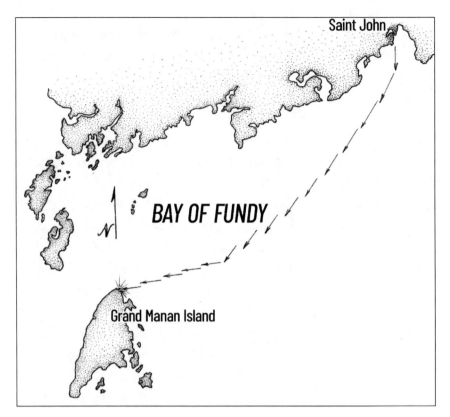

Against his instincts, the captain of the Sarah Sloan *sailed into rough seas, eventually crashing into Grand Manan island.*

Huddled behind the rock, he put in an awful night, his feet freezing in the icy wind and snow. The weekly paper, the *Eastport Sentinel*, reported that as soon as daylight came, "he scaled the cliff where it seemed impossible for a human being to go" and reached a camp inhabited by Indigenous Peoples.[52] What actually happened was a piece of unsung heroism that wouldn't come to light for two more decades.

There was an Indigenous man by the name of Newell who lived in the camp not far from the rocky shore where the tragedy unfolded. He sensed foreboding in that awful storm and told his wife that some white men were in trouble. In 1893, George Batson of Campobello, said:

Next morning at day break, Newell went out and looked over the cliff, 175 feet high. He saw a man half way up and went down after him. The man was a Negro, and Newell took him on his back, struggled with him to the camp and, finding he was frozen, put him on a tub and bathed his feet in snow water to take the frost out. Leaving his wife to take care of the sailor, Newell then hurried to Gaskell's for help. The white people came, but Newell got there first and picked up nine dead bodies. Could a white man have done more? Why has Newell never got a medal from the Canadian government?[53]

Batson wrote to ministers, members of parliament, and newspapers, seeking a suitable medal to honour Newell's bravery and unselfish actions.

Newell spread the news of the shipwreck to nearby North Head, returned to the site, and gathered up some of the bodies. Other men from North Head soon joined him, and they all worked together to gather up the remains. The bodies were frozen, encased in ice, and badly mutilated and dismembered. The men gathered up the frozen remains of Captain Sloan, mate King, and six of the sailors; the other officer's body was found after further searching. Meanwhile, residents of North Head took Turner to Captain Eben Gaskill's house, where they did their best to provide him with whatever comfort and medical help they could give him. On March 17, Captain Gaskill took Turner and the remains of Captain Sloan and his crew to Saint John on his schooner *Gould*. Hugh McQuiston's missing body was found on March 25, not far from the site of the wreck, and it too was taken to Saint John for burial.

Wreck master Lewis Kent took charge of what remained of the *Sarah Sloan*. The wreck was soon sold at auction for $490. The expenses incurred, by order of the wreck master, amounted to $334.05, leaving a balance of $155.95 for the owners, a rather pathetic return on their ambitious plan to set sail into the teeth of a gale. The shooks scattered along the beach were sold for $30.

The Sarah Sloan *struck the headland, broke up, and washed into the cove. No remnants of wreckage can be found there now.*

Forty bundles of hay were picked up at nearby Long Eddy, and they were bid at 80¢ a bundle. The ship itself broke up, and the wooden portions washed away; indeed, its hard pine bowsprit drifted all the way up the Bay of Fundy to Advocate, and went ashore near Captain William Morris's place, where it lay for many years.[54]

There is little wreckage left in the cove. On several occasions, I swam the shores of this site, keeping an eye out for any sign or remnant of the shipwreck, but I failed to find anything. Perhaps the *Sarah Sloan* can best be remembered for its story of the struggles of our working lives, of people pushing themselves to the limits for different reasons. On the one hand, we see the respectable and well-to-do push for commercial gain, pushing crew and their craft against the forces of nature, all in the interest of financial profit. On the other, a humble, compassionate Indigenous man pushed his physical limits to save the life of a poor, injured, and half frozen Black man. Life sometimes unfolds with cruel irony when it demonstrates to us what is really most noble in human ambitions, attitudes, and actions.

THE SCHOONER *VELMA*

The sea's changing moods fascinate those of us who live along the coast, but for those intimately involved with the sea, either in little wooden ships or struggling for survival in the water itself, the sea can be terrifying. I can recall working underwater and being frequently reminded that I needed a healthy respect for the power of the sea; even in moderate seas, it carried me about with no more regard than if I were a piece of seaweed. I had the benefit of a diving suit and air tanks, but I often wondered at the terror experienced by drowning sailors tumbled in the heavy surf and pummelled on the rocks as their wooden sailing ships were overwhelmed by the fearful power of the sea.

The boisterous weather in the fall of 1900 took its toll on Fundy shipping. Among the shipping casualties, three schooners in the bay were victims of this capricious nature of the sea, by which some people were destined to live, and others to die. Indeed, the circumstances that determined whether a person would live or die were no more than tiny opportunities seized or missed.

The coasting schooner *Velma* was making a routine trip up from Boston in the fall of 1900 when, on Tuesday, October 16, the southwest wind died out and its master, Captain Dunham, deemed it prudent to come to anchor below Grand Manan. Heading for its home port of Calais, ME, the *Velma* carried coal for the Calais Tug Boat Company. The *Velma* was a typical coasting schooner, about a hundred tons register, owned in Calais by James Murchie & Sons. No one on board felt any cause for concern as it lay at anchor to wait through uncertain weather. But that evening a northerly gale sprang up.

All sail was taken in, and the captain hoped to ride out the gale at anchor. In the surge of the sea and stiffening gale, however, the anchor cable parted, and the schooner was driven helplessly before the wind.

In the powerful northerly gale, the crew were unable to muster any sail to gain control of the vessel, and the *Velma* was dashed upon the Cross Jack Ledge, one of the Murr Ledges to the south of Grand Manan. The heavy surf pounded against the schooner frightfully, wrenching it back and smashing it against the rock. Before the crew could make it ashore on the ledge, the thirty-five-year-old cook, John Carver, was drowned. It was a dark and wild storm in the middle of the night, which made it more difficult and dangerous to try to escape from the wreck to the rock. In getting to the sea-swept ledge, Captain Dunham had one of his legs crushed. One of the crew, a Mr. Young, dislocated his shoulder. A third survivor made it to the rock, where the three of them recovered the body of their drowned shipmate.

As the tide rose, the rock offered less and less protection from the waves that swept over it, making it especially difficult to hang onto Carver's body and prevent it from washing away. The survivors had no food, and their wet clothes offered no protection from the cold wind. Unnerved by the stormy night, chilled through by the cold, stinging, windblown spray, and having to be vigilant against the sea sweeping over their desolate rock on the high tide—with the thundering surf threatening to tear them away at each pass—the three survivors put in a horrific night on the Cross Jack Ledge. As if this was not enough to fill their night with terror, the dead body they held constantly reminded them of both their responsibility to each other and also of their powerless frailty against these vicious whims of the elements.

During the morning of Wednesday, October 17, the sea subsided a little, and they were able to salvage a few wreck materials. On the bald ledge the survivors erected a makeshift flagstaff on which they flew their American flag upside down as a signal of distress. But there was a low mist over the ledge all day, and no one discovered their plight, although the lightkeeper at nearby Gannet Rock did

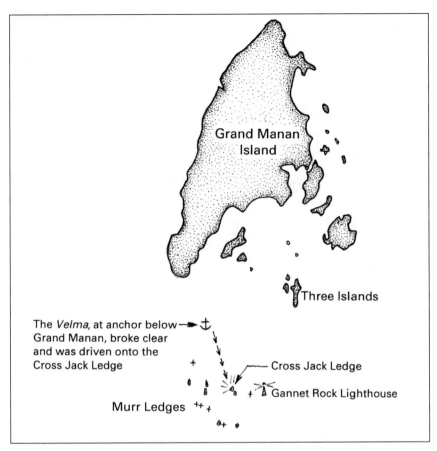

The following labels appear on the map:

Grand Manan Island

Three Islands

The *Velma*, at anchor below Grand Manan, broke clear and was driven onto the Cross Jack Ledge

Cross Jack Ledge

Gannet Rock Lighthouse

Murr Ledges

The Velma *was driven onto the Cross Jack Ledge.*

note in his journals that some flotsam from a wreck had drifted onto the ledge. But he saw no sign of life there, so did not fire the signal guns for a lifeboat to come to the ledges.

That night, as the sea was not running as high, the survivors succeeded in building a fire on the ledge without the fire being washed away. The fire not only warmed them, but it gave them hope, a possibility that they might be seen and saved from their forsaken rock. Early on the morning of Thursday, October 18, the weather cleared a little and at 2:00 A.M. one of the survivors' flares was seen from Gannet Rock Light Station. The lightkeeper, Willard Lincoln Harvey, immediately fired three guns as a wreck signal to the life-saving crew. When daylight came, he commenced repeating the signal almost hourly.

Captain Albert Cheney, who was at nearby Kent Island at the time, also noticed the wreck on the Cross Jack Ledge. He set out with his two sons, Lloyd and Arthur, to rescue the shipwrecked men. There was still a heavy sea running, and the wind was blowing hard, making it very difficult, especially under sail, for Captain Cheney to bring his craft close to the shipwrecked sailors. The captain skilfully kept his sloop as close to the ledge as the sea conditions would permit while his sons took the dory and rowed in through the surf to the rock and took off each of the crew, one at a time. They also succeeded in saving the body of the dead shipmate, Carver. But Captain Cheney and his sons saved nothing of the vessel, as the *Velma* had gone to pieces and was a complete wreck.

Rescued from their dangerous ordeal, the shipwreck survivors were cared for until they could be taken to Eastport two days later. Carver's body, which had been in their constant care for four days, was prepared for burial at Eastport and was taken on to Calais to be buried by relatives. The two injured sailors—Captain Dunham and crewmember Young—received medical treatment in Eastport and recovered fully. As a result of their heroic rescue, the Cheneys were later presented with medals from the Humane Societies of both Canada and the United States.

THE SCHOONER *ROWENA*

The ninety-six-ton schooner *Rowena* sailed from Westerly, Rhode Island, on October 4, 1900, bound for Saint John in ballast. It had a rough passage up the coast. Encountering easterly headwinds, the

Rowena took shelter in several New England ports along the way. On Tuesday morning, October 16, it set forth from Bass Harbor, ME, in a southwestern wind, passing Grand Manan about 6:30 that evening. The *Rowena* passed Point Lepreau, coming up the bay under full sail in a brisk southwest breeze, headed toward Saint John.

The *Rowena* had four men on board. The captain was forty-four-year-old William J. Stevens of Saint John, NB. He was married with three children, and a successful and experienced coasting master who owned a 50 percent interest in the vessel. The mate, John Leonard, was a thirty-eight-year-old from Deer Island, NB. He was single but had been working on coasting schooners for many years. There were two unmarried sailors aboard: twenty-four-year-old Jonas Stafford of Lepreau, and twenty-eight-year-old Arthur Davidson, who was born in the Netherlands but was a resident of Saint John.

Late that evening, within a couple of miles of Partridge Island just outside Saint John, the wind died out, and the schooner was unable to continue into the harbour. The calm did not last, for the wind radically changed, blowing a gale from the north. The schooner continued to carry all its sails, attempting to beat against the wind for the short distance to its destination. Within a few minutes, the captain prudently sent Davidson and Stafford to take in some sail. Davidson was attending to the foresheet and Stafford to the jib sheet. Before they could carry out the task, a particularly violent squall struck the schooner, and it capsized. This was the same gale that parted the *Velma* from its anchor many miles to the south.

As the vessel capsized, Stafford, who was on the side facing into the wind, climbed into the fore rigging. The vessel continued turning over, and he scrambled from the rigging along the chainplates and onto the upturned hull without even getting wet. The weight of the anchors and chain pulled the bow down but also gave the vessel some stability in its completely upside down position and, the hull being undamaged, the schooner remained afloat, with the bow down, and the stern raised slightly. As Stafford clung to the keel in the midnight darkness, he looked around and saw no sign of the other three men. They had been carried under and never appeared again.

That Stafford managed to get to his position on the bottom of the schooner without getting wet was most fortunate, for the weather throughout the rest of the night was terrible. Snow beat across the upturned hull where the keel offered scant protection. Stafford worked his way to the stern where he took up his position about four or five feet above the water, trying to find what shelter he could from the keel, which was a little deeper at the stern. He put in an awful night; sleepless, cold, wet, frightening. But at least he was protected somewhat from the weather with his oilskins and hat keeping the windblown snow and spray and the biting cold from cutting through to the bone.

When daylight came on Wednesday, October 17, hope sprang within Stafford that he might be seen by a passing vessel and be rescued. He was wet and cold, but too anxious to be hungry, and he spent most of Wednesday sitting astride the keel straining his eyes to every horizon, hoping for a sign of a vessel. All night and day, he had been drifting farther and farther away from land. About midday, a barquentine passed by about a mile away, but he was offshore from it and unable to attract the ship's attention. Several schooners also passed within a few miles but they too failed to see him waving his arms as he stood on the low, wallowing bilges. No one knew the schooner was missing, so no one had any reason to be looking for a wreck. The wind blew hard all day, and as the seas buffeted Stafford throughout the afternoon there were times when he narrowly avoided being washed off his cold, wet, and very precarious perch.

As night fell on Wednesday evening, Stafford felt discouraged, despairing that no one had spotted him or had even become aware of his predicament. Cold and alone, with nothing to do but think of surviving, he looked at his situation from every angle. His hope and strength were still strong, and he felt that if he could just hang on to the keel for another night, he would be discovered and rescued the

Jonas Stafford clung to the upside down hull of his schooner, the Rowena, *trying to attract the attention of passing vessels.*

next day. Looking toward the morning became the all-consuming goal of life. Suffering intensely from the cold, Wednesday night seemed like an eternity. He dared not, indeed could not, go to sleep. Every thought, every part of his being, was directed to the hope of the morrow. The cold bothered him the most, sapping and draining his energy.

Daylight brought bitterly cold winds and high seas. Stafford's hands and feet were sore and swollen from the wet and cold. Still, he clung to his perch on the keel and tried vainly to attract the attention of a fleet of schooners inshore from him. Their sails were readily visible to him, but the schooners could not see him.

On Thursday afternoon, October 18, the side-wheel steamer *City of Monticello* was working its way up on a regular run from Yarmouth to Saint John. Captain Harding was in the bridge of the steamer when Mate Newall sighted what he thought looked like the upside down hull of a schooner floating about nine miles southeast of Point Lepreau. As they came near, they were astonished to see something black moving on the keel, which they soon were able to discern to be a man.

They hastened over to the wreck and launched a boat that went along-side. In the heavy sea, the skilful boat crew succeeded in taking Stafford from the rolling, heaving hulk and quickly took him aboard the steamer where he was stripped of his wet clothes and put in a warm bunk.

Stafford had not noticed the steamer as he had been trying to attract the attention of the schooners in the opposite direction. When he discovered the steamer approaching and saw the boat launched for his rescue, the strength that had kept him going for thirty-eight hours gave way to a sense of overwhelming weakness. Well cared for on the steamer, Stafford, who was a strong and sturdy young man, seemed little the worse for his ordeal.

The *Rowena*, drifting about off Point Lepreau, posed a serious threat to navigation so tugs went out from Saint John to search for it and bring it in. They found it on Saturday morning, twelve miles below Point Lepreau. They succeeded in securing a line on it and towed the wallowing, upside down derelict back to Saint John, arriving that evening. In spite of the tragic loss of life and the ordeal of the survivor, the schooner was not badly damaged. When righted, it was easily repaired to sail again on its coastwise trade.

THE OBSOLETE STEAMER *CITY OF MONTICELLO*

The foundering of the old side-wheel steamer *City of Monticello* was one of those tragic disasters that goads regulatory authorities to improve the safety and accountability of those who provide seagoing transportation. The 478-ton *City of Monticello* was 232 feet long, 32 feet wide, and 10.9 feet deep—in other words, it was long, narrow, and with shallow draft. It was built in Wilmington, Delaware, in 1866 by Harlan & Hollingsworth, and was originally called the *City of Norfolk*. Overhauled with new boilers in 1886, the steamer was renamed, but became inactive.

In 1889, Howard D. Troop of Saint John purchased the steamer and had it thoroughly renovated in New York. Captain Robert H. Fleming took charge of it there and sailed it to Bermuda to procure a British registry. He returned with it to Saint John and operated it for the Bay of Fundy Steamship Company, running between Saint John and Annapolis with stops in Digby. Under Captain Fleming's command, the *City of Monticello* remained on this route until 1896, when the Dominion Atlantic steamer *Prince Rupert* replaced it.

On September 16, 1898, the side-wheel steamer *Express* was wrecked on Bon Portage Island, near Pubnico, while on a regular run from Yarmouth to Halifax with calls at ports along the way. The Yarmouth Steamship Company urgently needed a replacement and purchased the aging and mothballed *City of Monticello* to run the coast route between Yarmouth and Halifax, also connecting with Saint John.

The *Monticello* had large paddle wheels on each side of its hull and, equipped with a vertical beam steam engine, it was considered obsolete. The shipping world looked to propellers to serve their needs. Side-wheelers were harder to handle in rough weather and were considered structurally inferior, as the heavy paddles on either side of the hull placed greater stress on the hull than propellers. Furthermore, the loss of the side-wheel steamer *Portland* in the fall of 1898 had all but destroyed whatever reputation side-wheelers might still have had for ocean work. Nevertheless, the *Monticello* had been extensively rebuilt, and its route was never far from land, should the weather become threatening.

The *City of Monticello* arrived in Saint John on Thursday, November 8, 1900—less than a month after rescuing Jonas Stafford from the wreck of the *Rowena*. A gang of longshoremen worked through Thursday night aboard the steamer. After discharging the Saint John freight, they stowed aboard large quantities of oil, meal, feed, cement, nails, lime, and pitch pine, along with other general freight. By mid-morning the freight was all stowed.

Eight passengers boarded the *Monticello* on Friday morning. They represented a typical cross-section of people who travelled for a variety of reasons: A. E. S. Eldridge was a crockery merchant from Yarmouth; Rupert Olive, a native of Saint John and purser of the steamer *Prince Edward*, was returning from leave in Saint John; Elsie McDonald and Ida May Lawrence, both from Yarmouth, were returning home. There were three commercial travellers from New Brunswick on board: Odbur W. Coleman of Moncton, John Richmond of Sussex, and John C. Fripp of Woodstock. There was also another ship's captain on board, Captain Norman A. Smith, who had taken leave of his ship, *Pharsalia*, to visit his family in Nova Scotia.

The *City of Monticello* left Saint John at 11:15 A.M. on Friday. Although the wind was blowing moderately, the sea was not rough, and the steamer had fair passage across the Bay of Fundy. As they approached Petite Passage about four o'clock that afternoon, squalls struck with heavy rain showers. Smith was standing on the saloon deck when Captain Harding, the master of the *Monticello*, came up to him and asked him if he had ever been to Digby. Captain Harding contemplated going into Digby for the night as he felt a little uncertain about the weather and would be able to reach Digby before dark. Smith responded that he had been, and he felt that he could bring the steamer to a safe anchorage there. As the two captains discussed the situation, however, the squall passed, the wind veered to the northwest, the sky cleared, and it appeared that they would have fair wind all the way to Yarmouth. Captain Harding decided to continue his voyage.

The steamer churned its way down through Petite Passage and into St. Marys Bay. The wind died out, but the calm did not last, for the wind soon went to the south and started blowing harder. They reached Cape St. Mary between 7:00 and 8:00 P.M. and shortly after that the wind increased to a southerly gale, building up mountainous waves.

Two hours later, a heavy sea came over the bow and there was a thunderous crash. Steward Kate Smith came out of her room and found that the sea had smashed in the starboard side entrance and forward bulkhead partition of the forward saloon. This made the saloon unusable, but the damage was temporarily repaired by crewmembers using boat awnings. The steward kept a close check on the women throughout the night. Elsie McDonald, only sixteen years old and returning from her first trip to Saint John, stayed in her stateroom all night. Ida May Lawrence had no stateroom and had been in the forward saloon. She was forced back to the aft saloon after the wave had done its damage.

Steward Kate and others of the crew reassured passengers as the steamer laboured in the building seas. Captain Smith went into the wheelhouse and joined Captain Harding, who had decided to try to run for shelter somewhere. As Smith watched, Captain Harding attempted to bring his ship around, but it wallowed helplessly in the trough of the seas and would not respond to paddles or helm. The captain managed to keep the steamer's head to the wind, but it was unmanageable as far as bringing it around to another course. Captain Harding had no alternative but to keep his ship heading into the wind and working down the shore through the night.

About 7:00 A.M. on Saturday, the Yarmouth lighthouse could be seen off in the distance; the *City of Monticello* was about five miles off Cape Forchu. Captain Harding considered his position and was determined to try to run for Yarmouth if he could get his steamer to respond at all. All the pitching and rolling throughout the night had strained the old hull and it was leaking quite badly. The gaining water rolling about within the ship made it sluggish and it developed a bad list to port over the night. The steamer was equipped with powerful steam pumps that were capable of pumping over a thousand gallons of water a minute; these had been operating trying to keep the vessel clear of water. Second Engineer Herbert K. Poole reported to the captain that the steamer was leaking badly, leaking beyond the pump's capacity. As the water gained in the hold, the ship's list became worse, for the water rolling about inside the ship made it more unstable. The crew and passengers then worked together to jettison cargo. They emptied a number of casks of oil onto the water in an attempt to smooth the rough seas so that it might be brought about to try to steam for safety. All efforts failed. The steamer lay wallowing in the seas, wholly unmanageable, leaking badly, its incline to port worsening as the water gained inside its old hull.

At half past ten, the water rising in the engine room put out the fires, which brought the steam engines to a halt. As this also halted the steam pump, it would be only a short time before the rising water would overwhelm the ship. Captain Harding then ordered the boats to be manned and summoned the passengers up on deck. The steamer was equipped with four boats and, as it leaned badly to port, the boats on this side were easiest to launch. The port quarter boat was the first to be lowered under the charge of the captain. This was not a real lifeboat so there was not much enthusiasm about getting into it. As was customary, the women were placed in the first boat, which was manned by Second Officer Murphy, Third Officer Fleming, and Quartermaster Cook. Smith had not intended on getting into this boat, but, since few others seemed to want to get into it, he climbed aboard.

Passenger Rupert Olive assisted the women into the boat and, after helping Elsie McDonald, tossed her handbag into the boat after her. He declined an invitation into the boat, saying that he would wait for the next one. Lowered into the rolling seas, rising and falling under the davits, the waves gradually started to pick up the craft. With one tackle free, the boat tipped dangerously as the sea fell away, but Captain Harding deftly cleared away the tackle that had lowered the boat, allowing the boat's passengers then to pull it away from the steamer with the oars, just as the forward port boat was also lowered. This boat was being launched near the paddle box, in calmer water. Several men were aboard, and the boat was set to pull clear of the steamer when the *City of Monticello* suddenly laid down on its side, broke apart, and settled away to the bottom of the sea.

Steward Kate was in the first boat to be launched and was only about a hundred yards from the steamer when it sank, about seven or eight minutes after the boat were released from the tackle. From this vantage point, Kate described the scene that she witnessed:

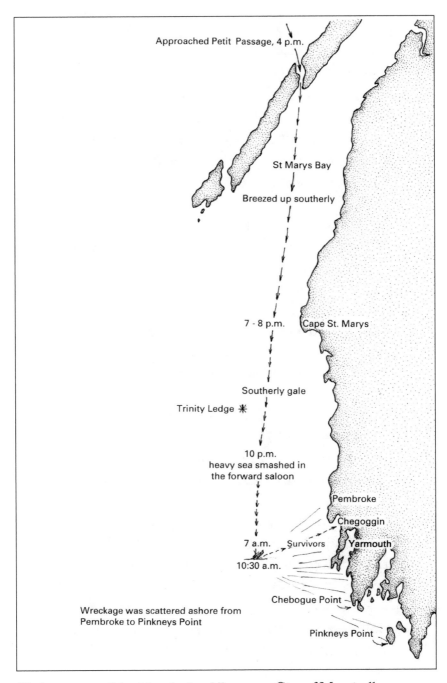

Approached Petit Passage, 4 p.m.

St Marys Bay

Breezed up southerly

7 - 8 p.m.   Cape St. Marys

Southerly gale

Trinity Ledge ✳

10 p.m.
heavy sea smashed in
the forward saloon

Pembroke

Chegoggin

7 a.m.   Survivors   Yarmouth

10:30 a.m.

Chebogue Point

Wreckage was scattered ashore from
Pembroke to Pinkneys Point

Pinkneys Point

The last voyage of the side-wheel paddle steamer City of Monticello.

When we left the steamer, the mate's boat was in the water and I saw persons in her, the boat being about full. The other boat was in the water and some men in her. She was still hanging to the davit hooks. In about five minutes the steamer rolled over and went down and both boats went with her. I heard someone in our boat say, "She's broken in two." We heard a crash... When the ship broke in two I heard a terrible scream, which I will never forget as long as I live.[55]

Captain Smith recalled someone in the boat crying out, "Those poor fellows are drowning!" But there was nothing they could do in the howling gale and crashing seas, for they had to concentrate on their own safety. Second Officer Murphy, distraught and in tears at being powerless to assist his comrades, grasped the boat's tiller with a desperate grip and worked gradually toward the Yarmouth coast, while keeping the little craft always before the wind.

Smith described what happened next:

When a short distance from the shore, we tried to run the boat into a small beach between the rocks. I saw a tremendous comber coming after us and I shouted to all to hold on for their lives. ... In an instant the boat was lifted like an eggshell to the angle of 45 degrees, my grasp on the boat was broken, and I found myself thrown violently to the earth and grass on the beach. ...I observed Miss [Kate] Smith and Mr. Flemming [sic] crawling up the beach, and afterwards was joined by Mr. Cook. I saw nothing of Mr. Murphy and the two girls after the comber struck us. They uttered no shout, and I do not know how they met their death. It seemed hard that after displaying so much courage and fortitude they should be lost when safety was so near.[56]

Steward Kate owed her life to Third Officer Fleming who, grasping a large rock, held her tightly to prevent her being washed back in the heavy undertow. As the sea fell back, they scrambled as best they could up the rocky beach before the next comber crashed with fearsome force onto the rugged shore. The cook and the steward had been injured in the landing, but all four sought refuge in the nearby homes of Captain George Vickery and his neighbour at Pembroke, where they were provided with dry clothes.

It was about 3:30 P.M. when Smith reached a telephone in Chegoggin, and he contacted Yarmouth to request medical assistance for the steward and also to report the loss of the steamer with all but four lives. Word spread quickly of the disaster, and by the time Smith arrived at the Yarmouth post office an immense crowd had congregated, filling the street, eager to hear the painful details. Smith patiently told them what had happened, being frequently interrupted by questions about the fate of friends and acquaintances who had been on board. Each tragic response was met with sobs, cries of disbelief, and tearful, stunned silence.

Over Saturday night and Sunday morning, wreckage strewed the shores from Pembroke to Pinkneys Point. In the early morning, word spread through Yarmouth that a large number of bodies had come on shore with wreckage at Chebogue Point, and soon over five hundred people gathered along the beaches to pick through the wreckage washed ashore in search of bodies. Fragments of the steamer's wooden superstructure lined the high tide mark.

Those who arrived at first light on Sunday morning discovered a boat on the beach near Chebogue Point. It proved to be the *Monticello*'s zinc lifeboat, considerably shattered. Not far from it were four bodies, which were later identified as those of the merchant, Eldridge; the second engineer, Poole; the Saint John salesman, Fripp; and a sailor. A half a mile away, toward the cove, the volunteers found eleven other bodies. The bodies were covered up until ox drags could be brought down, upon which they could be carried up the beach to awaiting undertakers' teams. On one drag, volunteers laid the bodies of seven strapping men, whose remains the sea had cast up on the beach after battering out their lives. It was generally believed that these fifteen men came ashore in the stranded lifeboat, but were killed when the towering combers dashed and tumbled the boat and its occupants in capricious fury onto the rocks. Many of them wore life belts, and other bloodstained belts were found nearby. Even the rocks around the zinc boat were stained with blood. Each revelation stirred thoughts too horrible to hold.

Everyone wanted to do something to help—anything that would help show the sorrow and compassion they felt for those lost and their families. When they recovered the mailbag near Pinkneys Point, Postmaster Hood took charge and carefully dried the 150 water-soaked letters and delivered them to their proper destinations. Certainly, the seafaring people of Yarmouth were accustomed to hearing of disasters at sea, but this one was so close to them, right on their own shore, many of the victims people they knew well, and the lives taken in such explicit horror.

The federal Department of Marine quickly appointed a Board of Inquiry to investigate the loss of the ship. The three-man board, made up of prominent marine captains, convened in Yarmouth within two weeks of the disaster, calling several witnesses to appear. The main witness was Smith, who, although he was a sea captain, had survived the disaster as a passenger aboard the *Monticello*. He recounted the passage and details of the foundering disaster. From his marine experience, he also concurred that a propeller "stood a better chance than a paddle-wheel steamer."[57]

The board rendered its findings. First, for that class of ship, the *Monticello* appeared to be seaworthy, but the board pointed out that it was authorized to carry 500 passengers while only having lifeboat capacity for 132. Secondly, Captain Harding was noted "to have had the ship in good discipline." They regretted, however, "that Captain Harding sailed from Saint John on the 9th of November, disregarding the storm signal and notice issued by the meteorological office, when navigating a ship of the class and description of the *City of Monticello* in the winter season."

The report determined that the loss was caused by bad weather, exonerated the crew, and made an important recommendation: "But in view of this disaster…the undersigned strongly and respectfully suggest that no side-wheeler paddle steamers, with more than one tier of deck houses, and those to be confined to the middle of upper or main deck with clear gangways fore and aft, shall be licensed or authorized to ply on the seacoast, excluding the Bay of Fundy and similarly protected locations, between the 1st of November and 1st of April inclusive."[58]

By the turn of the century, side-wheelers were considered obsolete for ocean use. Although their shallow draft gave them extended favour on rivers, structurally they were simply not up to the stresses of open seas. Nevertheless, several were still afloat and ongoing shipping losses continued to keep up demand for any vessels capable of fulfilling expectations of busy sea freight service. But the tragic loss of the side-wheel *City of Monticello* confirmed the propeller for steam trade and nailed the coffin shut for good on ocean-going side-wheel steamers along our North Atlantic coast.

THE TERN SCHOONER *LENA PICKUP*

Captain William Mattson of Lunenburg joined the tern schooner *Lena Pickup* in Halifax in mid-November 1900, where it had just discharged a cargo of hard pine from the southern United States. Joseph Hall had built the *Lena Pickup* at Granville Ferry, NS, in 1890 for S. W. W. Pickup. It weighed 292 tons. In Halifax, it had been purchased by Captain S. B. Robbins of Yarmouth, who obtained a charter for it to load a cargo of piling at Port Greville to be carried to New York.

The fifty-year-old skipper had had a lot of experience as a mariner and, with his fine A1-classed vessel, he was looking forward to his term with the *Lena Pickup*. Captain Mattson set out from Halifax in ballast, bound for the head of the Bay of Fundy to pick up the piling cargo. Running into contrary gales, it was a week later when the schooner rounded Cape Sable, and the wind veered to the east. The ensuing gale blew it across the Gulf of Maine throughout the rest of the day and night.

By the time the wind died out and the weather cleared, they spotted the Petit Manan lighthouse. An hour later, the fog set in. Under light southwest wind, the schooner headed into the Bay of Fundy. Sailing up through the Grand Manan Channel, the fog was thick; the helmsman could not even see the length of the schooner. Listening to the foghorns, the crew picked out the distinctive sounds of each station to determine their position and progress. About 8:00 P.M., they identified the deep and sonorous fog whistle at Long Eddy, Grand Manan, to their southeast. Captain Mattson set a confident course for his destination, Port Greville.

Sailing along in a moderate southerly wind with wet, dense fog, the schooner ambled up the bay until Wednesday morning, November 21, when the wind backed around to the southwest and strengthened, pushing the vessel onward more quickly toward Minas Basin. At 4:00 P.M. the captain considered his situation. He was heading for Minas Basin much faster than he had planned. The fog was still thick and, according to his dead reckoning and taking into account the wind and tides, Captain Mattson calculated that he would arrive at his destination before daylight. Not wanting to make a landfall in the night in thick weather, he brought his schooner around to drop back down the bay a bit, planning to return to his course up the bay a little later so that he would approach land well after daylight.

The wind increased and by early evening it had whipped up a heavy sea. At 6:30 P.M., the sailor on the bow lookout reported land ahead. The order was given immediately to bring the wheel hard around. Rolling and pitching, the vessel was starting to respond to its helm when it hit the rocks with such a heavy crash that the sturdy hull started to break apart.

It was clear to Captain Mattson that he would not be able to get his vessel off the rocks and, even if he did, it was breaking up so badly that it would quickly sink. His immediate concern, therefore, was to try to save the lives of all seven people on board. Being an experienced mariner, the captain knew that a vessel beached broadside to the shore usually leans over offshore as the seas surge against the hull and then draw back from it. Therefore, he ordered the offshore rigging to be cut so that as the vessel rolled back and forth in the surf, the masts would fall inshore, possibly providing sufficient leverage to roll the hull toward land and form a makeshift breakwater against the sea, which would give everyone a better chance to get ashore. He did not know exactly where he was, but his reckoning placed him in the vicinity of the rugged and rocky New Brunswick coast, east of Saint John.

The deck of the *Lena Pickup* was a fearful place to be. Daylight was gone in the stormy evening. The howling of the wind through the remnants of the rigging was all but drowned out by the roar of the heavy surf, a roar punctuated with the sharp cracking of timbers and the mournful groans of the wooden hull wrenching itself to pieces. The boatswain, Stephen Shiffon, went to his chest and took out his watch and a new pair of trousers, which he put on, remarking to his comrades that if the ship were to be totally lost, he wanted to save at least his watch and new trousers.

The schooner's boat was hanging from its davits at the stern, and the captain ordered it to be lowered. With Shiffon and Sailor Edward Norris in the boat, the crew lowered them to the heaving water. They were to work the boat around to the lee rail of the poop deck where the others would get aboard so that they could all try to get ashore. Just as they were unhooking the tackle that had lowered them, a heavy sea struck the small boat, swamping it and throwing the two men into the water. It was pitch-black and nothing was seen of Norris. Shiffon cried out in agony, "My God, save me! I am hurt!" A line was thrown to him, which he grasped, and his comrades pulled him over to the side of the vessel. They pulled him up and had him almost to the rail, almost within reach, when he yelled, "Save me! My God, I am hurt!"[59] And he let go of the line, fell back into the sea, and disappeared, never to be seen again.

The five men left on the wreck were badly shaken by the disappearance of their two comrades and terribly discouraged at the loss of their boat. But Captain Mattson was calm and determined that all the rest should be saved. He tied a light line to a lifebuoy to float a man ashore, after which the buoy could be drawn back to the ship to save the next man. As captain, it was his duty to be last to leave the ship, so he sought a volunteer from his crew to be the first to try to get to shore in the lifebuoy. The four other men on the wreck each refused to get to shore afloat in the life ring.

❖ The poop deck is the stern deck, usually the highest deck on a sailing ship, and typically includes the roof of the cabin.

The ghostly, phosphorescent "water fire" was all that could be seen of the wild crashing surf in the stormy night. Each preferred to take his chances on the breaking hull rather than be dashed onto the rocks.

When all refused the offer to use the lifebuoy, Captain Mattson took off his seaboots and jacket and pulled the life ring over his head and shoulders. Telling his crew to pay out the line, he jumped overboard, hoping that by reaching shore he would give the others the confidence they needed to get to shore themselves. The water was bitterly cold, numbing him to the bone, but he set out with determined strokes toward the thundering surf. Even buoyed up by the life ring, nearly every wave broke over him. Calm and confident, Mattson held his breath until the ring floated his head up through the wake of each comber. Not only was the sea crashing about him, but flotsam from the disintegrating schooner was also being hurled about. This was the swim of his life, but Mattson continued to make steady progress toward shore. About half way there, however, the line reaching back to the schooner became fouled by surging wreckage, pulling the ring under the water. He had the choice of leaving the lifebuoy or being drowned in it. So, without hesitation, he wriggled out of the lifebuoy, paddled for the surface, and stroked for shore.

A heavy sea picked Captain Mattson up, carried him in, and landed him on a large rock. He clung to the rock with all his might and succeeded in prevailing against the powerful undertow of the receding wave swirling back around him. He had landed on a point of ledge jutting out about 125 feet from shore. He scrambled up along the rocks about 60 feet, reaching a high shelf safe from the boiling surf. There he heard a voice hollering out of the darkness. It was Sailor Norris, who had disappeared when the boat was lost off the stern of the schooner. He shouted to the captain that he was safe, having successfully swum ashore after the failed attempt to launch the boat. He was perched on a large rock but could not get to the captain because of the turbulent water swelling and swirling between them.

The four men remaining on the schooner faced a bleak situation. They had no way of knowing the fate of their captain, for the line they held secured only an empty life ring, buffeted by surging flotsam. Certainly, what the captain had tried to do held little promise for them. They did not feel safe on the schooner either. The masts had gone over the side, opening up the hull. The timbers groaned and cracked as each swell pounded and ground the stalwart vessel's bilges into the rocks. Steward Henry Godley went to get something from the galley and while he was there, the bow broke out of the schooner, and he narrowly escaped drowning as the forecastle collapsed into the sea. Nevertheless, he succeeded in joining the rest of the crew back on the quarterdeck. By this time, the whole forward part of the vessel was submerged. About 8:00 P.M., an hour and a half after it had struck the rocks, the *Lena Pickup* broke completely in two.

Although this latest development looked bad for the four men, it was actually a blessing in disguise. The hull had been so weakened by this general disintegration that two big surges pounding successively against the remains of the hull washed the poop deck, with the four men on it, clear of the wreck. This unlikely and most opportune raft washed ashore against the side of the sheer and rugged ledges. With added good fortune, there was a ladder lashed on their piece of wreck, which they quickly released and placed against the side of the large, bluff outcropping, scrambling on top of it before the next heavy sea could carry them away from this one chance at safety.

Even though there was solid rock underfoot, they were still in danger, for a heavy sea came up and almost washed them away. Moments later, they heard their piece of poop deck below them being smashed against the rocks and pounded ashore on the beach.

The tide began to fall, taking with it the danger of being washed by heavy seas. Around 9:30 P.M. the six men were able to get to a cliff shelf about sixty feet above the water. They were a sorry-looking sight. Captain Mattson, Mate Howard Farrell, and one of the sailors had taken off their boots (so as not to be encumbered for swimming), Steward Godley had injured his back, and a plank thrown by the sea had cut sailor William Groves over his eye as he was scrambling ashore on the rocks. All were cold and hungry, battered, bruised, and exhausted. Their clothes were wet, and they feared death from exposure in the bitter, cold wind.

About 2:00 A.M., one of the men found some matches in one of his pockets. They scoured the sheltered crevices for scraps of dry driftwood and were able to start a fire around which they huddled for the rest of the night, gaining hope that they might survive their terrible ordeal. At daylight, they climbed to the top of the cliff and surveyed the scene of their shipwreck. Only fragments were left of their vessel: a couple of pieces of spars, part of the poop deck, and, amazingly, the two heavy anchors that had somehow been washed up against the base of the cliff. The rest of the schooner had drifted off or was scattered along the beach in small pieces.

The survivors who were barefoot found some scraps of canvas washed ashore and bound pieces of this around their feet. Then everyone headed inshore through the woods. They came to a road and, after having trudged about four miles, arrived at the house of William Evans. He took them in and gave them a warm breakfast and a chance to dry their clothes. After staying at Evans's house for an hour or so, their host found some shoes for the barefoot men and obtained a team of horses and a cart to take all six men to Saint John, some fifteen miles to the west. They arrived there about 4:30 P.M. and were taken to the Seaman's Mission.

William Corrigan of Gardner Creek found the body of Boatswain Shiffon two days later. He was gunning along the shore and discovered the body a short distance from the site of the shipwreck, which was on the rocks near Black River. The body was turned over to Coroner Gilmour of St. Martins. Shiffon was thirty years old, unmarried, and a native of Bay St. George, NL.

Most of the survivors came from Lunenburg: Captain Mattson, Steward Godley, and two seamen, Norris and William Wilmot. Mate Farrell came from Digby, and the other seaman, Groves, came from Newfoundland. Captain Mattson, who lost his charts, books, instruments, clothing—everything—in the wreck, summed up the feeling of his crew: "I am about as destitute as any man who has been shipwrecked, but I thank God that my life and those of my crew have been spared."[60]

HEROIC NORWEGIAN SAILOR: THE STEAMER *KINGS COUNTY*

NORWEGIAN SEAMAN HERO OF SHIPWRECK ON LORNEVILLE COAST

This newspaper headline in the *Saint John Telegraph-Journal* of December 12, 1936, introduced a story of bravery, of a young man who swam through a sea too rough for a lifeboat, to carry a heavy line ashore by which thirty-six lives could reach safety from their shipwrecked steamer.

The Norwegian *Kings County* was a cargo steamer of 3,252 tons. It was built in West Hartlepool, England, and had formerly been the *Bjornstjerne-Bjornson*, named for a Norwegian poet. Wilhelm Torkildsen of Bergen, Norway, owned the steamer.

Now, as a ship of the County Line, it was a frequent visitor to Saint John, but its voyage there in December 1936 was the first trip as captain for the skipper, Captain Egil Massoe. After loading six thousand tons of grain in Sorel, Québec, the *Kings County* put in at Sydney, NS, to fill its bunkers with coal before heading to Saint John to finish loading the cargo for overseas.

Coming up the Bay of Fundy in rain and thick fog, Captain Massoe reckoned he was ten miles offshore, but the heavy winds and a strong tide had carried him off course, and at 2:00 A.M., on Friday morning, December 11, there was a grinding crash as the *Kings County* ripped open its hull on the rocky shore just above Tyner's Point, down the coast below Lorneville, not far from Saint John.

Immediately the steamer began to list as the water poured through the jagged hole in its hull. The men who had been sleeping, and that was most of them, rushed up on deck from their quarters after the impact, many not even taking time to put on shoes. But so rapidly did the sea pour into the ship that they had no chance to return to their quarters to retrieve shoes, clothes, or anything else.

As soon as his ship struck, the captain sent out a wireless call for help. But he did not know exactly where he was, so the tug that set out to help inched down the shore, through the blowing fog and mist, carefully searching all along the shore below Lorneville.

Meanwhile, on the deck of the *Kings County*, the crew gathered. Not a hundred feet away, through the driving rain, the ship's spotlight showed a great rock cliff. But those hundred feet were white with the surge and reflux of heavy breakers crashing onto the rocks. It was far too rough to launch a lifeboat. They knew a lifeboat would be lifted up, thrown about, and dashed to pieces in the fury of the surf.

The Kings County *rested on the bottom alongside rugged cliffs, and broke up right there.*

The ship was listing and settling deeper as the water poured in through the hole. All hands knew that the deck itself would soon be awash in the waves. The situation looked hopeless indeed.

Then, almost before the crew knew what was happening, a sturdy young man stripped to his seaman's pants, tied a rope around his waist, and plunged into the icy and turbulent Bay of Fundy water. They watched as he swam with firm and confident strokes toward shore. A breaker covered him; he bobbed up again, swam hard, disappeared, bobbed to the surface, and swam purposefully toward the shore.

It was only a hundred feet, but after five minutes, he still had not even covered half the distance. Waves carried him in, pulled him back in the undertow, and picked him up again. With the light of the ship trained on his struggle and all sound drowned out by the roar of the heavy surf, all eyes were on the young man. After ten minutes, they were ready to concede that he couldn't do it. "He can't last," someone said. Chilly Bay of Fundy water taxes every bit of energy in the best of conditions, but in these heavy breakers…

But he finally reached the shore and clutched at the jagged rocks. Then the crew saw a large wave pick him up and fling him back into the sea. He struggled for the shore, caught the rocks, and was again flung back. And as the waves lifted him and dropped him, he was bumped and slammed against the rocks. But he finally won his struggle and managed to scramble up beyond the pull of the breakers.

The searchlights piercing through the blowing fog and rain showed him struggling up the rocks, dragging his rope as he went. The crew on the ship saw him tie the end of the rope to a big boulder. A collective cheer went up as he waved to tell them that the line was secure. The crew wasted no time in tightening the rope and tying their end firmly to the ship.

The steamer had settled lower into the water, with surf and waves splashing across its deck. The more physically fit of the crew set out hand over hand along the rope for shore. About a dozen made it ashore this way. And then the rest came one by one, carried on a makeshift breeches buoy, made from a stool cradled in ropes suspended from the taut line from ship to shore. The captain, first officer, and chief engineer waited until all the rest were ashore before finally abandoning the ship completely.

By this time, the tug *Foremost 43* had arrived on the scene and, pitching and tossing in the wind and heavy sea, it maintained its position under power, just off from the sinking ship. The sea was too rough for the tug to come alongside the freighter, so the tug stood by as the ship's crew took their lifeline to safety. The tug's skipper knew exactly where the *Kings County* had smashed into shore and sent a wireless message to Saint John. In short order, employees of the tugboat company went to Lorneville and set out through the woods to try to find the shipwrecked crew. Soaked to the skin, and many without shoes, the crew of the *Kings County* clawed and scrambled their way up the rocky cliff only to meet thick woods at the top, woods so dense that in the darkness the survivors were almost immediately lost. Some tore apart their life preservers and wrapped their feet in the canvas. Others had grabbed whatever fabric they could find as they left the ship to protect their feet.

Lost and soaked in the driving rain, they huddled and shivered through the remaining hours of darkness. At dawn, shaking with cold and with the sharp rocks and stubble cutting their feet, they wandered through the woods and out onto the Lorneville road. Cold, soaking wet, and exhausted, they found warmth—and breakfast—at the homes of the hospitable folks of Lorneville. All had made it safely to shore.

Harald Hansen was a hero. The young Norwegian, whose brave swim had saved the lives of thirty-six men, was carried on the shoulders of the others when they arrived in Saint John. They cheered him on as he posed reluctantly for a cameraman. The Seaman's Mission sought to get a Royal Humane Society medal for him for his courage and determination in swimming the heavy hawser ashore through numbing cold and the frenzy of surf and breakers and up the jagged, rocky cliffs.

News of the wreck spread quickly. And the curious by the score made their way through the woods to the clifftop to see the wrecked ship. There was still a heavy sea running and, even back in the woods, above the roar of the breakers, onlookers could hear the grinding of steel on rock and the heavy thud of the iron hull being lifted and dropped on the rocks.

The agents of the Norwegian underwriters and the insurers of the cargo visited the scene of the wreck and saw heavy seas sweeping over the ship. They expected the superstructure to be breaking up quickly, and so they proclaimed the ship to be a total wreck. Furthermore, they stated that no attempt would be made to salvage the *Kings County*.

Norwegian law required an inquiry into any such shipwreck. The inquiry was held at the office of the Norwegian consul in Saint John, who presided over the hearing. Two Norwegian captains in port officiated as nautical assessors. Most of the crew left Saint John that same weekend on a passenger liner headed back across the Atlantic, but several officers remained to give their statements. The findings of the inquiry were not released but sent directly to the Norwegian government first. But, unofficially, the wind and strong tide had drawn the *Kings County* off course and onto the rocks.

~

In the summer of 1970, I had just finished doing some salvage work on the wreck of the *Hada County* (see Chapter Nine), off Grand Manan, when I visited with an acquaintance, Les Kierstead, in Saint John. Les had dived on the *Kings County*. I had not yet researched the story of its stranding but had surmised that it would be a sister ship to the *Hada County*, and so, of course, I was very interested. Sam Maguire, a fisher from Lorneville, agreed to show us where the *Kings County* was wrecked. So, on the morning of September 15, 1970, I drove to Saint John, bought several cases of dynamite with prima cord and safety fuse, and then went to Lorneville to meet my partners in the expedition: fellow diver Carman Cook and Harry Johnson, who provided his little lobster boat *Debbie Sue* to be our work vessel.

After supper, Les and Sam came with us as we left Lorneville and sailed down the shore to Tyner's Point. This is a rocky, bold coast, with rugged cliffs plunging straight down into the depths. Sam showed us where he thought the wreck should be, very near the shore. I dropped over the side. I had a buoy line looped over my shoulder in case I should find something of the wreck. The water was dark and the visibility was terrible. I could not even see my luminous depth gauge when I reached 40 feet down. I drifted on down and landed in mud. I determined my direction by the slope of the mud, as I couldn't see my compass. In fact, to help concentrate, I worked with my eyes closed. I groped slowly about. Bumping into several large rocks, I felt the shape of one deck beam, but no more. As I went further inshore, I came to a very steep ledge bottom at about 40 feet depth.

This was, in fact, the bottom of the solid rock cliff, which made up most of the bold shoreline. By this time the sun was going down, so I quit exploring any further. But having found a deck beam, I was satisfied that Sam had given us good directions.

The next morning we returned to Tyner's Point. I swam down the side of the undersea cliff. When I reached the mud bottom, I worked slowly offshore and quickly ran into wreckage. Feeling my way around, I figured it was the bow section, with the stem aimed almost straight up. Broken off from the rest of the wreckage, it thrust upward about 30 feet from the bottom. I felt my way all over this bow section and then worked my way along the inshore side of the wreck for about 50 feet, and then tied my buoy line there and came to the surface.

Having a buoy line on the wreck, I could then put my efforts into trying to find out what was there. So I spent the rest of the dive slowly determining just what was to be found. The visibility was again poor, so we decided to wait on the mooring through the flood tide to see if the green water offshore would work inshore on the flood tide far enough to replace the brown water of the Saint John River, and give us better visibility. On the last of the flood tide, just before high tide, the green water reached us, so I went back down on the stern of the wreck. Though the visibility was better—four or five feet at best—and it was very dark, but this was much better than the zero visibility of low tide.

I set out across the wreck to find the engine, picking my way onward through the gloom. For correct direction I relied more or less equally on my compass, the layout of the wreckage, and basic instinct. What elation I felt when I came upon the familiar shapes of machinery in the engine room. I felt my way around trying to do some preliminary appraisal. The triple expansion steam engine was still standing bolt upright, jutting up from the bottom about twenty-five feet. Just inshore from the back of the engine, I found a large saltwater pump. I saw quite a few copper pipes and brass valves strewn about. Groping about in the darkness by the base of the engine, I found the condenser, which was very long. Having looked things over, I set several investigatory charges of dynamite about the engine room, to learn just what we had there in salvageable brass and copper.

The next day I was able to assess what the blast had done. Much of the cast iron case was blown off the condenser. The more I dug into the wreckage opened up by the dynamite, the more brass valves and copper pipes there seemed to be. I set out new mooring lines for the boat, fore and aft, to position the boat closer to the engine room and align the boat to ease the hoisting of brass and copper from the engine room area onto the boat. After lifting large pieces of copper pipe I set more dynamite around the condenser, to shatter its cast iron casing.

Over several days we worked on the shipwreck, removing brass and copper steam pipes and fittings. And at the end of each dive, I set up more dynamite charges to blast clear more brass and copper, to be recovered on the next dive. Carman and I both bundled up brass and copper that had been freed up by the previous blast. With the system we used, we made good progress salvaging. Later in the dive, while Carman continued to send up pieces of brass and copper, I studied the engine room area and set dynamite charges in strategic places about the condenser and engine room. Since the condenser was made up of about 750 brass pipes and was 22 feet long, secured to brass end plates with a brass plate midway along, I figured it would take careful planning and considerable dynamite to blow the whole thing clear. I set the dynamite charges to try to do just that.

The following morning, we returned to the wreck. Apart from moving the engine to expose the brass condenser for easier recovery, the overall damage done by the blast was quite impressive. It is almost unbelievable that a couple of innocent-looking cardboard boxes could contain such power, dormant in the paper-wrapped dynamite sticks. We managed to put in a pretty good tide's work picking up brass and copper, as the weather was fine, the swell was minimal, and the visibility surprisingly good, at least 6 or 8 feet. By the time we finished this dive, we had most of the loose brass and copper picked up and aboard the boat.

The next morning, back at the wharf with a full boatload of brass, Harry and I donned old work clothes and started to unload the boat, piling the brass on the wharf. All this wreck stuff was black with salts of iron, and this was pretty dirty work. While we were doing this, Carman duded up in a white shirt, all clean and spiffy, took my Jeep, and set out to do a little dealing with our good friend Len Kaplansky, of Dominion Metal in Saint John. Prices for brass and copper were not very good at that time, but we had a good quantity, so Kaplansky gave us a fair deal. Following Carman's return, the Dominion Metal truck came, which we succeeded in loading in time to get back out to the wreck for an afternoon of diving on the high water and ebb to pick up condenser tubes.

We had been plagued with the problem of handling these brass tubes, which were twenty-two feet long. We overcame this in our customary makeshift manner by lashing a pole to the corner of the awning of the boat. We fastened the upper block of a four-fall block and tackle to the top of the pole, which was stayed off suitably for support. When the regular four-fall tackle had come to its limit at the trap hauler pulley, we hooked on the high four-fall, slacked up the main one, and raised the loads of long tubes high enough to be able to swing them over the side of the boat more easily. The outfit was crude, but it worked well.

I took the first turn on the bottom. I had good visibility for the first hour, but then had to use a light for the next couple of hours. I sent up close to four hundred tubes, but the cold was getting through the wetsuit, and I was becoming chilled and inefficient. So I surfaced and warmed up a bit while Carman suited up. Carman went down and spent a couple of hours on the bottom, during which time the lifts came along very smoothly. When he finally came on board to call it quits, he announced that our condenser was now all aboard the boat.

After supper, we went to the wharf in Lorneville to unload the condenser tubes on the flood tide. In a short time, we had all the condenser tubes—over four thousand pounds of them—all on the wharf. It was a long and hard day, and the clammy bunk in the fore peak of the *Debbie Sue* sure felt good.

The next morning we called Dominion Metal for a truck to pick up the condenser tubes and bought a barrel of gas for the boat. With the gas aboard, we went back to the wreck. I went down and cleaned up enough stray condenser tubes to send up to the boat in a couple of lifts. I also recovered a couple of brass coolers, deliciously heavy for their size. I checked over the forward part of the engine room, but there was little else that could be easily seen and obtained. So I cleared our mooring lines and we wrapped up our *Kings County* expedition.

We sailed back to Lorneville and picked up the auxiliary steering wheel off the floating slip, putting it aboard Harry's boat. We didn't have enough additional brass to call in the truck, so opted to take it home with us and add to the brass from the next wreck salvage. So Carman and Harry set out in the boat for Grand Manan, and I took my Jeep and headed over to Dominion Metal to pick up our cheque, which was, after all, the whole point of our expedition to the wreck of the steamship *Kings County*.

～

In August 1999, three Hansen brothers—Leif Harald, Helge, and Thor—made the trip from Norway to the shores of Saint John to see where their father, Harald Hansen, had made his heroic swim to save the lives of the thirty-six seamen on the *Kings County*.

When they arrived in Saint John on Sunday night, August 15, they were thrilled to see for themselves the strange place, half a world away from their home, where their father had been part of such a thrilling experience, which they must have heard of often as they were growing up.

"We're very excited," said Thor Hansen. "We talked about this for many, many years. But we had families. We were building houses, building our lives."[61]

The next day, local fisher David McCavour took them and about twenty Lorneville old-timers in his boat for a sail along the coast to come to the spot where the remnants of the *Kings County* lay hidden beneath the dark waters of Fundy. It was a beautiful summer day as the three brothers sat on the front of the wheelhouse, atop the foredeck of the fishing boat, heaving gently in the swell. As they looked at the rugged, rocky shore, it was of course, a very different scene from the stormy December night when the heroic swim took place. Still, they were there in person, able to see for themselves the massive and austere rocky coast, to imagine for themselves the cold, unforgiving, crashing breakers and foaming sea into which their father had plunged.

They returned to shore satisfied with the fulfilling of their life-long dream. They visited the mayor of Saint John and made a presentation to the city on behalf of their hometown in Norway. They attended a special presentation at the Lorneville Community Centre. And they returned to Norway filled with memories of the breathtaking Bay of Fundy coast, and the warmth and hospitality of its people.

Meanwhile the bones of the *Kings County* lie deep under the dark water, cold and still, slowly disintegrating as time and tide pass unrelentingly along.

CHAPTER SEVEN

INCOMPETENCE

∽

THE *HUMBER* LUMBER BONANZA

U sually the complete story of a shipwreck must be pieced together from the different recollections of those who were there. Each person remembers what was most personally striking, and by piecing together what each recalls, a mosaic of the event can be reconstructed. Occasionally we have the good fortune to discover a fairly complete story. Such is the case with the loss of the ship *Humber* on January 27, 1873. The log of the pilot, George Mulherrin, who was engaged to take the ship from Saint John to the mouth of the Bay of Fundy, records for us the day-to-day events, ineptitudes, and misfortunes leading up to the ship's loss. In our twenty-first-century need for efficient travel, the meandering trail of the *Humber* about the bay is indeed mystifying.

The 1,403-ton *Humber* was a full-rigged ship built in Kennebunk, ME, in 1861. In the early 1870s, it was under British registry, giving its hail as London, England, where John Lidgett & Sons owned it. In early January 1873, the *Humber* loaded the cargo hold and deck full of deals in Saint John, intended for Liverpool and being shipped by New Brunswick lumber baron Alex Gibson.

The ship was laden carelessly and trimmed poorly (too much of the cargo was stowed forward and not enough aft). Furthermore, a dozen new crewmen had just shipped aboard in Saint John the very day it was to sail. The hastily-acquired Saint John crew would later prove to be the undoing of the ship's voyage. Nevertheless, the *Humber* put to sea, under the command of a forty-eight-year-old Englishman, Captain Thomas Atkins. The pilot, George Mulherrin, was clearly frustrated with the gross incompetence of the crew, as was evident in his writing of trying fruitlessly to get the ship out to the open ocean.

According to Mulherrin's log, the ship left "St. John on Monday, Jan 13, 1873. The crew being mostly drunk and sails frozen could not get sail on the ship.... At midnight attempted to wear ship off the Nova Scotia shore and were two hours in accomplishing it. Suppose it was due to her being out of trim." On Tuesday, January 14th, it was "very dirty weather and snowy. [The *Humber*] drifted along the shore with the flood tide until she reached Quaco (St. Martins)."

On Wednesday, with the ship poorly laden and unresponsive, the crew had to throw overboard lumber on the forward deck to try to enable steering with the rudder. On Thursday, with the ship still not responding well, when the crew saw Grand Manan Island in the distance, they headed for Bliss Harbour, near what is now Blacks Harbour, to seek shelter to move more cargo toward the stern. On their way there, with the bow deep in the water, they lost control and veered sideways, and the ship rolled down and became unmanageable. But they eventually managed to reach shelter in Bliss Harbour that afternoon as a heavy gale struck.

The gale continued on Friday, the weather being too severe to work on shifting cargo. Finally, on Saturday, the crew was able to spend all day "trimming the ship" (bringing the heavy lumber from forward aft) to raise the bow and lower the stern so that the rudder would have more effect steering the ship.

Ready to continue the voyage, they had to wait almost a week for a wind that would allow them to safely leave Bliss Harbour. Finally, on Friday, January 24, they were able to raise the anchors

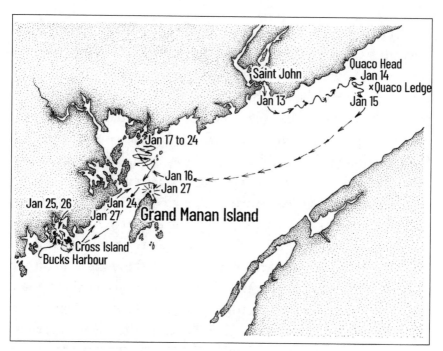

The Humber *meandered from Saint John to Quaco to Bucks Harbour and back up to Grand Manan.*

and leave the harbour. Once out in the Bay of Fundy, the weather worsened, but the pilot, Mulherrin, noted that the ship steered much better than before.

With the wind blowing hard, Mulherrin felt it prudent to take the large ship past smaller harbours and seek shelter in the more spacious Machias Bay on the Maine coast. About five o'clock in the afternoon, while passing Cross Island, the ship oversteered in the heavy seas and briefly touched bottom at the outer end of a ledge there. The ship did not stop, but headed up into the bay and anchored off Bucksport, on the west side of Machias Bay.

The weather worsened, as the pilot noted in his log: "no land visible though close inshore, owing to the snowstorm, crew unable to stow sails." On Saturday, January 25, Mulherrin writes: "The crew refused to proceed in the ship until she was taken back to St. John and had her bottom examined (although she was not making a drop of water in consequence of her touching). At 3 p.m. after getting the second anchor, the crew shipped in St. John came aft and refused to lift the other anchor until the Captain promised to comply with their demand, which he refused them; went into the forecastle, although a fine, fair wind was blowing. At 5 p.m. I left the ship."

With the crew in a state of mutiny, the pilot left the ship, picked up by his pilot boat. The next morning, with fair wind, the captain flew flags signalling his intention to sail again and his need for a pilot. As Mulherrin continued in his log on Sunday, January 26: "I returned to her and found the crew in the same mutinous state. On the captain complying with their demand they returned to duty, and at noon proceeded for St. John."

The next day, Monday, January 27, the *Humber* slowly worked its way up the Bay of Fundy. But the wind increased, and visibility was cut with drifting snow. The progress the ship had been making was reduced by the ebb tide carrying it back down the bay. By 4:30 p.m., the wind and snow were increasing and very thick.

By six o'clock, it was dark with a heavy northeast gale and thick snow. Nothing could be seen beyond the forecastle on the ship. At 6:10 p.m.—with the captain wiping the snow off one side of the binnacle, the mate and pilot working on the other side, and two men at the helm—they peered into the darkness, hoping for the best. As Mulherrin noted in his log:

> *Owing to the want of a light and a whistle on the Bishop's Head, at 7 p.m. saw the land over our heads, like an umbrella, and at the same time the ship struck the self same rock as the doomed ships Sarah Sloan and Lord Ashburton [see Chapter Six]. Owing to the coolness of the Captain and his officers we succeeded in getting out three boats, and I succeeded in landing in the first boat with a line, although the sea was breaking*

over the ship and the breakers on the rocks were like a seething cauldron. The boat returned to the ship and brought part of the crew, but in the act of sending they were precipitated out of the boat, and the boat smashed to pieces on the rocks.

Some of the crew launched a lifeboat from the deck of the ship and, with a line back to the ship, they worked their way to shore. After getting out of the lifeboat onto shore, the boat was hauled back to the ship to transfer more crew until everyone was safely ashore, off the ship's deck being washed by heavy waves. The captain was the last to leave.

Everyone was wet and cold, and a strong wind was blowing with heavy snow. Fortunately, the mate had placed a lighted lamp in each boat and had filled his pockets with candles and a box of matches, and Mulherrin noted in his log how they survived the night: "With broken pieces of the two boats, and some small fragments of the *Sarah Sloan* (that was wrecked [there] the previous year) we succeeded in kindling a fire, and thus saved our lives. Some of us after the fire was lit commenced to sing, keeping time with our feet, to keep them warm; others again walking briskly at the base of the mountain to the edge of the surf; others searching the rocks for firewood."

By daylight the next morning, the fire was out and their clothing was frozen stiff. The tide was down, and some of the men were able to get back on the ship for a few minutes to get some provisions, but they had little time there as the seas were washing over the deck.

With daylight, others tried to find their way up the cliff. Some succeeded and reached a nearby Indigenous camp where they were helped and cared for. Then one of the men from the camp took a rope to the cliff and succeeded in helping all the crew escape up the cliff. Word soon spread, and other Island residents opened their homes to care for members of the crew too, for which all were thankful.

Pilot Mulherrin concluded his log entry by saying, "I feel so completely fatigued, and having swollen feet, I cannot get on my boots but with difficulty, and the Captain and his officers are nearly worn out walking through the heavy snow, climbing the rocks, and over-exerting themselves to save all they can, as the ship is breaking up, and will go to pieces the first heavy blow."[62]

And the incompetent crew who joined the ship in Saint John drunk, mutinied in Machias Bay, demanding to return to Saint John? They managed to get back on the ship and plundered the cabins of the captain and first mate, even robbing the Seaman's Orphan Asylum Box of its contents.

The American Revenue Cutter *Mosswood* arrived and pulled the *Humber* off the rocks on Sunday, February 2, but being unable to take it to a harbour, anchored it in nearby Long Eddy. The ship's hull was badly beaten in and it was full of water, floating on its lumber cargo. The Canadian steamer *Stroud* went to Grand Manan on Tuesday and succeeded in towing the hulk into Whale Cove, Grand Manan, where it was beached.

In spite of the fact that the *Humber* was a wreck, it was, neverthe-less, resting on a beach in a partly sheltered cove, and the sale of the wreck attracted a lot of interest. The hull had within its construction two hundred tons of iron knees to strengthen it, giving entrepreneurs ideas of being able to patch up and rebuild the ship or, failing that, reuse the knees in another hull. There was a steam donkey engine on deck that was quite valuable, much of the ship's outfit was still there, and the below-deck cargo of deals was still contained within the ship.

The steamer *Stroud* made a special trip to Grand Manan on Sunday, February 16, to take people there to attend the sale the next day. Businessmen came from all over to look over the wreck and make their bids at the auction. At the end of the day, Captain Gaskill of Grand Manan bought the hull for $1,075. The anchors and chain sold for $600, and the deals yielded another $4,000. Proceeds from the sale of the ship, materials, and cargo came to a grand total of $5,529.80.

Captain Gaskill considered the situation carefully, thinking of the precarious exposure of the wreck to easterly winds. He and others who had interest in the wreck sold out to parties in Eastport and Machias, ME, who intended to tow the ship to Machias and unload the million feet of deals that was within her. The resale grossed $9,286.57 giving the entrepreneurs a quick and handsome net profit of $3,713.57 for their enterprise.

The decision was a timely one, for an easterly storm on March 3 demolished the wreck, along with a thousand dollars worth of property on deck: the donkey engine, winch, and more were all lost. The *Eastport Sentinel* of March 19, 1873, printed the local correspondent's report of this loss:

> *The storm of the 3rd and 4th raged fearfully here. The old ship "Humber" could not stand the shock. She went to pieces on the night of the 3rd, scattering the deals along the shore in a very grateful manner, laying it in every way and shape that the imagination could conceive of. A beholder viewing the scene remarked, "is it possible that such an extensive pile of lumber as this could be taken from one ship! Anyone would naturally suppose that there was enough to load three such vessels. The scene is worthy an artist's attention and would pay any one who never saw a wreck of such gigantic magnitude as this."*

This windfall on the shores of Whale Cove was seen as a providential dispensation to offset a dull season in the local fishery. Local contractor John Ingalls paid men two dollars per day to assist him in gathering up the lumber and piling and securing it above high water. Over the rest of the month, wreckers completed taking apart what was left of the ship, gathering up any of the fastenings and iron knees that were fit for reuse.

Although the deals were damaged to varying extent, with corners and edges scuffed and chafed on the rocks, they sold readily for anywhere from two dollars and fifty cents to five dollars per thousand. The sudden good fortune of a month's steady wages along with the ready supply of lumber sparked a building boom in the Grand Manan village of North Head, including the construction of a large schoolhouse. Though nothing at all remains of the wreck, a great many houses of North Head today trace their origins to the hold of the old ship *Humber*.

And perhaps an even greater legacy of the old ship arrived the following year: a new steam fog alarm was built at nearby Long Eddy, put into operation on July 1, 1874. Its deep and sonorous tone boomed out across the north channel to give comfort to many a mariner for over a hundred years, riding Fundy's currents enveloped in fog. Indeed, that headland has ever since been called "The Whistle."

THE WANDERING BARQUE *GEORGE W. HUNTER*

On December 21, 1872, under the command of Captain John C. Grace, the 793-ton barque *George W. Hunter* sailed from Saint John, bound for Dublin, Ireland, with a cargo of lumber. A new vessel, it had been launched at Tusket, near Yarmouth, just over a year before. With a hull fully braced with iron knees, it was a well-built vessel that had been optimistically consigned to the lumber trade. The owners—from Tusket, Yarmouth, and Saint John—looked forward to a profitable venture in the bulky but dependable shipping of large, squared lumber deals.

After the tug left, the barque worked its way down the Bay of Fundy. The wind started blowing hard and the captain decided to seek shelter in Bliss Harbour. It was at this point that fortunes turned for the worse for the *Hunter*. Whether or not a more competent captain might have been better able to cope with conditions, we will never know.

In the wind, the barque heeled over "on beam ends," that is, it laid down on its side, no doubt partly because of the large load of deals it carried on deck. Lying down like this, it would not respond to its rudder and the captain could not steer it clear of Man of War Rock in Bliss Harbour. The captain dropped the port bower anchor

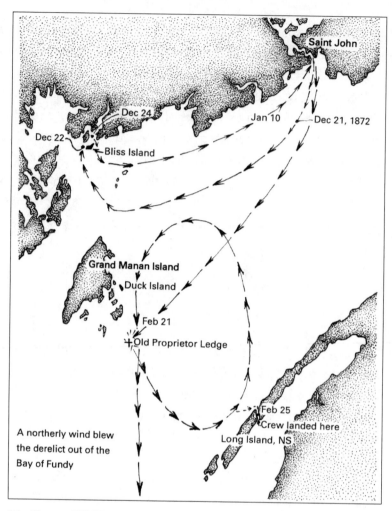

The George W. Hunter *wandered aimlessly through the Bay of Fundy.*

to try to stop the ship from drifting onto the rock. Captain Grace was ultimately responsible for gross crew incompetence: the sailors had been careless in stowing the anchor chain, and it jammed before the anchor could take hold on the bottom. So this port anchor was hanging useless below the ship—not digging into the bottom to hold the ship, but weighing down the chain, preventing the crew from untangling it. Before the starboard anchor could be let go, the ship grounded on rocky bottom on the west side of Man of War Rock on the morning of December 22.

When it struck ground, the tide was on its way out, at about half tide. So the *Hunter* waited there as the tide continued down and then came back up again. On the next flood tide, the *Hunter* floated on its lumber cargo as the tide rose toward high tide. Before the captain could move the ship away from the rocks, the wind veered northwest and blew a terrific squall. Swinging around in this strong wind, the ship dragged both anchors, and went aground again on the north side of Bliss Island, on Crab Rock. When the tide dropped, it left the ship in about 2 fathoms (12 feet) of water. The *Hunter* lay there on its starboard side, filling with the tide, until the afternoon of December 23.

The captain engaged the steamer *Glendon* to tow his barque to a safe anchorage, where it was surveyed. It was towed back to Saint John on January 10, to have the deck load discharged. It was put on Halyard blocks so shipwrights could replace the damaged planks and re-caulk the ship.

The *George W. Hunter* was laden again with deals, and then under the continued command of Captain Grace, it sailed from Saint John for

❋ "Scantling" are rough remnants of lumber.

Dublin with its cargo of deals and scantling. This time, however, heading down the south channel of the Bay of Fundy, it struck Old Proprietor Ledge southeast of Grand Manan on Friday night, February 21. The cause of the shipwreck, according to the report of the Department of the Marine, was "drunken crew." Again, one wonders at the captain's leadership.

Soon after stranding, the crew was able to back the *Hunter* off on the flooding tide, which created a strong current pushing it back up the bay, off the treacherous reef, and into the deep water north of the rock. The *Hunter* was leaking badly and soon became waterlogged, but it was in no real danger, as it floated on its lumber cargo. It drifted toward the Nova Scotia shore and, not far off Long Island, NS, the undisciplined crew abandoned it the next morning and eagerly landed at Petit Passage on Tuesday, February 25.

In this derelict state, the *George W. Hunter* drifted northward and a tug went to look for it but was unsuccessful. It then drifted back near Duck Island, Grand Manan, but there was too heavy a sea running to permit small boats to go out to it. A northerly wind took it out of the bay and the *George W. Hunter* was next seen three hundred miles south of Cape Sable.[63]

On March 2, at 2:00 P.M., the steamship *Hansa* saw the water-logged and abandoned *Hunter*.[64] On March 14, the crew of the *Winged Hunter*—bound from New York for Liverpool—boarded the derelict. It was full of water and its rudder gone, but they found a little dog and a cat on board, obviously left behind by the crew of the *Hunter*. The crew of the *Winged Hunter* tied their ship alongside the wreck with a thick rope, intending to take some things off the wreck. The first officer brought away the dog, but the cat escaped. They also took some charts, some nautical books, the octant, and the quadrant. There were hawsers and ropes and a fresh quarter of beef in the stores. The anchors and chains were still on the bow, and the ship held a full deck load of deals. The *Hunter* had a three-foot list to port, and the remnants of a British ensign flew atop the mizzen-mast.[65]

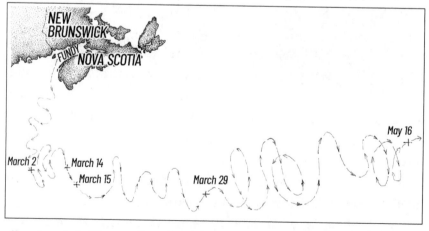

Abandoned, the Hunter *floated and drifted about the Atlantic Ocean.*

A few days later, the brigantine *Arthur* encountered the *Hunter*.[66] On March 29, the *Selma* reported taking a cable, four new ropes, two compasses, and a bell from the wreck.[67] The *Hunter* then continued to drift off eastward on the prevailing current. The *Dauntless* was the last to see it, on May 16, waterlogged and fast breaking up.[68] This was the last report of the wandering derelict. The *George W. Hunter* was insured for $20,250, and for a total loss, $28,000—clearly a major setback for the optimistic investors of only two years before, investors who had placed their business venture in the hands of an incompetent captain and crew.

THE UNMANAGEABLE SHIP: THE *TURKISH EMPIRE*

At the zenith of square sail, the British full rig ship *Turkish Empire* must have been a proud command for an ambitious young captain trading on the world's shipping routes. Registered at 1,502 tons, it was a wooden ship with an iron top and copper-sheathed bottom and was built in England in 1856 as the steamer *Stamboul*. It survived to be a veteran, by nineteenth-century merchant marine standards, and was converted to square sail for global, long-range trade across the world's oceans.

In the late 1870s, Captain Alden J. West, a young man from Harvey, NB, commanded the *Turkish Empire*. He was only twenty-nine when he brought the ship into Saint John in early winter 1879 to load timber for Dublin, Ireland.

Rough, squared deals were stowed under the ship's deck and were also piled and lashed securely on top of the deck. When ready to sail, the ship had on board about 1.1 million board feet of deals. As they prepared to sail, three new men joined the crew. On departure the ship's company consisted of Captain West, twenty-four men, and a boy. The captain's wife and two-year-old daughter had been sailing with the ship but returned to their home in Albert County before the ship set out on this March voyage. As was common practice, a pilot accompanied the ship to the mouth of the Bay of Fundy and past the treacherous Grand Manan archipelago—so pilot Richard Cline of Saint John was also aboard.

When the *Turkish Empire* left the port of Saint John on the afternoon of Thursday, March 6, 1879, people on board and ashore noticed that it was leaning over with a bad starboard list, a result of careless stowing of the lumber cargo on deck. But a tug nevertheless towed the ship out of the harbour and six miles below Partridge Island. There the ship cast off the tug's towing hawser to proceed under sail. Off Point Lepreau, at 10:00 P.M. Thursday evening, the weather was threatening, and some thought was given to returning to Saint John, no doubt to re-stow the cargo and correct the list to float on an even keel again.

The young captain decided, however, to proceed on the voyage. This ultimately proved to have been a fatal error in judgment. The worsening weather that evening prompted the captain to lighten the ship by jettisoning the deck load. This was not easy, with the ship lurching and rolling in the heavy sea, sliding the unsecured, heavy deals about dangerously to roll off over the side. A scow load of deals and ends were thrown overboard, but with little effect, as the gale had become a full and furious snowstorm blowing from the northeast, a direction that increased the starboard list. The ship was thrown down so far at times that the sea was washing up the deck as far as the hatch coamings.

Lifelines were rigged and all sail was taken in as the ship lay over so badly on its side that it became completely unmanageable. The ebb tide through the night took the ship down the Bay of Fundy toward Grand Manan, as the ship wallowing on its side responded little to its southeast heading. It became evident to Pilot Cline that it would be impossible to save the ship from going ashore. With the seas washing the leeward deck, the men were forced to spend the night clinging to the topsides of the ship.

Through the early morning flood tide of Friday, March 7, the wind buffeted the helpless ship against the current until it turned at high tide. At 10:00 A.M. any hope of saving the ship was lost. The captain, who had been standing on deck near the pilot, went below and got his watch and returned to the deck. The hostile rocky shore was imminent, and each man stared his own death directly in the face.

A few minutes later, listing heavily to starboard, the *Turkish Empire* was thrown broadside onto the shore at the northern end of Big Duck Island, Grand Manan. The heavy breaker dropped back, and the next swell surged against the huge hull and then rolled it over on the other side, breaking off all the masts and splitting the ship in two. Captain West, wearing hip rubber boots and a heavy coat, was never seen again. The cargo of deals spewed out of the broken hull and reeled wildly back and forth and up and down in this massive maelstrom that tossed flotsam and men about like toothpicks.

The pilot was washed overboard on the offshore side. The next sea threw him back over the steering wheel. The deck was breaking apart from the side of the ship, and Pilot Cline caught himself in the opening split. A third sea washed him toward shore, clear of the wreck. Grasping a floating deal, he kept his head above water and reached for more deals to hold himself up as he drifted to shore, where he scrambled up the beach among tumbling and rolling timbers. Within five minutes of striking the rocks, the *Turkish Empire* was reduced to chunks of hull and a frenzy of floating heavy timbers.

Sixteen sailors, each with a different story to tell, managed to make it ashore. The first mate said that from the time the ship struck until he found himself ashore on the bank seemed to be but a moment. Seven lives were lost. Along with Captain West, all three men who joined the ship in Saint John were lost: Charles Dwyer of Halifax; Anthony MacPherson of Newfoundland; and Burton Raymond of Yarmouth. The other three lost were James Irvine of Shetland, Scotland; Dan MacIntosh of Pictou, NS; and William Magee of Ireland.

The story of Anthony MacPherson is particularly unusual. Within three months, he was shipwrecked three times. Originally a school-teacher, MacPherson decided to go to sea. When the Saint John schooner *Welcome Home* sailed from Inagua, West Indies, for Baltimore, Maryland, MacPherson was a member of the crew. The schooner foundered on December 30, 1878, but MacPherson was rescued, along with the rest of the crew, and landed at Bermuda. He went back to Saint John, where he shipped on the Saint John barque *Canada West*, bound for Barcelona. Off the southern part of Nova Scotia, the vessel sprang a leak and became disabled and waterlogged. The crew abandoned the sinking ship on February 13, 1879, was rescued by the *Lina*, and landed at New York. Undaunted by these experiences, MacPherson returned to Saint John and joined the *Turkish Empire*. This time, on the rocky shore of Big Duck Island, he experienced his final shipwreck.

The storm spent out its fury and eventually subsided, permitting survey of the awful scene. Big Duck Island is treeless and flat, the low-lying bank giving away to a rugged, rocky beach. The tidal shore is a two-hundred-yard band of rocks and ledges. Low tide at Big Duck Island offered a catastrophic spectacle. A million feet of deals lay in an unbroken windrow at high tide level for a third of a mile, piled up as high as twenty feet.

Wreckage was strewn in all directions: spars, sails, rigging. The largest piece of the ship was a seventy-foot chunk of the bottom of the hull. The top of the ship was constructed of iron, and one side of this lay at half tide, while the other was further up the beach, partly covered with deals. Its anchors lay at low water, with the chains twisted back and forth in all directions, running under wreckage and huge boulders. The lower masts, also made of iron, were badly bent and smashed.

Of the seven men lost, only one body was found in relative entirety. The badly bruised body, with part of the leg gone below the knee, was found nearly half a mile away down the shore of the island. Survivors identified it as that of the cook, a man of about fifty years of age—probably Charles Dwyer of Halifax. Dr. Cameron, of Grand Manan, came to the scene, took charge of the body, and removed it to Grand Manan for burial. Not far away, a lump of human flesh was discovered; only because the doctor was present could it be identified as a human heart.

In a few days, the floating remnants of the ship and cargo were spread along the Grand Manan shores from Swallow Tail to Three Islands. The *Turkish Empire* had been copper-sheathed and copper-fastened. This—along with the iron topsides and masts, and the sizeable cargo of deals—generated considerable interest in the sale of the wreckage, which took place by auction at Grand Manan on March 19. Several people came to the island by steamers and boats to attend. After lively bidding, the ship was sold for $2,150 and the cargo for $800, all purchased by parties from Saint John. The salvage work provided welcome winter and spring employment, as locals gathered lumber and broke up copper and iron pieces of the wreck for reshipment to the scrapyard. All through the summer and into the fall, salvage work continued.

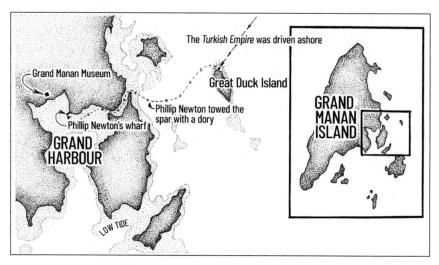

After the Turkish Empire *was wrecked, Phillip Newton salvaged a spar and towed it to his property in Grand Harbour.*

In a century's retrospect, the most interesting salvage was that done by Phillip Newton, of Grand Manan. Shortly after the ship was wrecked, Newton tied a drifting spar to his dory, which proved to be the yard that supported the mainsail for the ship. Using tidal currents to his advantage, he rowed and towed the massive spar through a tidal passage known as "The Thoroughfare" onto his shore property in Grand Harbour, about three miles from the wreck. He used the entire spar in one piece when he built it into his wharf. It remained there until 1970, when the owner of the property at the time, Reverend David Romig, donated the spar to the Grand Manan Museum. High school boys and their teachers carefully dislodged the spar and floated it across Grand Harbour on the incoming tide, where it was beached on skids the boys had made. A tow truck brought the spar, on its skids, to lie on squat supports beside the Grand Manan Museum.

Two tapered pieces of yellow pine carefully spliced together make up this spar, which is about seventy feet in length and once carried the ship's great mainsail. Now, prone and unmoving, this huge wooden spar remains a massive and silent reminder of the tragic shipping catastrophe on a wild March morning in 1879, when the age of sail was starting to wane in Atlantic Canada.

THE STEAMER *CORINTHIAN* ON NORTHWEST LEDGE

The Canadian Pacific steamship *Corinthian* left Saint John at seven o'clock on Saturday morning, December 14, 1918, under the command of Captain David H. Tannock and carrying a large cargo for the British government. As the *Corinthian* steamed out past Partridge Island, NB, there was fog and a moderately heavy sea running.

Heading down the Bay of Fundy, the engineers could not bring the ship up to its top speed of twelve knots. The stokers worked harder than usual, but the quality of coal was poor, with clay and stones in it. The engines were only turning about forty-eight to fifty revolutions per minute on the poor coal, which gave the ship a speed of seven and a half knots. Operating at this slower speed in the tidal currents of the bay proved to be a costly error.

The bridge of the steamer was above the thickest of the fog, and by 1:00 P.M. the sailor on watch saw Boars Head, at the upper end of Long Island, NS, some nine miles away. The weather was clearing slightly, but the sea was choppy as a southeast wind was breezing up. Soon after passing Boars Head, the higher ground of Brier Island was seen over the fog. The lookout was watching for the Northwest Ledge buoy, which he expected to see over the port bow.

When he saw the buoy, it was off the starboard bow, which meant that the ship was on the wrong side of the buoy. The helmsman immediately turned the rudder to try to turn the ship, but the ship did not respond in time and about a minute later, at 2:20 P.M., the ship struck with a slight lurch and remained hard aground.

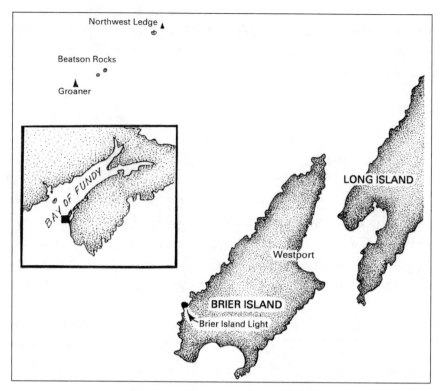

The Corinthian *was wrecked on Beatson Rocks off Brier Island, the western tip of Nova Scotia.*

It had hit Beatson Rocks, just southwest of Northwest Ledge, off Brier Island. Immediately, the captain ordered the engineers to put the engine full astern, which they did. But Captain Tannock soon realized that this would be futile, and ordered the engineers to stop the engine, although they kept the pumps going until about 7:30 P.M., when the rising water threatened to extinguish the fires.

When the Partridge Island wireless station picked up the distress signals from the *Corinthian,* the government steamer *Aberdeen* was on the way from Westport toward Saint John. It turned around and went to the wreck. The *Aberdeen* arrived at the scene before midnight, and the *Festubert,* of the Canadian naval service, arrived shortly after. In the thick fog, they were unable to see anything. The sea conditions had worsened, making it difficult for the ships to rescue the *Corinthian*'s crew. By 2:00 A.M., eight had been rescued in a lifeboat from Westport. Fishers bravely set out from the nearby coves and ports and nimbly rescued men from the stranded steamer and landed them ashore at Westport.

By noon on Sunday, authorities in Saint John received a wireless message that Captain Tannock was safely aboard the *Aberdeen*, and that his entire crew of eighty-seven was all accounted for. The *Aberdeen* and the *Festubert* divided up the crew and carried them to Saint John, leaving Captain Tannock in Westport to attend to the survey of the wreck. The captain reported that the holds of the steamer were full of water and that the ship would be a total loss. Indeed, as the *Aberdeen* passed the *Corinthian* on its way to Saint John at 8:30 A.M. on Monday, it was high tide and the decks of the ship were awash. Only the bridge, masts, and funnel were showing above the surface of the water.

The 7,332-ton *Corinthian* was built at Belfast, Ireland, in 1900 by Workman & Clark for the Allan Line, and was, about three years earlier, taken over by the Canadian Pacific. It carried a large cargo for the British government, including 120,000 bushels of wheat, a lot of Douglas fir lumber for the construction of airplanes for the war effort, 106 standards of deals, and a big shipment of apples, condensed milk, nails, packages of flour, and boxed meats.

At the inquiry that followed the stranding, Captain Tannock noted that when he set his courses, he had made no allowance for the wind or the tidal current. Furthermore, with the very poor quality coal, the ship could not reach normal operating speed and so was subjected even more to the effects of the current—all significant errors in judgment, indeed.

On the Monday after the stranding, boats from Westport salvaged what they could of the cargo, but the next day, a heavy gale swept over the Bay of Fundy and kept boats away for several days. A week later, the little steamer *La Tour* recovered several thousand dollars worth of cargo and took it to Yarmouth. Westport boats continued working at the wreck. The sea was taking its toll on the steamer and as it started breaking up, boxes of bacon, pork, and canned goods floated around the bay. Within a month, the steamer had broken up in the gales and disappeared beneath the waves. It was estimated that goods valued at a total of 3 million dollars were lost in the wreck of the *Corinthian*.

~

Within a few months, the Yarmouth Salvage Co. Ltd. was formed with the intention of salvaging valuable machinery from the wrecked ships around this part of the bay and, in particular, from the *Corinthian*. The promoter who formed the company, David A. Saunders, had bought the hull as it lay, together with all the cargo on board. With a salvage boat, crew, and an experienced diver, Fred Doyle of Saint John, Saunders visited the wreck in June. Doyle surveyed the wreck and noted the tidal slacks and working conditions. He felt conditions to be satisfactory for salvage work, which was carried out on the wrecked steamer that summer.

I visited the wreck of the *Corinthian* in August 1970. Carman Cook and I took a lobster boat to Westport, which was to be our base. On Tuesday morning, August 25, we left Westport and went out to Northwest Ledge to be there before the low water slack. Arriving there, we went over to the Beatson Rocks groaner buoy. We asked some of the handline fishers there where the ledge was to be found and they pointed us to it, so we went over and dropped anchor.

I donned diving gear, judged where I might expect to find the ship, dropped over the side of the boat, and swam down through the swiftly flowing tidal current, plunging for the bottom. I pulled myself across the bottom against the current until I came to the wreckage of the *Corinthian*. Securing my float line to a connecting rod in the engine, I checked all the crank bearings, hoping they might be brass. But they were iron bearings, worthless in salt water—disappointing.

I found the wreck to be lying roughly east to west, with the stern to the east. I checked over the area to the north of the four boilers and found very little. I then swam down toward the stern and back, again finding very little, so I probed around south of the boilers and found a few pieces of brass and copper there. I returned to the anchor line that went up to the boat. We moored the boat over the remnants of the wreck, and I took down some dynamite to set some exploratory charges on wreckage to the south of the boilers. After setting off the dynamite, we returned to Westport.

That afternoon, we returned to the wreck for the high water slack. The tide was still running hard when we got there, and it took some hunting to find our buoys in the current. Carman went down and explored the wreck too, while I tended on the surface. After a while he came up and took down lines to lift any salvageable materials. Before it became too dark to work, we picked up a few hundred pounds of brass and copper.

The next morning, Wednesday, after an early breakfast, we left for Northwest Ledge. Shortly after leaving the northern point of Brier Island, the fog started to shut in, and by the time we reached the Beatson groaner, it was thick. Setting out from the groaner by compass, we found our lobster buoys marking the wreck a half mile away. I went down and set up new work lines. The visibility underwater was good; although I was working in about 40 feet of water, I could see the bottom of the boat plainly. I sent up the remainder of the brass and copper that I could readily find, and then our bow anchor.

I took a final swim around the wreck to have another look, and after towing out a final copper pipe with our stern line we left the wreck. It looked to me like the ship had been well picked over before, so there was no point in spending any more time there. But we had picked up close to half a ton of brass and copper, so it wasn't a wasted trip. And besides, it was an interesting shipwreck and location to dive, so we felt some pleasant satisfaction as we sailed back across the bay to Grand Manan.

CHAPTER EIGHT

FOG

∽

Fog has often been blamed for the many shipwrecks about the Bay of Fundy. Indeed, in fog, not being able to see familiar landmarks, mariners can become anxious and apprehensive, and this makes matters worse. When I was working out on the bay without radar, I listened to what the old-timers told me: observe your compass course and times under different tide conditions in clear weather, and then when the fog shuts in, follow the very same courses, at the same speeds, and mark the same time. It is hard to have the confidence to do that while running along in thick fog. But stopping to listen for foghorns or slowing down just adds to the uncertainty. The mariners who followed their courses with steely confidence generally fared better than those who timidly slowed down and were carried farther off course by the tidal currents.

Grand Manan is often surrounded by fog, most particularly during the early summer, but also at other times of the year when warm, moist air blows over cooler water. Winds from the southwest usually bring this moist air with them, and blowing over the cool Bay of Fundy, the moisture condenses into tiny drops that drift along with the wind. Fog is basically a cloud that forms right at sea level.

In thick fog, sailors often take turns on lookout at the bow, looking for hazards—other vessels, unexpected rocks. Fog was dreaded, but a fact of Fundy.

Interestingly, the northern end of Grand Manan experiences less fog. By the time the fog reaches that point, the southwest wind has blown over warm land for the twenty-mile length of the island, drying out before it reaches North Head. This was recognized early in Admiralty charts, which valued the harbour at North Head for its relatively fog-free atmosphere.

The hazardous reefs and ledges that are strung out below Grand Manan, on the other hand, lie directly exposed to the "out winds," as the island's residents refer to winds from the southerly quadrant. These ledges, low lying and hidden from view until almost upon them, have regularly collected more than their share of shipping, piled up and haplessly stranded.

Fog usually occurs in warmer weather, in spring and summer, and the odds of successful salvage then are much better than during the heavier winds of winter. But some ships hit the rocks so hard that their hulls crack and break up beyond repair.

THE STEAMSHIP *TYNE*

The Bay of Fundy's demand for more rigorous care in navigation was brought to a head after a veteran sea captain who, in spite of many years in charge of ships at sea, was severely censured for taking too casual an approach when navigating out of the bay on his first visit to these waters.

Captain Herbert William Robson had been in charge of the Royal Mail Steam Packet *Tyne* for four years, but he had never been in the Bay of Fundy until he brought the *Tyne* to Herring Cove, near Alma, NB, in the early summer of 1916. Anchored just off-shore, lighters loaded the steamer with heavy timbers to be taken to Cherbourg, France, to be used to shore up Allied trenches in the Great War.

The *Tyne* weighed anchor and left Herring Cove at 4:20 P.M. on Saturday, July 22, and set out down the bay into a southwest wind. It ran into a dense fog at 5:00 P.M. Captain Robson was rather casual in reckoning his position, computing his progress solely on the basis of the revolutions of the propeller shaft. This might have been adequate in ordinary conditions, but in the strong tidal currents of the Bay of Fundy, to his ultimate chagrin, his reckoning did not at all agree with the ship's actual position.

At 8:27 P.M. Robson reduced the speed of the steamer to about six knots. This, in fact, worsened his reckoning error, for at the slower speed the current exercised its influence for a longer period of time, carrying him even further off course. At 10:00 P.M. he stopped and took soundings, finding 47 fathoms. The crew continued to take soundings throughout the night, and at 6:00 A.M. they had 100 fathoms.

At 7:20 A.M. the captain noticed a disturbance in the sea—possibly a tide rip—and immediately the lead was cast, to find only 27 fathoms. Robson gave the order to stop the steamer. Another sounding found 8.5 fathoms. The engines were ordered full astern and the anchor let go. At 8:20 A.M. the anchor was dragging and at 8:30 on Sunday morning, July 23, the *Tyne* ran on the rocks on a shoal about three hundred yards north of Old Proprietor Ledge, off Grand Manan. It struck about two hours after high tide, when the powerful tidal current was running out of the Bay of Fundy. The engines were put hard astern, but the ship could not be moved against the powerful current and as the tide ebbed, the ship's bow ground and strained on the rocks.

> ✸ A kedge anchor is carried away from the ship and dropped to the bottom to enable the crew to winch the ship toward this anchor.

The *Tyne*, weighing 1,821 tons, was an old steamer, built in 1880. But it was a steel ship and took the stranding in stride. The bottom was punctured, and the forepeak and first hold filled with water. The crew ran out a kedge anchor to hold it in position, in an attempt to contain the damages while they awaited assistance. The lifeboat from the Outer Wood Island life-saving station discovered the stranded steamer that evening and came alongside at 2:00 A.M. on July 24. The life-saving crew made three trips to Seal Cove with the *Tyne*'s officers and crew, thirty-five men in all. The lifeboat then waited by the stranded steamer until 6:00 P.M. on Tuesday, July 25, when the services were no longer needed, the salvage tugs having all well in hand.

The Coastguard steamer *Helena* arrived at Old Proprietor Ledge on Tuesday afternoon and stretched heavy hawsers to the stranded steamer. During the day, Captain Robson and some of the crew had jettisoned the deck load of timber on the fore part of the ship to lighten the bow. The tug *Neptune* arrived at 8:00 P.M. and picked up a hawser to tow the ship. At 9:30 P.M.—with the tide high and both steamers straining, along with the stranded steamer's own engines running full astern—the *Tyne* slid off the ledge into deep water.

With the two tugs towing, the *Tyne* was taken to Saint John to be berthed, surveyed, and repaired. Although the forepeak and forehold were full of water, the rest of the ship was tight and there was little to suggest the recent ordeal to the casual observer. But, on its port anchor, two great streamers of seaweed hung as souvenirs of the adventure.

~

At the inquiry into the stranding, when all the witnesses had been questioned, the court concluded that Captain Robson "did not adopt all the prudence that was required in navigating his ship; taking into consideration the fact that he was a stranger in these waters…" The court stated: "To navigate a vessel meeting conditions existing in the Bay of Fundy, such as tides, by basing himself only on the number of revolutions the ship was making notwithstanding the fact that he stopped occasionally to take soundings, is not a very reliable method to adopt."[69]

The court noted other errors in judgment made by the captain and determined the following:

> *For the above reasons we feel that the master deserves that the court should deal with his certificates, but after taking into consideration the honesty displayed in giving his evidence as it was quite apparent he did not endeavour to*

hide any particulars or shortcomings of his; and the able manner in which he succeeded in getting his vessel from the rocks, for which, the court is aware, few vessels have heretofore escaped after striking; also the shortage of masters and officers under present conditions; the court thinks it will meet the justice of the case by reprimanding and severely censuring the master for failing to adopt the precautionary measures mentioned above.

The lasting legacy of this event is the naming of the treacherous rocky shoal that the steamer ignobly struck. Fishers and sailors have since come to call it the "Tyne Rock."

THE STEEL BARQUE *ASHMORE*

Less than a year later, at 9:00 A.M. on Tuesday, April 2, 1918, and again in thick fog, the Norwegian iron barque *Ashmore* struck the Dixon Rocks—one of the treacherous Murr Ledges to the south of Grand Manan Island. The *Ashmore* was a steel barque of 1,043 tons, built in 1877 at Port Glasgow, Scotland. It was bound from Saint Vincent, Cape Verde, for Saint John in ballast, intending to load a cargo for Australia. Sailing all the way from Africa and by dead reckoning up into the Bay of Fundy, at about 8:30 on the morning it struck, Captain Leknesund had obtained a sounding of 52 fathoms. He sounded again at about 9:00 A.M. and had 16 feet (2.5 fathoms)—and almost immediately grazed a rock, then within a minute or two was stranded on the Dixon Rocks. Looking around his grounded vessel, the captain noted that to the windward, ahead, and to the lee, snarling rocks were angrily breaking in the heavy swell. From the moment his sounding alerted him to a problem, he could do nothing to avert the stranding.

The Ashmore had two decks, but its steel construction was no match for the rocks and heavy swell of Fundy. Two minutes after the barque struck, the bottom was torn out and the *Ashmore* was a total loss, unsalvageable. Captain Leknesund quickly realized that his vessel was doomed, so he made preparations to abandon the ship, and accordingly a boat was launched.

The small craft was smashed against the rocks, but a second was launched without mishap. All fourteen of the crew succeeded in boarding their frail craft and, with considerable difficulty, made their way among the breakers and out into the long roll of the outer Bay of Fundy. They rowed to the Gannet Rock light, where they remained for three hours until they were rescued by the Outer Wood Island lifeboat, arriving back at the life-saving station at 2:10 P.M. After spending a comfortable night at Outer Wood Island, they were picked up by a government steamer and taken to Saint John the next day. Besides Captain Leknesund, there were two officers and eleven crewmembers. An international crew, there were two Swedes, two Danes, two Finns, and the rest were Norwegian.

~

Walter and Leavitt Benson were brothers who fished out of Seal Cove, the nearest village to the wreck. Being experienced in the waters around these ledges, they were the first ones to visit the *Ashmore* after it struck. In the late 1960s, when I was living in Seal Cove, I spoke with Leavitt who was, by that time, an elderly man. He was quiet and kindly, and he enjoyed the opportunity to tell me his story. When Leavitt and his brother arrived at the wreck, the crew had already abandoned the ship and had rowed away to seek land. Leavitt described the wreck as a large steel barque that had a steam engine on deck for handling freight.

Leavitt smiled as he told me how they found two monkeys aboard the wreck (no doubt brought aboard in Africa). They were

The Ashmore's *name was made of brass letters fixed to the hull. This "S" was found lying on the rocky bottom near the remains of the hull.*

obviously pets and needed care, so the Benson brothers brought them back to Seal Cove and gave them to Tom Foster, the lighthouse keeper at Southwest Head.

The captain had said to Leavitt that he was sorry to lose his ship, as so many had recently been lost (this wreck taking place during the Great War). The captain also said he hadn't seen land since he left Africa until he struck the ledge in the fog.

The steel barque quickly broke up and disappeared. I visited the remains of the *Ashmore* in the exposed shallows among the Dixon Rocks. There were recognizable sections of the hull on the bottom along with large pieces of rigging hardware, but the ship was badly beaten up by heavy seas from every direction, so very little is left intact. Perhaps the most interesting item I found was a brass "S" that had been fastened to the hull to form part of the name.

THE STEAMSHIP *TROJA*

Less than a year after the loss of the *Ashmore*, Old Proprietor Ledge claimed another stranding. The steam collier *Troja* was bound from Louisbourg, Cape Breton, for Saint John, NB, with a cargo of 3,650 tons of coal. While running through a dense fog in a heavy southeast wind, it struck a sunken ledge about 150 yards due west of Old Proprietor Ledge at 10:50 in the morning, about high tide, on Tuesday, March 18, 1919.

Captain John C. Caine, the master of the *Troja*, stated that after leaving Louisbourg, the weather was quite fine until they reached Cape Sable. When he figured, by dead reckoning, that he was abreast the Lurcher Shoal, about two o'clock on Tuesday morning, he altered course again to take his ship up the south channel, midway between Grand Manan and Brier Island. At 7:15 A.M. he ordered half speed and gave orders to cast the lead for a sounding, and at that moment, the man on lookout reported breakers ahead. The captain had thought he was mid-channel, but obviously he was not. He ordered the ship hard to port. The *Troja* had a deep draft for a small steamer and it steered poorly—its top speed was only seven and a half knots. With the ship not responding well to the helm, Caine could not control it, and at 10:50 A.M. the *Troja* ran aground on a sunken ledge.

After striking, the ship swung around about three points (approximately 18 degrees) to the west before settling in its stranded position. Caine ordered the boats to be readied, and a hand foghorn was sounded. Water entered the engine room, but the engines kept going until being put out by the rising water. The fog settled in more densely with a strong southeast breeze and a heavy sea running. The crew of twenty-eight men stayed aboard the *Troja* until noon the following day, when the weather cleared sufficiently for them to see the Old Proprietor buoy to know where they were.

~

When he was an elderly man many years later, White Head fisher Quint Small told me that he had been there to help take the crew off the *Troja*. He described the seas washing over the decks, fore and aft. Some of the crew left the ship in a small boat, with the ship's carpenter in charge. With four rowing on each side and two pushing it off, Small thought the little boat would be smashed against the steel hull in the seas, but luckily the seas subsided for a few minutes to allow them to get clear and pull away. They went into White Head Harbour. Shortly afterwards, the Outer Wood Island lifeboat came alongside the ship and took off the captain and rest of the crew.

The crew stayed at the life-saving station for two days and then went to Saint John, with the exception of the mate, Mr. Wayte, who stayed on at the station to attend to the stranded ship. The lifeboat made eight trips out to Old Proprietor to visit the stranded ship with the mate, the owner's representatives, and the underwriters to inspect the ship's condition.

The *Troja* was an iron screw steamer of 1,653 tons, built in 1896 in Stockton, England, by Richardson, Duck & Co. The Troja S. S. Company of Montréal owned the ship. Due to the exposed location, it being filled with water and laden with coal, the ship was sure to be a total loss.

But Captain Henry Black of New York, representing Lloyd's underwriters, decided after a survey of the scene and an examination of the hull that the *Troja* could be floated. In April, he awarded a salvaging contract to the Maritime Wrecking and Salvage Company. Accordingly, the wrecking tug *Sarnia City* left Halifax, towing along the wrecking barge *Maggie Marshall*, bound for Grand Manan to work with the tug *Hercules* in the effort to float the *Troja*. Fortunately, the weather remained reasonably calm over the next few weeks. As the cargo was discharged into lighters, salvors temporarily repaired the stranded steamer.

At 10:15 on Thursday morning, May 29, 1919, the *Troja* was floated and towed into White Head, where it was beached on flats.

Over successive low tides during the weeks that followed, the hull of the *Troja* was repaired and with the hull reasonably tight, the ship was towed to Halifax to be docked, arriving in the latter part of July.

At the investigation that followed the stranding, Captain Caine was severely censured for not using the deep-sea lead to take soundings, considering the weather conditions in which he was sailing. Once all the activity of the spring had subsided, the only reminder of the incident was the name "Troja Rock," applied to the culprit ledge and known by that name since.

THE STEAMER *COBAN*

At the end of May 1927, the 689-ton steamer *Coban* had just started carrying coal from Parrsboro, NS, at the head of the Bay of Fundy, to Saint John, NB, arriving on May 30 at Dominion Coal pockets in Saint John to discharge. On another coal run, it left Sydney, Cape Breton, on Thursday afternoon, June 16, with a full cargo of 1,168 tons of coal. Captain Benjamin Pope sailed in good weather until early morning on June 19, when he encountered thick fog.

Pope anchored off Partridge Island, just outside Saint John, at 3:00 A.M. and picked up the anchor shortly after 8:00 A.M. as the fog lifted. He had just started to enter Saint John Harbour when the fog shut in very thick. He had not gone far when he sighted land, and within a few minutes the steamer ran ashore on rocks off the southeast point of Partridge Island. The captain and his crew of twenty-one made it ashore and went into the city. It was nearly low tide when the *Coban* struck; the sharp rocks pierced the hull and it filled rapidly, being entirely submerged on the high tide.

With the tide flowing freely in and out of the hull, the *Coban* remained hard aground, its heavy cargo holding it there solidly. A lighter—a flat-bottomed barge—went to the wreck and commenced removing the coal from the holds. After remaining ashore several weeks, and with most of the coal cargo removed, the Saint John dry dock considered attempting to float the ship. Although the bridge and wheelhouse were washed away, along with almost everything on deck, the hull remained intact. Dry dock workers planned to pump the ship out on the low tide, lash large empty lighters on either side, and float it on the rising tide.

Meanwhile, at the inquiry investigating the stranding, the court reprimanded Captain Pope for not using his sounding lead in the fog. No doubt, when the fog had lifted briefly and he had seen Partridge Island and figured out where he was, he had been confident of his course across the short distance into the harbour. But Pope hadn't reckoned on the strong current out of the harbour on the last of the ebb. His captain's certificate was suspended for six months, although he would be permitted to sail as a mate on a coasting steamer.

There were a few attempts to raise the ship, but these were unsuccessful. The wreck and what remained of the cargo were sold at auction on September 2, where James H. McPartland, a Saint John junk dealer, was the successful bidder. McPartland managed to salvage the anchors and a considerable amount of gear and fittings. During the heavy gales that struck Saint John on Wednesday, January 25, and Thursday, January 26, 1928, the remnants of the *Coban* broke up and it disappeared, leaving no visible trace of its existence.

~

On August 19, 1971, Carman Cook and I went to Saint John and met with Lawrence Benson, a lighthouse keeper. While stationed at Partridge Island, Benson had done a little lobster fishing. Southeast of the island, just off from the keepers' houses, he had found a bad catch that snagged his traps and he suspected that it might be a shipwreck. He had heard about my shipwreck exploration work with Carman, and reached out. Carman and I had recently built a submarine, planning to use it to explore deeper water, but it didn't prove to be practical in strong currents. It sat, a novelty, in my front yard, with debt accumulating on a loan we had taken out to build it. We weren't actively looking for shipwreck profits to pay off the loan, but it appears Benson and the *Coban* crossed our paths at exactly the right time.

In the early evening, we boarded a boat and went out to the site. In diving gear, I dropped down onto the muddy bottom and started a compass search of the area. In a short time, I found the remains of a steamer, with its engine room reasonably intact at a depth of 20 feet. The condenser, pumps, and other machinery were all perfectly in place. The shipwreck appeared never to have been stripped at all: an exciting discovery to someone looking to salvage brass and copper! Looking around further, I found a steel shaft and propeller. The visibility wasn't too bad either, about eight to ten feet.

❀ When the tide is rising, the current flows into the harbour from the open sea, bringing clearer water with it. When the tide is falling, the current flowing out of the harbour brings muddy harbour water.

We returned to Grand Manan to prepare for a salvage expedition—at this point we had no clue as to the wreck's identity. We engaged a lobster boat and invited a couple of friends to work on deck, taking a week off their work to come to Saint John on this expedition just for the adventure of it. I picked up several cases of dynamite and other blasting supplies. On August 23, we returned to the wreck. I went down and set up our operation there.

I secured mooring lines on the bottom to tie up fore and aft, to position the boat over the work area on the flood tide (when we anticipated the best visibility). I then set up a ring line in the middle of the work area. With a large ring secured into the ship, a line through the ring allowed the lifting straps to be lowered to the work area from the boat, and bundles of copper to be raised on this continuous, endless line; a sort of conveyor belt for lifting scrap copper. Using the ring line, the first thing I did was send up any loose copper pipes. We prepared several charges of dynamite, and I secured these to critical points about the steam engine, places where I wanted to blow the iron and steel away from the brass and copper. Returning aboard the boat, we set off this charge. Since the blast stirred things up on the bottom, rendering the visibility to zero, we sailed up inside Partridge Island and remained anchored for the night.

After a day of windy weather, we returned to the wreck. I went down, where the visibility was poor due to the mud being stirred up by the windblown seas. I was able to make out the work done by the blast, even in the murky water. Some of the machinery was opened up, but it needed to be broken apart even more, so I set another series of charges on the places needing extra impact to break apart. Due to the poor visibility, this was very slow work, as I wanted to be thorough about what I was doing. I did not relish the notion of forgotten charges of dynamite lying around the work area of the steamer's engine room. I finally secured in place and tied together all the charges I wanted. I surfaced, boarded the boat, and we set another blast.

We returned to the wreck the next day and raised several pumps, pipes, and valves—about 3,000 pounds of brass. I set up more charges of dynamite on the appropriate places to pry out the main bearings of the engine, to blow apart the condenser ends, and around the port engine room fittings. After I surfaced, we set off the blast and returned to our mooring.

We returned the next day and raised quite a few crank bearings and a boatload of condenser tubes. We now had about 9,000 pounds of brass and copper aboard, and it was time to get a truck from a dealer and sell what we had before going back for more. The engine room was pretty much flattened by this time, and we were able to pry clear whatever brass and copper we wanted, but this took time. Using up the last of our dynamite, we went back the next morning and cleaned up the remnants of the brass found on the wreck. Picking up our mooring lines, our ring line, and all the rest, we bid farewell to this wreck site.

After returning home, Carman and I settled our accounts for the *Coban* expedition. After the expenses for our week at Saint John, we gave our boatman his share (for himself and the boat), paid off a former salvage partner, paid off the rest of the loan we had taken out at the bank to build our submarine, bought a case of whisky apiece for our buddies for their help on deck for the week, and when we looked everything over we wound up with fifty-seven dollars apiece for our efforts. A bit of a laugh, but thanks to the *Coban*, our submarine was paid for, free and clear.

CHAPTER NINE

A DANGEROUS BAY

⤳

A SALVAGE TRAGEDY: THE STEAMSHIP *HUMACAO*

The first steamship to be wrecked in the waters around Grand
Manan Island was the 1,714-ton Spanish steamer *Humacao*.
In August 1885, under the command of Captain Izaguirre,
it was bound from Hampton Roads, VA, for Saint John in ballast,
intending to load a cargo of deals for Liverpool. The *Humacao* was a
relatively new ship, built in Glasgow, Scotland, by G. Connell & Co.
and was registered in Bilboa, Spain.

Approaching the Bay of Fundy on August 4, the ship steamed
along in a fresh breeze, accompanied by rain and stormy weather.
The wind strengthened, and the visibility worsened as thick fog and
driving rain blackened the night and obscured everything around
the steamer, pitching and churning its way up the bay. Thinking he
was acting prudently, the captain slowed to half speed, adjusting his
reckoning accordingly. Slowing the steamer only worsened the errors
made in reckoning, and the flood tide and the southerly wind carried
the ship badly off its intended course.

At 2:30 A.M. on Wednesday, August 5, the *Humacao* struck a ledge unseen in the darkness, wind, rain, and fog. Although the ship was not travelling at full speed, its enormous momentum carried it onto the rocks to such an extent that it was immediately apparent to Captain Izaguirre that there was no hope of backing off. However, as there was no immediate danger for those on board, the captain felt it would be prudent to await light a

The wind and heavy rain ceased by four o'clock in the morning, but thick fog continued throughout the day, so the captain and crew stayed aboard the ship; they had no idea where they were stranded. About midday, the engineer managed to get up enough steam to blow the steam whistle continuously as a distress signal. The lighthouse keeper at Southwest Head light station, Walter B. McLaughlin, heard this. He duly noted it in his journal, figuring that it represented distress, but with no visibility in the thick fog, he had no way of knowing what the problem might be.

Late that night the wind changed to northwest and the fog cleared, and the lightkeeper thought he could see a light near the Western Murr Ledge. At first light, he discerned through his telescope the shape of a steamship ashore on the Wallace Rocks, and keeper McLaughlin cabled his superintendent J. H. Harding in Saint John to report it. He carefully recorded his discovery in his journal with the following entry for Thursday, August 6:

> *At midnight A.M. wind N. fresh breeze and clear weather. We think we can see a light near, or on, W. Murr ledge.*
>
> *At 4 A.M. we can see a Steam Ship ashore on Wallace Rocks. Cabled J. H. Harding to that effect.*
>
> *At 7 A.M. ships boat with officer and four men brought on shore by William J. Benson. The officer says the wreck is S.S. Humacao of Bilboa, Spain from Baltimore for St. John, N.B. and went on the Rocks at 2:30 yesterday morning in the fog storm. I cabled the fact to J. H. Harding and*

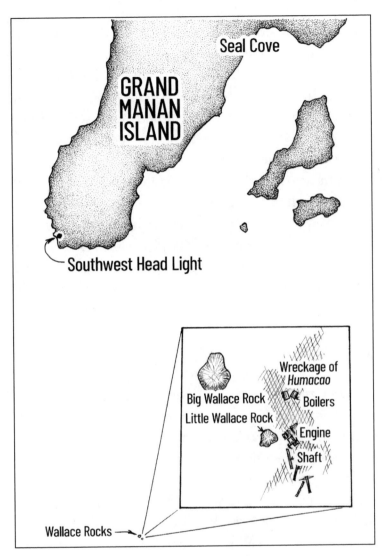

The Humacao *shipwrecked on the Wallace Rocks.*

offered my services to the officer, sent my son and hired man
with them to the ship, then dispatched for Turner Wooster
to come and take charge of the wreck. Weather continues
fine all day.[70]

The Wallace Rocks (named for the loss of the barque *Wallace* in 1841; see Chapter Three) are two inner rocks of the chain of Murr Ledges that ring the southern approaches to the Grand Manan archipelago. These treacherous rocks are covered at half tide, so a ship steaming along at high tide would hardly be aware of the rocks on a clear day, let alone on a windy, stormy, foggy night.

Local fishers sailed out to the stranded steamer and safely took the rest of the crew off the wreck, along with their personal effects, and brought them to Seal Cove before the end of the day. The crew stayed in Seal Cove all night, being well cared for by the hospitable people in the little village. Early on Friday morning, the tug *Storm King* arrived at Seal Cove, gathered aboard all the crew of the *Humacao*, and set out for Saint John. With the crew safely delivered, the tug returned to Seal Cove late Saturday evening, bringing the ship's agent.

On Sunday morning, the *Storm King* went off to the wrecked *Humacao*, and the ship's agent reviewed the situation. The steamer was stranded on the southeast side of the smaller of the Wallace Rocks, with its bow aimed about north-northeast. The submerged ledge on which it lay was almost amidships. Riding out on the rock abreast of the engine room, the ship's bottom was soon badly broken, and the tide ebbed and flowed within. Having struck with the tide high, the ship had filled with water, but the afterdeck was only awash on the high tide and the foredeck was well out of the water. The agent felt that, given the exposed location of the wreck and the strain of being grounded amidships, the steamer was in grave danger of breaking in two, particularly with the bow section sliding off into deeper water to the eastward of the ledge. The agent returned to Saint John having decided to abandon the wreck to the underwriters.

~

On Tuesday, August 18, 1885, the New York underwriters and a Halifax contractor steamed off to the wreck from Saint John, taking along a diver to check the underwater condition of the hull of the *Humacao*. They spent the next two days working at the wreck, assessing its condition. They returned to Saint John with the recommendation that arrangements be made to save everything possible from the stranded steamer. They carried out salvage operations over the next few weeks. With the salvaged materials and cargo being sold separately, the remains of the *Humacao* were sold at auction: the hull for $2,000 and what was left of the cargo in the ship for $500.

A consortium of Donald McNeil from New York and James Griffiths and others from Saint John purchased the wreck. They came up with a bold plan to try to build airtight wooden tanks inside the ship and lift the iron hull off the rocks. If successful, they could recoup their investment with a tidy profit, for the *Humacao* was quite new, with valuable engine machinery.

Early Sunday morning, September 20, the tug *Dirigo*, with Messrs. Griffiths and Napier and a gang of Saint John carpenters, left the port city towing a large scow bound for the wreck of the *Humacao*. They arrived at the stranded steamer about midday. Loaded on the scow were lumber and deals to be used in constructing the floatation tanks inside the hull of the wreck. The scow was tied up alongside the wreck, and the twelve workers went aboard the *Humacao*, where they would remain while they built the airtight wooden tanks that would be used to lift the ship off the rocks. The tug returned to Saint John late that afternoon.

The Saint John crew went about their work over the next two days, having set up sleeping quarters aboard the ship to allow them to take advantage of the low tides, both day and night, for the hull was so badly broken that the ship filled with each high tide. On Tuesday afternoon, the wind went to the south and the weather started to look threatening. About four o'clock in the afternoon, the tug *Dirigo* went out to the wreck to take some fresh water to the crew. The tide was down, so the tug could not go alongside the steamer. Furthermore, in the heavy swell, they could not launch the small boat from the tug to transfer the water either. Griffiths called out to the tug to go back to Seal Cove and return on the high water later in the evening, at which time the tug could come directly alongside the ship and transfer the water. The tug returned to Seal Cove, and the men at the wreck continued their work with the lumber in the ship's hold.

By the time the tug returned to the wreck at ten o'clock in the evening, the wind was out to the southeast, blowing a strong gale with rain. The wind was blowing directly on the offshore side of the ship, the side facing the deeper water. It was a very dark night and, as the captain considered the lee side of the wreck, there was great danger of the tug itself being stranded on the Wallace Rocks, which, while covered with water, were breaking menacingly the heavy sea. The afterdeck of the *Humacao* was awash in the high tide swells and, while the foredeck was well out, the lee side was dangerously close to the big Wallace Rock. It was apparent that it would be difficult and risky to try to bring the tug alongside. Those aboard the tug discussed among themselves that it was indeed a dirty night, but the men on the wreck felt secure where they were, and no one considered attempting to get aboard the tug to go ashore. So Griffiths called out once again to the *Dirigo* to go back to Seal Cove and return in the morning.

The men at the wreck went to bed in their quarters on the steamer without much concern for the situation. Certainly a strong gale was blowing, but a southeaster doesn't usually last long, and if the wind shifted to the northwest in the morning, the weather would improve. And even if it did stay rough, the deeper water would be on the lee side of the wreck, and the tug could come alongside to provide help should they need it. Besides, there was much work to be done to build the floatation tanks in the steamer's holds before the heavy fall winds did further damage to the steamer.

The feeling ashore, however, was very different; local mariners know well that at the Murr Ledges, a strong westerly following an "out wind"—a wind blowing from the outer bay—gives the roughest of sea conditions. There was grave concern at Seal Cove. At his light station at Southwest Head, lightkeeper McLaughlin wrote in his journal, "God help anyone who may be on the *Humacao* tonight."

As daylight arrived on Wednesday, September 23, the gale was changing direction, blowing from the south and continuing to shift in toward the west. As the tide rose, the wind increased from the west and the heavy ground-sea swelled and heaved against the ship, solid and immovable on the ledge. The men on the *Humacao* spent the first few hours of the day down in the hold, trying to secure the lumber that was being heaved about by the swell rolling through the ship. The *Dirigo* attempted to leave Seal Cove to go out to the Wallace Rocks, but the sea was running so high that they could not make it. Until the wind went westerly, they had not feared for the safety of those aboard the wreck, but now as the gale intensified, they became alarmed. Unable to go out to help, all they could do was go to the cliffs and watch off the ledges to see how the iron steamship weathered the storm.

By ten o'clock that morning, with the gale a full-blown westerly, on the last of the flood tide, the seas were making a clean breach of the ship, rolling up the unprotected stern deck and smashing against the central superstructure. The work in the holds had to be halted as the tide rose inside the ship, and the men looked about to see what they could do to try to assure their own safety. As the powerful seas swept the ship, there was nothing anyone could do but try to seek shelter in the wheelhouse amidships. They remained there until a particularly heavy sea struck the ship and broke it open just forward of the frightened men. The groans and loud bangs of shearing steel and fractured rivets were all but inaudible in the howling wind, the roaring seas, and thundering surf.

Another enormous wave swept the whole forward end of the ship off the ledge and into deeper water. Lumber and deals tumbled out and popped to the surface, and surged and rolled about madly in the surf. The men gazed in horror as their immediate peril became so suddenly clear. All hands scrambled up onto the upper bridge. There was no conversation as the men held on for their lives against the howling gale and the seas crashing about the ship.

As the men clung for their lives, the smokestack sheared off at the deck and washed away over the starboard side of the ship. A few minutes later the mainmast fell with a crash, and it too went over the side. A big sea hit Napier and knocked him down. He barely had time to scream to the others in a voice of plaintive desperation, "My leg is broken!" when a couple more seas tore the bridge apart and all were floundering about in the water. Napier was never seen again.

The wooden roof of the chart room was afloat nearby, and five men swam to it and scrambled up on it. A short distance away, Griffiths was on another makeshift raft of floating wreckage. Others crawled aboard whatever pieces of substantial flotsam could be found, for there was no shortage of lumber floating about the wreckage. For an hour, they paddled with pieces of boards, trying to avoid getting caught up in the breaking up wreck, or getting hit with heaving lumber and deals. The gale blew furiously, and the seas pounded the disintegrating steamer.

The sorry group of exhausted men struggled with the great waves cresting and troughing, as huge combers roared and crashed on the Wallace Rocks and smashed at the iron ship with unforgiving vengeance. They could not keep track of one another in the blowing spray, their tiny rafts disappearing from view in the troughs but rising to reassure one another on the next crest. Then, without warning, Griffiths's raft rose empty; he was gone beneath the waves. A few minutes later, another man was missed. No one knew when he drowned; in all the heaving turmoil he was just suddenly missed.

The Humacao *broke apart just forward of the bridge, and eleven people drowned.*

The five men on the drifting chart room roof were all that were left. Two of them soon died of exhaustion and slid off the raft, disappearing into the deep. Three were left: Jeremiah Daley, Hartley Stackhouse, and Sam Scribner. The strain of all that had happened had a profound effect on Stackhouse, and he became frenzied and distressed. Scribner and Daley restrained him and secured him to their raft with a piece of rope. They had been drifting about to the east of the wreck on the high tide slack, but the current of the ebb tide carried them around the Wallace Rocks and slowly to the west, against the wind. They soon came into the ebb tide eddy of the rock, and the relentless gale pushed them gradually back toward the wreck.

In among the breakers of the Wallace Rocks and the wreck, the little raft overturned, and Stackhouse and Scribner disappeared. Daley, a sturdy young man, only eighteen years old, came to the surface and swam over to a larger piece of wreckage floating nearby. He climbed aboard a piece of the bridge that had just broken clear and, catching the wind, he drifted eastward.

The gale abated on the ebb and, at about three o'clock, the tug *Dirigo* weighed anchor and steamed off to the ledges to search for any possible survivors of the terrible disaster that they had watched unfold from the top of the cliffs at Southern Head. Before the tug sailed, a large dory had gone out from Deep Cove, manned by local sailors who braved the waves in their sturdy and seaworthy little craft to do their part to try to save lives. On their way to the ledges, the tug caught up with the dory, threw it a line, and towed the local lifesavers the rest of the way to the Wallace Rocks. There, they carefully looked all over for any signs of survivors, but none were seen in the flotsam around the wreck. Saddened, they were about to give up and return to Seal Cove when someone on the tug spotted a large piece of floating wreckage about a mile to the east. The captain turned the tug and headed over. As they neared the wreckage, they realized there was a huddled form clinging to it, being tossed by the waves.

"It's a man, Cap, it's a man!" was the cry from the lookout on the bow of the tug. The *Dirigo* neared the wreckage, but in the heavy sea could not come too close for fear of smashing into it or being thrown upon it in the tossing seas. The small boat set off from the tug, manned by Grand Manan men, and they pulled alongside the heaving piece of bridge. With the expert skill of seafarers whose livelihoods depend on dealing with a capricious sea, they deftly plucked young Jerry Daley from his cold, wet, and precarious raft. In a few minutes, the dorymen were back alongside the tug, and the tough young survivor was helped aboard. Amazingly, in spite of his terrifying and enervating ordeal, Daley was still able to walk and, when sheltered and warmed aboard the tug, was soon able to relay his frightful experience. The tug and dory remained among the vestiges of the wreck for some time, searching through the flotsam for bodies, or possibly, against all odds, another survivor. But there were none to be found.

Over the next couple of days, boats visited the broken remains of the *Humacao*, searching for bodies of the victims of the fatal gale, but the sea did not give up any of the dead. As time went on, the remaining structural pieces of the iron hull gradually broke apart and slid under the waves. The *Humacao* and its tragic sequel faded into the background of local lore.

~

I first visited the wreck in December 1966, sailing there with Deverne Green, who fished lobster traps in the vicinity. I located the wreckage right up against the rocks, obscured by a thick forest of kelp. As we had visited on the low water slack, Deverne couldn't bring his lobster boat in close to the wreckage against the ledge, so he anchored off and came over in a dory. I tied chunks of copper pipe and red brass fittings from the ship's engine room to scraps of lobster trap line and Deverne hauled them into the dory. The thick kelp made it difficult to move about or find pieces of wreckage. But it was a nice calm day, and we had a good slack, so we were able to pull up a good haul of scrap brass and copper for our day's effort.

I didn't return to the *Humacao* for over a year, but spent several days working on the site during the summer of 1968. Carman Cook joined Deverne and me, and we systematically tore the heavy iron remains of the engine and shaft apart with dynamite to free up the brass and copper there. Early steam engines used brass more liberally than later models. The main crank bearings were just the sort of thing we wanted: each bearing half was made of 215 pounds of solid brass, so we were delighted with the several tons of brass and copper we raised from the wreck.

It was several years later when I returned to the *Humacao*. In the mid-1970s, I was a partner in a number of herring weirs, and we needed some heavy anchors to secure stays to run to weir stakes and hold one of the weirs against the strong tidal current. I recalled some large anchors at the *Humacao*, so we went there. This was some time after the Groundhog Gale of February 2, 1976 (more on that in Chapter Ten), which had had an enormous impact on the ocean floor around Grand Manan, moving about rocks and wreckage like toys. The iron wreckage on the Wallace Rocks had been stirred up and moved about and, much to my surprise, in the midst of this steamship wreckage were some old iron cannons. They were not in good condition, but appeared to be from a century previous to the *Humacao*. I was puzzled. The only explanation I could come up with was that they might have been there as ballast. Old cannons were obsolete and plentiful in the late nineteenth century, so it would make sense that their great weight would be put to good use as ballast. As far as I know, the cannons are still there, waiting for someone who wants one badly enough to venture there and pick one up.

The *Humacao* is not a shipwreck that attracts divers. It lies in very shallow water, with an almost incessant swell heaving over the rocks, making it difficult to bring a boat in on the low tide. And when the tide is up, a strong current flows over and around the submerged rock. Kelp usually covers the shallow rock in profuse abundance, which makes it difficult to move through the thick seaweed or see much wreckage. As inhospitable as the shipwreck is, its most indelible legacy is the tragic story of the failed salvage enterprise that cost so many Saint John tradesmen their lives.

THE U-BOAT RAID

In 1918, Allied forces were gradually winning the Great War. They were making advances, and there was an optimism that the worst was over. Nevertheless, German U-boats were still wreaking havoc with shipping in the North Atlantic and even on the doorstep of the coasts in New England and Atlantic Canada.

The Bay of Fundy was not in prime target territory for U-boat activity, but for a few days in August of 1918, local fishing and merchant shipping suffered significant losses at the hands of a U-boat in its short foray into these waters.

A submarine sank the eighty-four-ton fishing schooner *Muriel*, sailing out of Boston and bound for the Grand Banks, shortly before noon on Saturday, August 3, about forty-five miles west of Seal Island. After the submarine crew allowed the crew of the *Muriel* to set off in a boat, a bomb was exploded amidships, and the schooner sank. The crew rowed to the Nova Scotia coast and landed safely.

At three o'clock the same afternoon, the same submarine overhauled the seventy-five-ton schooner *Annie M. Perry*, also fishing out of Boston, about thirty miles west of Seal Island and destroyed it the same way. The schooner's American crew rowed for many hours in their dories and finally reached Woods Harbour, near Cape Sable, where kindly Nova Scotians helped them.

The seventy-nine-ton American fishing trawler *Rob Roy*, also out of Boston, was blown up by the submarine five hours later, at 8:00 P.M., some thirty-five miles west of Seal Island. Gorton-Pew Fisheries Co., the owner, suffered a loss of $14,000. As with the other ambushes, the captain and crew were allowed to leave in their dories. Some of the crew spent the night at Seal Island, while others continued to Clarks Harbour and landed there. All of the crewmembers then made their way to Yarmouth.

Captain John Simms, of the *Nelson A.*, had spent a successful week fishing on the LaHave fishing banks and, with the weather being favourable on Saturday, decided to head home to Lockeport with his catch of seven thousand pounds of halibut and seventy thousand pounds of mixed groundfish.

When about twenty-five miles south of Lockeport at 11:20 on Sunday morning, the crew on watch spotted a submarine about seven miles away coming toward them. The U-boat did not fire on them but came toward them at full speed until, about fifteen minutes later

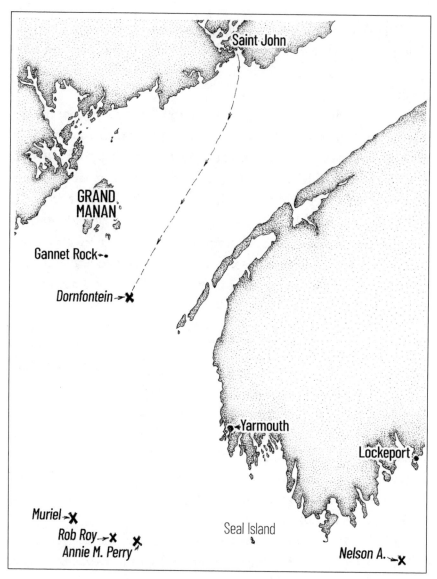

Saint John

GRAND
MANAN

Gannet Rock

Dornfontein

Yarmouth

Lockeport

Muriel

Rob Roy

Annie M. Perry

Seal Island

Nelson A.

In August 1918, U-boats sank multiple sailing vessels in the Bay of Fundy.

it stopped within hailing distance, just off their stern. The fishers were ordered to take to their boats as quickly as possible. This they did, launching four dories.

Captain Simms later told his story:

Acting under the instruction of the commander of the submarine, I took one dory with two men alongside the U-boat, and we rowed the commander and two of his men over to the Nelson A. They had with them several bags, containing bombs, I suppose. The Germans went aboard and ordered me to come with them. They took our log line and hauled one end of it under the ship's stern, making it fast to the main rigging. Then they proceeded to "keel haul" one of their bombs. It was evidently timed, as the Germans seemed in no hurry to leave the ship.

The German skipper demanded my papers and flag, which I gave. He then asked what fish we had on board and demanded some halibut, which he took and put in the dory. Then he took me into the forecastle and took all the provisions there that he considered worth taking.

After he had removed about everything that was movable, he ordered us to leave and take him back to the submarine. I asked him if he would allow me to get a pair of boots and he granted permission. We then rowed off from the Nelson A. The other dories had proceeded a half a mile or so and they waited for us. When we gathered together we rested on our oars to see the end of the poor old Nelson A., but nothing happened. The bomb evidently failed to explode.

The Germans got out a boat of their own, rowed to the schooner and stayed on board a minute, then returned to the submarine. Three minutes later (at 12 noon, to be exact) we saw our ship split in two, and in a few minutes there was nothing left on the surface but wreckage.

The last we saw of the submarine she was heading east southeast. At first, we thought she was making for a small Lockeport schooner which could be seen about five miles away. But the smoke of a steamer could be seen on the horizon due south and the U-boat immediately headed for her. Whether she sunk the steamer or not I do not know, as a haze shut down and we were unable to see any distance.[71]

~

The story of the *Dornfontein* is a most unusual one. This four-masted schooner had just been launched in Saint John and was on its maiden voyage. Great hopes had been expressed for this vessel, as it was seen as sparking a rebirth in shipbuilding in Saint John.

During the 1850s and 1860s, the port of Saint John launched a prolific tonnage of wooden shipping. Full-rigged ships were launched every week, sometimes several in one week. The port city was bustling with the business of building wooden ships. But the decline in wooden shipping hit Saint John hard, and since 1890, little had been built in the port.

Ironically, it was the activity of German U-boats that spurred a renewed interest in wooden shipbuilding. Ruinous ship losses to enemy submarines had seriously disrupted vital ocean trade, so there was an urgent demand for wooden ships. And so, in October 1917, on the Strait Shore in Saint John Harbour, the keel was laid for a large wooden ship.

The *Dornfontein* was a large four-masted schooner, registered at 695 tons. It was too big to launch in the conventional manner into the narrow channel of the harbour at that location, and so was launched sideways. It was an exciting day on June 11, 1918, when the *Dornfontein* slid sideways from the yard of the Marine Construction Company into Saint John Harbour. A large crowd witnessed the event with enthusiasm, and no doubt many an old-timer watching the ship slide into the water thought wistfully of the heady days when Saint John ships were launched routinely and could be found in any port on the globe.

The four-masted schooner Dornfontein *was maneuvered by a tug in Saint John Harbour just after being launched in 1918, preparing for its maiden voyage.*

The 185-foot schooner was well built. Its keel was of Douglas fir; stern and rudder posts were of Virginia oak. Outside, it was planked with birch. D. A. Saker built it, and took great pains to make it a strong ship to ply the oceans of the world.

The *Dornfontein* was heavily laden in Saint John Harbour with a cargo of lumber and construction board. On July 30, 1918, under the command of Captain Charles E. Dagwell, an Irishman from Belfast, it set out on its maiden voyage from Saint John, bound for South Africa. The crew was truly international, coming from England, Sweden, Denmark, Norway, and Portugal, not to mention three able seamen from New Brunswick: John Newman and Robert London of Saint John, and James Oliver of New River.

Relying entirely on wind, the *Dornfontein* made little headway out of the bay on the first two days of summer southwest winds. At eleven o'clock on Thursday morning, August 1, the lookout sighted a dark object far to the leeward. No one gave any thought to a submarine being in the vicinity and continued without concern. At this moment, a large black bird circled the ship and landed on the rail. A black bird at sea is regarded as an omen of misfortune, but, although noting the bird, no one thought of disaster.

A few minutes before twelve noon, while several members of the crew were below eating dinner, there was a loud explosion near the *Dornfontein*, and then another which showered splinters onto the deck. A submarine rose a few yards away and six officers stood on its deck. Using a megaphone, one ordered, "Come aboard, be quick also."

The crew of the *Dornfontein* wasted no time taking to the boats and rowing to the submarine, leaving all their clothes and effects behind. Arriving at the submarine, the six officers ordered them aboard. Following orders, the crewmembers descended into the submarine through a hatch and down steep iron steps. Afraid at first, they were gratefully surprised at how pleasant and hospitable the German sailors were. They were proud of their submarine and showed the crew around through the engine room and fed them well in the crew's mess.

Meanwhile, a party from the submarine rowed over to the *Dornfontein*, boarded, and took in the sails, slacked the rigging, and threw the lifeboats overboard. They took provisions and ship's stores from the schooner to the submarine, making seven trips before they had all that they wanted. The *Dornfontein* was well stocked, being provisioned for its months-long voyage to South Africa and back. The U-boat had been at sea for some time and was running low on supplies, so the German sailors were delighted at the windfall.

It was late afternoon when the submarine crewmembers were done, and they poured oil and gasoline all over the deck of the schooner. The schooner crew were then ordered up on the deck and told to take to their boat, which had been mounted at the stern, and row for shore. At 5:00 P.M., timed charges exploded and set the *Dornfontein* on fire.

People on Grand Manan, some twenty or twenty-five miles away, heard the explosion, but had no idea what had happened. The wind breezed up and the *Dornfontein* crew had to pull hard on the oars to reach Gannet Rock, the nearest point for them to reach, in the early hours of the next morning. They were picked up from there by the Wood Island life-saving crew and taken to the life-saving station, from which they were taken to Saint John.

When word of the disaster came up from Gannet Rock, Fletcher and Russell Harvey took their fishing boat and set out to see if there were any remains of the schooner to be found. After a two-and-a-half-hour sail, they came upon the *Dornfontein*, still in flames and burning to the waterline. There were four men on the Harvey boat, and they thought they would try to take the schooner in tow, and so they threw a tow line over the charred wheel at the stern.

They could make no headway towing the schooner. With spars hanging alongside, resisting towing, and a heavy anchor hanging from the bow, the remains of the massive schooner simply could not be moved by one mere fishing boat. Soon, however, two more Grand Manan fishing crafts arrived on the scene. Several of the men from the three boats boarded the schooner and worked at putting out the flames. The Harveys decided they could salvage the remains if they had another larger boat to help with the towing, so they returned to Grand Manan for fuel, food, and rope.

Once they had arrived back in Seal Cove and had brought together all the supplies they needed, the Harveys enlisted the help of Albert Cook and his boat. At dusk the two boats set out. The night was calm, and the moon was full. When abreast of the Gannet Rock lighthouse, the light suddenly went out. They shut their engines down and drifted in silence. No one spoke, but all were thinking the same thing: that the German sub had shot out the light. With no light to guide them, it would be risky to go down among the treacherous Murr Ledges and would be impossible to try to work the derelict back up through the ledges. But within an hour, the light was back on again. They later found out that the blackout was a mechanical problem.

The two boats arrived at the *Dornfontein* about 11:00 P.M. and found it still smouldering. Cook and the Harveys cut away most of the rigging and threw more water on the burning embers. Instead of trying to tow it directly, they headed south to go below the Murr Ledges and up to the west of them. Because the ship was filled with water, and there was no wind that night, it was a painfully slow trip. With a hacksaw, the salvors cut through the anchor chain. With the anchor cut clear, they would be able to tow the massive schooner into shallower water.

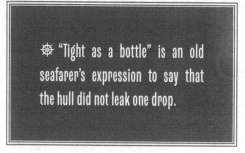

❈ "Tight as a bottle" is an old seafarer's expression to say that the hull did not leak one drop.

After a tow of some fourteen hours, Cook and the Harveys arrived back at Seal Cove the next afternoon, and people from all over the island came to see their prize. They pumped the water out of the schooner's hull and found the bottom to be tight as a bottle. There was also a quantity of lumber that had been submerged and not burned, which they salvaged from the schooner. Fletcher Harvey, the Receiver of Wreck—the wreck's caretaker in the absence of its owners—contacted the owners in Saint John, but they wanted nothing to do with it. So the salvors claimed their wreck and sold the derelict to Job Brothers, a New York shipbuilding firm that had an operation in Dennysville, ME.

The charred remnants of the *Dornfontein* were towed to Dennysville, where the large schooner was rebuilt and renamed the *Netherton*, this time under American register. But for many years the name *Dornfontein* stirred in the minds of old-timers thoughts of the brief encounter in the Bay of Fundy with the German U-boats of the First World War.

RUM-RUNNERS

The 1916 presidential election in the United States was expected to be a close race, so neither Democratic incumbent Woodrow Wilson nor Republican candidate Charles Evans Hughes wished to alienate any part of their political base by taking a position on the controversial issue of prohibition. In January 1917, however, when the sixty-fifth Congress convened, the "dries" heavily outnumbered the "wets" in both parties, so an amendment calling for nationwide Prohibition was introduced and was passed in both houses that December. Over the course of the next year, the amendment was ratified by thirty-six of the forty-eight states. A law was drafted, the Volstead Act, and with its passage, Prohibition in the United States began on January 17, 1920.

Prohibition was a peculiar law. While avidly supported outwardly, secret defiance was rampant. Chicago became notorious as a haven for Prohibition dodgers and Al Capone made millions of dollars heading organized crime's lucrative trade in illegal booze. The hypocrisy of the issue was commonly accepted. American actor Will Rogers often quipped, "The South is dry and will vote dry. That is, everybody sober enough to stagger to the polls."

With this kind of an attitude prevailing, demand for liquor was strong, and it did not take long for people in countries surrounding the United States to recognize a risky but lucrative opportunity: rum-running.

The jurisdiction of the Prohibition law only extended three miles offshore within the waters of the United States. Early rum-runners risked bringing their cargoes ashore through these waters, but the coastguard soon caught up with some of them. A Florida rum-runner, William McCoy, was credited with the idea of lying just off the three-mile limit and allowing small boats to come to his schooner and transport the rum into secluded coves under the cover of darkness. (Incidentally, McCoy was an honest rum-runner: he had the

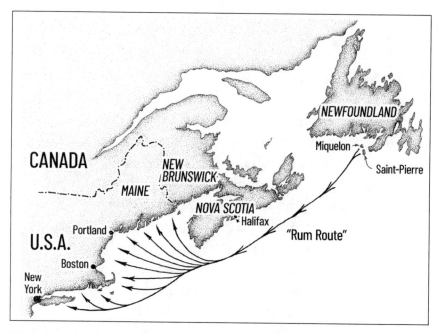

Rum-runners travelled along a "Rum Route" running from Saint-Pierre and Miquelon, France, down to New England.

reputation for excellent product; he never watered down his rum and sold only high-quality brands, thus giving rise to the term, "the real McCoy".)

It did not take long to recognize this same potential off the coast of New England. With a long, heavily indented coastline subject to frequent fog, New England provided great opportunity for rum-running. Saint-Pierre and Miquelon, a French enclave off Newfoundland, became a well-known source for liquors of all kinds. Enterprising captains along the Atlantic coast made good money transporting liquor to "Rum Row," the collection of vessels loaded with alcohol lying just off the "Rum Line," the three-mile limit.

Naturally, with rum-runners sailing back and forth past the Bay of Fundy to the Rum Line just off the United States, it was only a matter of time before some would be shipwrecked in these waters.

~

In 1924, the Lunenburg auxiliary schooner *George M. Cook*, bound for Lunenburg in ballast from the American coast, ran ashore on the west side of Race Point, Seal Island, NS, at nine o'clock on a foggy Sunday night, June 29, and became a total loss. The 133-ton schooner, built in 1919 by Smith & Rhuland of Lunenburg, was a fishing schooner and was among the highliners on the Grand Banks. But five months before its loss, it was chartered to American parties. Under Captain Abram Cook, the *George M. Cook* had been employed in the "coasting trade" (a euphemism, being in actual fact a rum-runner). Following the stranding, Winifred Hamilton, living on Seal Island, in her records simply stated, "Everybody happy."

Winifred Hamilton was a remarkable lady who lived her life on Seal Island. In 1973, when I was working on the shipwreck research project for the National Museums of Canada, I engaged a boat from Pubnico, went to Seal Island, and spent the afternoon visiting Hamilton, who was, by that time, an elderly lady. She gave me her list of shipwrecks around Seal Island, which she had typed and copied and made into a little booklet. And I was able to give her some shipwreck information that I had but she didn't. We continued to correspond back and forth by letter. In her booklet, Hamilton also noted her personal impressions of the wrecks that had occurred in her lifetime. In some tragic stories, she noted dealing with the bodies of deceased crewmembers with tender sadness. But you could see a smile and twinkle in her eye as she told of the stranding of this rum-runner with its "happy" crew.

~

On November 4, 1924, Captain Fred L. Boone sailed the schooner *Robert & Arthur* from Yarmouth, bound (ostensibly) for Honduras, with 1,300 cases of alcohol on board. I expect that most people who saw them sail away didn't believe the Honduras destination, but assumed the schooner was bound for Rum Row, and never gave much more thought to its fate. It was probably somewhat of a surprise to find the schooner stranded at Northwest Ledge, off Brier Island, at 2:30 p.m. on November 25. Fishers nearby assisted the crew in taking as much of the cargo ashore as possible before the schooner sank at 9:30 that evening in 35 fathoms (210 feet) of water.

We are not told what the cargo was or where the schooner had been for the intervening three weeks. But we might speculate that the cargo was unsold alcohol (which local fishers would readily try to save from the wreck). It was easy for rum-runners to get alcohol as far as Rum Row, but the risky part was the role of the small powerboats, which, under the cover of darkness, tried to evade coastguard vessels and run from outside the three-mile limit into remote coves and creeks.

What likely happened is that the *Robert & Arthur* had been waiting off Rum Row for close to three weeks for a small boat to approach with the cash to take some of the alcohol cargo. But the coastguard vessels had done such a good job patrolling their waters that few boats could get through. With fresh water and provisions running low (this wasn't supposed to be a long voyage), they would have to return to a Canadian port, which would explain why the *Robert & Arthur* was back in the Bay of Fundy with a cargo when three weeks out of Yarmouth.

~

In 1925, Captain Gee was caught out in an October storm in the twenty-four-ton schooner *Cora Gertie*. Attempting to enter the harbour, his schooner was wrecked on the Little White Horse Ledges off Bliss Island, Charlotte County, NB, at 3:00 p.m. on Saturday, October 10. After pounding on the rocks for a time, it slid off and sank in about 75 feet of water, along with its cargo—reported to be five hundred cases of liquor. The crew reached the shore safely.

And so, apparently, did ten gallons of alcohol, later found in a bog on nearby Spruce Island by Prohibition inspectors. Naturally, this shipwreck generated considerable interest. About seventy-five motorboats from New Brunswick and Maine stood by over the next several days while a large wrecking tug attempted to raise the wreck.

~

During the early winter of 1927, the fifty-seven-ton auxiliary schooner *Marion Phyllis* put in at Yarmouth with a crew of six men and a cargo of liquor. If anyone wondered about the profitability of rum-running, the extent to which rum-runners were willing to endure hardship and risk might well have provided a measure. Captain T. King cleared Yarmouth on February 3, ostensibly bound for Nassau in The Bahamas, but more likely for Rum Row. After battling a blizzard day and night on February 4 in the mouth of the Bay of Fundy, during which the *Marion Phyllis* lost its main boom and its sails were split, Captain King decided to try to make for Digby under engine power. But the engine became disabled and stopped.

> ⚙ The "shoe" is a heavy plank secured to the bottom of the keel, intended to take the wear and tear of the ship.

Considering the cargo under deck, the captain declined to seek a tug or otherwise solicit a tow. Early on Saturday morning, February 5, skilfully manoeuvring with a small sail taken from the locker, the vessel crept into Digby Gut. Before reaching the safety of the Annapolis Basin, the *Marion Phyllis* was blown across the gap, struck a sunken sandbar, and driven up onto a beach in Victoria Beach. On the flood tide, a tug towed the ship into Digby, with its shoe badly damaged and the hull considerably strained.

After repairing hastily at Digby, the schooner set out again around the first of March. But with the vessel strained and the patching relatively temporary, there were fears for its safety in the heavy gale of March 4. No further concerns were reported in shipping journals, which suggests that the old vessel reached a port safely. Under its Halifax ownership—the grandly named British and Colonial Transportation Company, Ltd.—the registry of the forty-two-year-old schooner was closed in 1930.

~

On November 23, 1927, the 115-ton steam/sail schooner *Retour* left Saint-Pierre and Miquelon with a full cargo of over two thousand cases of liquor. The *Retour*, under command of Captain Louis LeBlanc of Yarmouth, came up into the Bay of Fundy on its way south, perhaps to make arrangements for this valuable cargo. However, the schooner ran ashore in a cove just south of the Cape St. Marys lighthouse in Nova Scotia, in thick snow on Friday night, December 23. The tide was high when it struck, and at low tide the schooner was high and dry, well up on the beach.

Of course, the cargo piqued local interest. The liquor was seized under the Preventive Officers' Act, but by the time the crew of eight preventive officers arrived on the scene, some two hundred cases had already been removed from under the hatches. During the official removal, several attempts were made to steal liquor, and the officers were kept busy guarding their charge. Several unofficial salvage teams and trucks made off with liquor, and the officers scrambled to keep it from disappearing.

On December 28, Yarmouth witnessed a strange parade of trucks roll through town with a vehicle containing preventive officers at the front of the parade and a preventive officer placed on the back of each truck. The cases of liquor were stored in the strong room in the basement of the public building in Yarmouth.

The Preventive Officers charged Captain LeBlanc with trying to smuggle liquor ashore, but on February 27, 1928, the court in Yarmouth found that the vessel had been forced ashore by stress of the weather and, though circumstances were suspicious, LeBlanc was found not guilty of smuggling.

Meanwhile, at Cape St. Marys, the schooner settled deep in the sand, with the tide ebbing and flowing in, with seams opening up, becoming a total loss.

~

In the dead of night, very early on Thursday, May 10, 1928, a large motorboat came in from the Bay of Fundy and proceeded up the river through Saint John Harbour. The revenue cutter stationed in the port, under command of Captain McGinnis, gave chase. The unidentified boat caught fire, was beached, and burned with a great blaze near Fort La Tour, and when the firemen arrived at 1:50 A.M. they were surprised to find eighty cases of liquor on board the blazing craft, and no one around to claim responsibility. I suppose that the rum-runner was shipping liquor from a schooner to some point up the Saint John River.

Prohibition became increasingly unpopular and clearly did not work, as the law was so widely circumvented. Many social problems arose through Prohibition, not the least being the black market for alcoholic beverages and the profitable organized crime that was the result. Because it had to be smuggled, stronger liquor surged in popularity. A small bottle of 151-proof was easier to hide than an equivalent amount of alcohol in regular strength liquor. In 1933, Congress passed amendments to begin the dismantling of Prohibition. And into history went a bizarre and curious period in seafaring: the heyday of the rum-runner.

Early in the Second World War, the steamship *Hada County* was no stranger to the port of Saint John. A ship of the Norwegian County Line, it regularly moved large freights back and forth across the Atlantic. Craig, Taylor & Co. built it at Stockton-on-Tees, in the northeast of England, in 1921. A large iron steamer, it measured 386 feet long with a beam of 53 feet and depth of 26.6 feet.

On Saturday, December 6, 1941, thick fog had descended upon the Bay of Fundy. The *Hada County* was making a voyage from Swansea, Wales, to Saint John with four thousand tons of Welsh coal when it ran aground on Brazil Shoal, off White Head, Grand Manan. Striking hard in a moderate sea, it quickly filled with water. With the vessel sitting erect on a shoal in 24 feet of water at high tide, the forty-one men in the crew were in no danger, and lifesavers from Grand Manan easily rescued them along with their belongings.

Since this occurred during the war, an event that might otherwise have been a big news story was reported in only vague terms, the details being censored in the interests of national security. The story in the *Saint John Telegraph-Journal* of December 8 stated:

> *A freighter struck a ledge on the New Brunswick coast Saturday afternoon and remained hard aground last night after most of her crew of 41 had been removed by men from a lifesaving station when residents opened their homes to them. The captain and officers remained aboard.*
>
> *Rough weather held up refloating attempts by a tug from Saint John. Water was reported entering three holds and flooding the engine room. A favorable opportunity to resume refloating operations was awaited.*
>
> *The grounding occurred while the coal-laden freighter after a westward crossing, was groping her way through thick weather.*[72]

The local weekly, the *Saint Croix Courier*, offered more details, identifying the nationalities of the crew: one Nova Scotian, one Dane, four Britons, and the rest Norwegian. This paper further outlined plans to lighten the cargo, re-float the ship, and tow it to the dry dock in Saint John for repairs. The shallow depth of its stranding led people to believe that re-floating was all but a fait accompli.

The *Hada County* was in fact re-floated, but before the ship could be taken to safer waters, the powerful current stranded it again, even more securely than before, a defeat for those undertaking the salvage: the sea won, indeed.

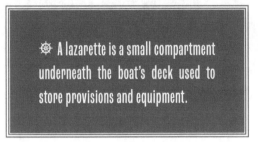

⚓ A lazarette is a small compartment underneath the boat's deck used to store provisions and equipment.

The following week, the paper told a different story, noting that the *Hada County* had been abandoned as a total wreck: "this luckless ship has been a Mecca for souvenir hunters on every suitable day since. The ship's stores and lazarette were the first to be raided…and then the ship was looted from stem to stern until everything of any value had been either taken or destroyed."[73]

A salvage tug and barge arrived for guns, wireless equipment, charts, and any other valuables left on the ship, but they had no interest in trying to salvage the cargo. What was not reported, probably for security reasons, was the prime target of the salvage tug: the degaussing cable. This was a heavy copper cable that encircled the *Hada County* at the waterline to demagnetize the magnetic field of the iron hull, to prevent magnetic mines from being attracted to and attaching themselves to the ship. This was a valuable cable, and an important piece to salvage. Along with collecting the cable, local diver Sheldon "Snooks" Green planted dynamite around the propeller shaft to blow the propeller clear. This too was picked up and taken by the salvage tug.

Over the winter of 1942, the Hada County *broke up where it lay, hard aground on the ledge.*

The *Hada County* broke in two during the southerly gale of January 6, 1942. Even after the ship broke apart, local boats ventured out to the wreck on fair-weather days to attempt to grapple and gather coals from its bunkers and holds. But in spite of the shallow water, this is not an easy place to work, for it is very exposed to out winds (winds from a southerly quarter) and lies in a powerful tidal current, making expert seamanship essential to work there. Storms continued to break up the ship and scatter the remnants of the cargo until the once mighty steamer had disappeared from the face of the sea.

$\sim$

I first visited the wreck of the *Hada County* in September 1967. I had been working on salvaging brass and copper from shipwrecks, teamed up with lobster fisher Deverne Green. Arriving at Brazil Shoal on the latter part of the ebb, just before the low water slack, I dropped down and quickly found the remains of the engine room, a large triple expansion engine, and condensers, all as they should be. I put out a mooring line to secure his boat in position when the tide turned to flood. I noticed that the slack tide was short, perhaps five or ten minutes, and then the current started running very hard.

On the bottom, in the engine room, I was out of the strong current, but I could see the effects as it raced by. Looking up at the boat from the bottom was quite striking: the current made a wake streaking by the moored boat. Even though the engine was off, the tidal current spun the propeller rather fast. It was an odd sensation on the bottom, hearing the rumbling of the spinning prop, but no engine noise. I looked around, noting that dynamite would be needed to gain access to much of the brass and copper there. Deverne and I returned a week later with dynamite, which I set in charges carefully placed around the engine room.

Returning to the wreck several days later, I found the condenser uncovered, and brass pumps and copper pipes all broken clear. So I spent an hour picking up the brass and copper; we felt it to be a productive trip. Another blast freed the condenser tubes, but these were a disappointment. Even though they were quite long, the brass was thin and they weighed less than three pounds apiece: a lot of work, for not much brass.

Deverne returned to lobster fishing in the fall season, but we went back to the *Hada County* the next spring. Over several days of diving during the spring, I took apart the engine room with dynamite and we removed several tons of brass and copper. Carman Cook joined me to help with the diving, which increased our productivity on the site.

We didn't return to the *Hada County* for another two years. In the fall of 1970, after the *Kings County* expedition, we came back to the *Hada County* and located more brass and copper. By the time we were done, we had removed several more tons and felt we had stripped what was profitable from the wreck.

As a shipwreck to visit, the *Hada County* lies in very shallow water, and being on rocky bottom, it offers excellent underwater visibility. It is however, exposed to winds from most directions. But the biggest challenge is the powerful tidal current that flows there. There is a short slack tide, and the current wastes no time in resuming strength in the opposite direction. Any diver wishing to visit the site needs to be prepared with sturdy mooring lines, to arrive just before the slack, and to quickly secure mooring lines for the tending vessel. I found it to be prudent to secure a line from the work area on the bottom to the boat on which to pull back to the boat to get back aboard at the end of the dive. Another good idea is to have second small boat along with an extra person to tend it, to pick up any diver inadvertently swept away in the current.

This powerful current is not for the inexperienced. The current prevailed over a mighty iron steamship, dooming its salvage chances; the same current would have no qualms doing this to an unwitting diver.

CHAPTER TEN

GREAT GALES

$\backsim$

Are there any eyes that are not glued in awed fascination to images of storm-blown waves tossing boats and smashing up harbours? Strong winds whip up the sea, hurling tons of water about with awesome power. We sometimes think of water as being soft and fluid, gently giving way as we swim and slide delightfully through it. But water in motion has enormous momentum—a big, breaking wave hits like a sledgehammer. And who can resist the powerful pull of a massive wave in reflux? There are stretches of the coast today where people, fascinated by the powerful breakers, are warned not to stray too close to the edge of the sea. In spite of the warnings, newscasts report surf watchers being swept out to sea to their death by the powerful waves.

During the age of sail, when ships relied on wind to propel them where they wanted to go, the same wind that carried the ship on its gainful endeavour could turn on the craft and tear it apart at sea or dash it ashore on the rocks with a vicious disregard for the sanctity of life. Masts, spars, and sails were built to capture the wind and propel the ship. Seafarers knew the power of gale-force winds; they knew that gales spared no one in their path. If wind was gaining strength, sailors cautiously took in the sail and ran under bare poles to cut the resistance to the wind to the bare minimum, but a sudden unexpected squall could capsize a ship or tear the rigging apart.

While vessels were lost to storms every year, there are some particularly powerful gales that stand out in the annals of our Atlantic coast. They stand out for their widespread devastation: vessels and harbours destroyed, and scores, sometimes hundreds, of lives lost.

The storms that hurled their fury at the Bay of Fundy generally fell into one of two categories: either tropical hurricanes, which usually occurred from August through the fall, or severe winter storms, December through early February. The tropical hurricanes did their damage by sheer force of wind. The winter storms had the added complications of snow, severe cold, and icing conditions. Furthermore, mariners talk of the wind being "heavier" in winter; that is, the denser winter air whips up bigger waves than the same velocity of summer wind. A forty-knot wind in February will generate heavy waves more quickly than a forty-knot wind in August.

Reviewing lists of shipping losses on our Fundy coast, some interesting patterns emerge. It would appear that, over the decades, severe storms have been occurring in clusters. A series of years would spawn major, devastating storms, followed by several years in which storms lacked as much ferocity. And then another cluster of storms would hammer the region once again.

Even as we look at these patterns, we must remember that back in the early days, just as today, the economy drove the overall traffic volume: when the economy was strong, more ships sailed. If fewer ships were sailing, fewer ships were wrecked. Nevertheless, even considering the economic booms and depressions, severe storms arrived in clusters.

In the early years, this cluster pattern is less apparent, probably because information coming to us from those years was less complete. Furthermore, there was less shipping traffic overall, especially during the winter months, when much of early shipping shut down.

A cluster of severe storms struck the Maritimes in the early 1850s. November 1850 saw a bad storm hit Prince Edward Island and the Northumberland Strait, resulting in the loss of many lives and much local shipping. In December, however, it was the Bay of Fundy that suffered at the hands of a vicious gale that struck on December 23, wrecking another six vessels on both coasts of the bay. Certainly, there were severe storms that overwhelmed ships and snuffed out lives during the ensuing years—some of these shipwrecks have been dealt with elsewhere in the book—but the widespread damage of the really great gales was not to occur until over a decade later.

THE SAXBY CLUSTER

The most famous storm to sweep across the Bay of Fundy was the Saxby Gale, which struck on October 4, 1869. Rather interestingly, in the years just preceding Saxby and the years immediately following, other severe storms did widespread damage and extinguished many, many lives.

The first great gale of the Saxby cluster was a hurricane that swept into the Bay of Fundy in August 1867. On Friday night, August 2, and the following morning, a heavy southeast gale struck the Bay of Fundy, bringing with it a tremendous sea and high tide. Several Grand Manan boats and vessels were wrecked or damaged. Other harbours around the Bay of Fundy also reported damages. Two fishing schooners were wrecked off Grand Manan; one was lost along with its entire crew of nine men.

Westport, Brier Island, saw a pair of schooners driven ashore. Five schooners, a pair of brigs, and two brigantines were wrecked around various parts of Minas Basin. A fishing smack was wrecked off Brier Island and two dead bodies were found in its cabin.

The year 1868 saw another severe gale damage shipping on the Nova Scotia side of the Bay of Fundy on Saturday night, October 17. The schooner *Belle* (owned at Shag Harbour, NS) left Boston, MA, on October 15, bound for Barrington, NS, and was not heard of afterwards. It was supposed that it sank with all on board during the severe gale, probably off southwestern Nova Scotia. There were about twelve passengers on board, all lost. Another half dozen schooners were lost along the Nova Scotia coast, mostly from above Digby to the Tusket Islands. One schooner took four men to their death, but in all other wrecks the crews survived.

THE SAXBY GALE

The Saxby Gale on October 4, 1869, was an unusually severe storm, breezing up to a violent southerly gale between six and eight o'clock that evening. The storm was named for Lieutenant Stephen Saxby, a Royal Navy instructor and amateur astronomer. He predicted—in a letter of warning published on December 25, 1868, in London's the *Standard*—that based on his observations of the anticipated relative positions of the sun and moon, October 5, 1869, would see unusually high tides in the western North Atlantic. The *Standard* published a reminder on September 16, 1869. Saxby expressed concern that, due to it being hurricane season, devastating storm surges could occur. And they did.

The storm was at its heaviest in the western Bay of Fundy, striking Charlotte County, NB, in the evening. Winds of over 100 mph (161 km/h) damaged, capsized, or beached a total of 160 vessels in the Passamaquoddy Bay area. Ten vessels went ashore between Robbinston and Eastport, ME, seven at Eastport, and twenty-three at West Quoddy. *Lloyd's List* reported, "Great damage was done on the 4th October by storm and high tides at New Brunswick. Eastport,

Maine, was entirely destroyed."[74] The *Lloyd's List* report cited the high tides as contributing, along with the storm surge, to the destruction of the Eastport waterfront, which must have been built precariously close to the sea. Most of the vessels lost were probably at anchor and were broken from their anchors by the storm surge.

All around the Bay of Fundy, major damage to shipping was reported. The federal government *Sessional Papers* publication reported, "No blame can be attached. 19 vessels were at anchor in the harbour of Westport when the gale commenced, 11 were driven on shore, 1 foundered at anchor."[75] One can visualize the hurricane winds and powerful storm surge overwhelming Brier Island's Westport. The Saxby Gale swept up the Memramcook Valley, propelling a storm surge that raised the tide eight feet over the dykes. Two schooners, the *Ida May* and the *Independence*, were carried over the marsh and stranded by the storm surge a half a mile from the riverbank.

Shipping caught at sea in the bay sustained damages too. A schooner belonging to Jonesport, ME, was found after the gale, drifting on beam-ends, all hands lost. Another caught out in the bay in the gale was badly strained, disabled, and leaky. It was located by a tug and taken to Saint John for repairs. Meanwhile, the brig *M. T. Ellsworth* was dismasted in the bay and later towed in, and the brig *Raven* capsized off the mouth of the Bay of Fundy, losing the mate overboard. A storm surge would not be the factor out in the bay. The damage was caused by the sheer power of the hurricane-force winds.

At Saint John, a dozen ships, brigs, and schooners were damaged in the gale—some pounded at the wharves, others broken away and driven ashore and smashed up. The schooner *Arrow*, lying at Wishart's Wharf, Saint John, laden with lumber, had the stern beaten off and the bow stove in. There was nothing worth saving but the spars and rigging. The schooner yacht *Emma F.* was smashed up by debris from the breakwater at Saint John. Much of the wheelhouse and captain's stateroom were blown off the river steamer *Fawn* into the Saint John River.

The new, five-hundred-ton barque *Genii* had arrived at New River (down the shore from Saint John) on Saturday, October 2, to load deals for Liverpool. When the Saxby Gale struck on Monday, some of the crew were ashore, but seven stevedores from Mascarene (near St. George) were on board. That night, in the fury of the gale and powerful storm surge swelling into New River from the bay, the barque broke from its anchors, struck New River Ledge broadside, and rolled over, hurling all on board to their death. The new barque ended up on shore, smashed up and upside down. The victims were Captain Bayley of Westport, Brier Island; First Mate John M. Straton of Fredericton; Second Mate James McGill of Saint Andrews; Steward John Wilson of Mascarene; and the seven stevedores also from Mascarene: Peter McVicar, George McVicar, Eben Green, Harvey McNichol, Daniel Hoyt, John Roix, and George Henderson. The *Genii*, insured for $15,000, had been launched at Saint Andrews only three weeks earlier.

In Saint Andrews, a dozen schooners in port at the time sustained damages in the gale and accompanying surge. The Saint Andrews packet sloop *Matilda* was picked up by the storm surge and set on top of the wharf, high and dry, smashing the lower part of the hull. The Saint Andrews schooner *Julia Clinch*, under the command of Captain H. Maloney, broke away from the steamboat wharf while loading iron for Wilmington, swung around, and crushed its bowsprit and masts. The captain was aboard, trying to secure his vessel, but fortunately escaped injury. The Digby brigantine *Mary Budd* broke adrift and was badly damaged beating against the wharf.

Eastport, ME, saw havoc along the waterfront, with several schooners smashed up and wrecked. The schooner *Speedwell*, owned by Messrs. J. & S. Griffin of Eastport, was totally lost there. The brig *Phoebe Ellen*, from Londonderry, NS, under the command of Captain Robert Dill, took shelter in West Quoddy Bay as the Saxby Gale breezed up, along with twenty-three other vessels. During the gale, several vessels' anchors dragged, and the brig was struck first by a barque, then by the schooner *D. Sawyer*, and finally by the brig *Whittier*, each adding to the damage from the last. The next morning, only thirteen vessels were left at anchor, all the others having blown ashore or sunk.

The schooner *Rialto* capsized in Passamaquoddy Bay and all on board perished. After the gale, salvors towed the *Rialto* into Northern Harbour, Deer Island, upside down. At nearby Spruce Island, the Saint John schooner *Guide*, with a cargo of shingles, was totally wrecked. Meanwhile, the schooner *Rio*, under command of Captain Young and bound for Boston with a cargo of pilings, was lost at Campobello along with the entire crew. The wreck floated off and drifted about Saint Andrews Bay.

The schooner *Rechab*, under command of Captain Mowatt from St. Stephen and with a cargo of axes bound for Saint John, had left Saint Andrews that morning and was totally lost in Bliss Harbour during the gale. The captain swung ashore from the peak halyards—ropes attached to the top of the masts—as the vessel lurched back and forth. Also wrecked there was the schooner *Ellen McLeod*, and the schooner *Gipsey*, bound for Boston, tore out its keel in this spot. The schooner *Rosilla B.* was also driven ashore in Bliss Harbour with the keel torn out.

At nearby Letang, a vessel went ashore and a young man drowned. Not far away, in Back Bay, a schooner sank. Up the shore at Beaver Harbour, the brigantine *E. W. Ross* was wrecked and lost; three men drowned, and the captain broke his leg. Wrecks were strewn along the shore from Beaver Harbour through Lepreau, Dipper Harbour, and Musquash. John Campbell's sloop *Nautilus*, owned in Dipper Harbour, went to pieces there in the storm. The fishing schooner *Renown*, under the command of Captain Dean, went ashore at the narrows at Musquash and became a total wreck. Captain Dean and two of his crew drowned.

Grand Manan Island felt the full force of the gale. The light-keeper at the Gannet Rock light, Walter B. McLaughlin, secure in his lonely fortress of a lighthouse, noted in his journal on

October 4, 1869, "At Noon, wind SSE strong gale and misty. From 6 to 8 violent gale and storming with rain. At 9, wind S, the gale continues."[76] At noon, the spring tide would be at its highest, so the south-southeast wind direction at that time accounts for much of the storm surge damage on the New Brunswick shore.

Meanwhile, around Grand Manan, seven schooners were driven ashore at Flagg Cove, including the schooner *Van Tromp*. The vessel was a total loss, but the captain and crew, though in great peril, were saved. Two schooners went ashore at Pettes Cove, at the northeast end of Grand Manan, where nine bodies later washed up on the shore. The Deer Island schooner *Echo* was lost off Pettes Cove, along with three lives—two of which were a father-son duo. Just down the shore at Bancroft Point, the Eastport schooner *Leader* was totally lost, along with another Eastport schooner *Romp*. The captain and crew were saved, but the captain broke his leg. Wreckage from two small vessels came ashore between Grand Harbour and Seal Cove; the crews assumed to be lost. Just off Grand Manan in Three Island Harbour, the schooner *I. Cooke*, owned by Jacob Cooke of Letete, was totally lost.

The Saxby Gale was one of those storms that makes a lasting impression. It was the stuff of legends, and for decades stories were told of that eventful day and the powerful acts of nature both along the shore and on the water. I recall old-timers—who had heard the stories from old-timers when they were young—telling me of the road across Deep Cove Brook, near the southern end of Grand Manan, being totally washed out in the storm, which required the community to build a new road. I have watched heavy breakers roll into that cove, and considering the storm surge of Saxby, that would be quite believable.

THE AUGUST GALE

Possibly the most destructive storm within written history in the general area of the Atlantic Canadian provinces, the August Gale whirled across the region on Sunday, August 24, 1873, and left in its wake enormous damage, especially in the Cape Breton area and the Gulf of St. Lawrence.

An estimated one thousand Nova Scotians lost their lives in the wreckage of their wooden vessels. Striking the Bay of Fundy on the evening of Saturday, August 23, the gale did not do much damage until it reached its heights of fury on Sunday, doing its greatest damage in eastern Nova Scotia and Cape Breton. The storm continued up through the Gulf of St. Lawrence, striking Labrador a couple of days later. Excerpts from local reports need few words to tell much:

> "The greatest gale ever experienced since 1810...25 vessels strewn along our shore."[77]
> –*North Sydney Herald*

> "[A]ll the wharves and many of the stores were destroyed and every vessel in the harbour driven ashore"[78]
> –*Halifax Morning Chronicle* (referring to Cape Canso)

> "A number of dead bodies have been washed ashore in various parts of the Island."[79]
> –*Halifax Morning Chronicle* (referring to Prince Edward Island)

In 1973, to commemorate the one hundredth anniversary of this great storm, I compiled and published a list of vessels wrecked or damaged in this storm. There were 330 vessels named in this list.

However, losses in the Bay of Fundy were remarkably light, certainly compared to eastern Nova Scotia, Cape Breton, and the Gulf of St. Lawrence.

AFTER THE SAXBY CLUSTER

The Saxby cluster wound down with a vicious winter storm that slammed into the Bay of Fundy on January 24 and 25, 1874.

The new American three-masted schooner *Levi Hart* went ashore on Bliss Island, near Blacks Harbour, during the thick snowstorm on January 24. It was trying to enter a harbour, but struck on the rocks and filled. The schooner *Escape* was stranded and totally wrecked within two miles of Digby Gut in the snowstorm during the night of January 25. All six crewmembers drowned.

The brigantine *Rover* went ashore at Money Cove, Grand Manan, during this snowstorm and became a total loss. During the same storm, the brigantine *Willie Maud* was stranded and bilged at Beals Eddy, Grand Manan, just a couple miles up the shore from the *Rover*. Both crews reached shore safely, climbed the bank, and shared the same fire, which kept them alive until George T. Tatton, who lived nearby, discovered them.

～

The remaining years of the 1870s certainly saw some storms, but the Bay of Fundy was spared the widespread devastation of another Saxby. Similarly, through the 1880s and most of the 1890s the same situation prevailed. In the 1880s, there were, however, a couple of December gales that merit brief mention.

In 1882, a winter storm blew through on December 13, doing its greatest damage in the lower part of the Bay of Fundy. Three schooners were wrecked at Grand Manan. A schooner and all its cargo was totally lost when it struck on Johns Island Ledge, near Pubnico. Another dragged its anchors and was driven ashore on the southern point of Ellenwoods Island, one of the Tuskets, in the gale on December 14, and went to pieces. The crew barely escaped with their lives.

The 921-ton barque *Scotia* was stranded about three hundred yards off Allen Point in Maine, two and a half miles west of the West Quoddy lighthouse. In the early hours of December 14, it capsized and lost its mast. The Quoddy Life-saving Crew rescued the fifteen crewmembers by breeches buoy to bring them ashore.

Another 1880s storm of note struck the Bay of Fundy three years later. On December 26, 1885, a vicious storm hit the Bay of Fundy, with temperatures near −18°C (0°F) and driving vapour and snow, carried by the strongest northeast gale in years. During this storm, several schooners were wrecked around Grand Manan. One of these, the *Sabra Killam*, dragged its anchors at Flagg Cove, Grand Manan, and fouled the *Adelia Hartwell*, forcing it to cast adrift from its anchorage also. The *Adelia Hartwell* then drifted ashore 150 yards below Drake's Dock, broke in two, and became a total wreck.

A quarter mile away, the *Sabra Killam* drove ashore. The crew succeeded in launching a boat and landed safely, but the captain, Alfred Amero—bareheaded, confused, and numb from exposure—at first would not leave his vessel. He jumped overboard after the boat, but then swam back to the schooner, put his arm around the foresheet traveller (rigging that controls the sail on the front mast), and refused to let go. The men tried to persuade him to go ashore, but he would not. Two of the men remained on board with him through many hours of intense suffering, until 2:00 A.M. when, totally exhausted, they went ashore. When they boarded the vessel again at daylight, they found Captain Amero frozen solid, his arms still around the foresheet traveller. Unmarried, he was twenty-six years of age and on his first trip as a captain.

The schooner *F. Christine*, lying at Oakes' Wharf, Digby, was driven broadside onto the shore in the storm. The building movers, J. B. Chute & Son, were engaged to get it off. Using jack screws, they raised the vessel four feet and, with the aid of rollers under the bilge and ways built under the bow and stern, they moved it about a hundred feet to the water.

The schooner *R. Leach* sailed from Weymouth just before this severe storm, bound for Boston with a cargo of cordwood. It went missing and was supposed lost in the storm, along with six lives. The wreck was passed on January 4, 1886, about ninety miles west of Cape Sable, "on beam ends" (lying on its side), with masts hanging alongside.

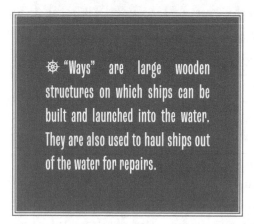

❋ "Ways" are large wooden structures on which ships can be built and launched into the water. They are also used to haul ships out of the water for repairs.

The schooner *Sea Flower* dragged ashore near the Life-saving Station at West Quoddy Head during the storm of December 26, and the crew was saved by the Quoddy Head Life-saving Crew, without whose assistance the captain believed they all would have perished.

THE PORTLAND BREEZE

The rest of the 1880s and most of the 1890s proved quieter in terms of major storm damage. The severe gale of November 27, 1898, however, was a storm to be remembered and is recalled whenever yarns are swapped by seafarers. The storm was named the "Portland Breeze" following the loss of the steamship *Portland*, which foundered with all hands during this storm off Cape Cod.

The side-wheel paddle steamer *Portland* left Boston, MA, at 7 o'clock on the evening of November 26, 1898, bound for Portland, ME, with sixty-five passengers and forty-nine crewmembers. That evening an exceptionally violent storm swept the New England coast, in which it is presumed that the obsolete steamer foundered with all hands about 9:00 P.M. By midnight, pieces of wreckage and bodies washed ashore around Cape Cod.

Many vessels about the Bay of Fundy were driven ashore and damaged. At Westport, Brier Island, nine vessels went ashore. The schooner *Sarah E. Ells* went ashore at Parrsboro during the gale. The schooner *Berma* filled and sank at Apple River; the vessel was a total loss, but everyone survived.

The ten-year-old schooner *Seraphine* parted from its mooring cable and drove ashore on the north side of Bear Island, Digby Basin, during the gale. The schooner *Silver Cloud* broke from its moorings and came ashore behind the store of E. Turnbull. Its jib-boom (a spar used to extend the bowsprit at the front of a sailing ship) crashed through a small building and broke off when it swung around and came ashore, side on, badly damaged. Three small schooners were also wrecked on the Bay of Fundy shore outside Digby Gut.

The schooner *Annie G.* set out from Bridgetown, NS, the evening before the gale, bound for New York with a cargo of piling. Out in the Bay of Fundy, it met with the severe gale on the morning of November 27. Crashing waves washed Captain Benjamin Robinson overboard at 11:00 A.M. and he was never seen again. Adding to the tragedy, that evening, Job Porter (likely the cook onboard the *Annie G.*) dropped into the flooded cabin and drowned. The three remaining members of the crew lashed themselves to the house on the vessel's deck to avoid the fates of their captain and crewmate. Suffering terribly in the cold, bitter wind, the three men were not rescued until December 1, when the steamer *Sarmatian* discovered them and took them off the waterlogged, dismasted schooner. The derelict *Annie G.*

was later picked up near Mud Island (west of Woods Harbour), and was probably condemned and sold as the vessel's registry was then closed.

Captain McKiel lost two schooners on the Saint John River: the *Estella R.* was stranded at Upper Greenwich, and the schooner *Relief* went ashore below Catons Island. Also driven ashore on Catons Island was the sixty-ton schooner *Sultan*. The schooner *Daisy* went ashore near the farm of its owner, Captain James H. Day. Other schooners and wood boats were reported (but not named) to be ashore at different points along the river as a result of the gale.

The schooner *Rebecca W.* sailed from Saint John on November 26, bound for Quaco (St. Martins) via Gardner Creek, where it discharged part of its general cargo and then set sail again for Quaco. It met with the strong winds and heavy seas of the gale and was forced to run down to Partridge Island, where it anchored. The gale tore away the *Rebecca W.*'s chains and drove it down the coast until it went ashore at Dipper Harbour and became a total wreck.

The schooner *Levuka* dragged its anchors and went ashore at Big Head, on the south side of Gleason Cove, ME, at high tide on Sunday morning, November 27, and became a constructive total loss. The wreck and cargo were sold at auction on November 28 to Captain James Taylor of Economy, NS, for $150. He had the vessel repaired.

The American tern schooner *Charles J. Willard* went ashore in Quoddy Bay, in the Narrows just below Lubec, at 4:00 A.M. on November 27. It lay on its side with the bottom ground out, but was still in a salvageable condition. The brigantine *Champion* parted from its chains and was stranded on Crowell's Ledge, near the life-saving station in Quoddy Bay. While members of the crew were being cared for at the life-saving station, thieves stole everything moveable from the wreck, including the stern and keel. As a result, it became a total wreck.

Grand Manan reported several shipping casualties during the Portland Breeze. The schooner *River Rose* went ashore and was badly damaged at Woodwards Cove, along with the schooner *Alert*. The *Flora* and the *Nettie Gaskill*, owned at Eastport, went ashore at Grand Harbour. Twelve boats owned at White Head were lost along with all the herring weirs in the area. The sloop *Uncle Sam* was driven out to sea from Two Island Harbour and lost. At Cheney Island, Captain Warren Cheney's new racing boat *Rough Rider* went ashore and its bottom was completely destroyed.

The schooner *Narcissus*—built in Lunenburg in 1883—was bound from Boston for Shelburne and Liverpool, NS, with passengers and a general cargo, when it became disabled during the gale and was abandoned off Seal Island, NS. The fishing schooner *Hiram Lowell* rescued the crew and passengers, twenty-three people in all, and landed at Gloucester, MA, on November 29. The disabled *Narcissus* foundered and became a total loss.

The 155-ton schooner *Saarbruck*, built in Machias in 1871, was bound from Portland, ME, for Saint John. It was transporting a digester valued at $5,000 and intended for the M. F. Mooney pulp mill in Mispec. It lost its anchor chains and went ashore near Milbridge, ME. The vessel was a total wreck; however, the digester was saved.

THE GROUNDHOG GALE

The biggest storm in the twentieth century to strike the Bay of Fundy hit on February 2, 1976 (Groundhog Day). It was, in fact, the convergence of two storms at the mouth of the Bay of Fundy. Amazingly, no lives were lost, but a million dollars in damage was done on the island of Grand Manan alone.

This storm has particular significance to me, as my business partner Carman Cook and I had bought a fishing boat on Thursday and lost it on the following Monday in the Groundhog Gale.

The *Miss Web* was a small herring purse seiner, which was offered for sale as the owners wanted to upgrade in size. We thought it would be great for tending our deepwater herring weir on the back of Grand Manan. We looked the vessel all over, and the price was reasonable, so we made the necessary arrangements and bought it.

On Thursday, January 29, 1976, we took delivery of the *Miss Web*. We were pretty pleased as we set out from the port of Ingalls Head, and took our vessel to its new home, the harbour of Seal Cove. This seiner was equipped with a scanner, which could peer through the water at an angle to find fish. So we examined a couple of weirs near Seal Cove to see what they looked like in a scanner. As we tied our craft up in Seal Cove, we were decidedly excited. Even though we didn't plan to use our boat until the spring, Carman called an insurance company on Friday to have the vessel insured. That proved to be a very wise move.

On Monday morning, February 2, the wind awoke me about four o'clock. A little after seven o'clock, I went to the Seal Cove breakwater and met Carman there. We checked the lines on the *Miss Web*. We had bought new nylon lines, but it was blowing hard, so we put out an extra set. With six lines out, and tied to both the wharf and the nearby herring carrier *Irene Greenlaw*, surely the *Miss Web* would be secure.

I returned to my office to work on a report. The wind outside was blowing harder all the time. About 11:30 A.M. Carman came by, and we took a drive to take a look at the havoc the storm was wreaking. The powerful southerly gale continued to blow harder. I took some movie footage of the huge waves breaking over the back of the Seal Cove breakwater and filling the boats tied up in the harbour. There was nothing anyone could do, as it would have been impossible to go down onto the wharf.

The power went out around noon. Our little house was shaking so badly, my wife bundled up our one-year-old daughter and went to the next village to her parents' house, which was much bigger and more solidly built.

About 1:20 P.M., the wharf pilings broke away from the Seal Cove breakwater; they simply peeled away. After a few minutes of dangling on lines in the heavy seas, the *Miss Web* and the *Irene Greenlaw* broke away, still tied together, and drifted ashore on the Seal Cove Sand Beach, washing up on the rocks. Within half an hour, the herring carrier *Strathaven* was ashore too. But the tide had ebbed some, so it lay in a better position further down the beach.

Later in the afternoon, after the tide had gone down some and with the help of some volunteers, I stripped all the major electronic equipment out of the *Miss Web* and stored it in my garage. At eight o'clock in the evening, I was finally able to get aboard our other boat in Seal Cove, the *James Burton*. It had been moored out in the middle of Seal Cove harbour, next to a lobster car. It weathered the storm well, far better than the boats tied up at the wharf that had been filled by the heavy waves and sank right there at the dock.

As I wrote in my diary that evening: "Certainly the worst storm in the recent history of Grand Manan. Winds blowing steadily at over 120 knots [218 km/h]; at Ingalls Head, [on the wind gauge at the Co-op Store] for one and a half hours it never dropped below 108 knots [196 km/h]. Many boats were swamped at Seal Cove; a lot of herring stands were flattened around the shores of Grand Harbour. The Groundhog Gale will go down in history as a storm to be remembered."

The next day I went down to the boats and wharves to view and photograph the damages. The shores were strewn with debris. After taking time to look around at the devastation, people set to work starting to clean up the mess.

The *Miss Web* and the *Irene Greenlaw* had come ashore still tied and when they came to rest, they were jammed tightly together, with

After the storm had gone by, we were able to board the Miss Web, *jammed in place on the rocks by the* Irene Greenlaw, *and assess the situation.*

the *Greenlaw* outside. Carman and I had to wait until it was moved before we could get at our boat. The Connors Bros., the owner of the *Greenlaw*, hired workers to jack and block the *Web* away from the *Greenlaw* in order to pull off their old carrier. Progress was slow, but the vessels were separated.

On Friday, February 13, a strong southerly gale struck, driving the *Greenlaw* back in against the *Web*. This put more of a hog in the hull of the *Web*. It broke the *Greenlaw's* skeg and rudder, bent the shaft, split the stern, and strained the hull even more. This added to our fear for the safety of the vessels. Carman relayed this to the insurance adjusters, putting pressure on them for a speedy settlement.

On Monday, February 16, we stripped the *Miss Web*, having bought it back from the insurance company for $3,000. We took off the batteries, power block, scanner transponder, and electrical components from the engine room, and unfastened the engine. In the afternoon, using chain hoists secured to the beams overhead, we hoisted the heavy diesel engine and worked it over to the inshore side of the boat and secured it there.

The next day, using a large wharf ladder (made of ten-by-tens) that had gone adrift in the gale and which we salvaged from the shore, we made up a skidway for the engine. With various pieces of machinery, we managed to remove the engine from the boat and work it along to the bow where it could be picked up by a large front-end loader.

The tides were springing, so on the high tide a large Connors Bros. carrier hauled the *Greenlaw* off the shore. It was clear they had no intention of trying to repair it, for it sustained quite a twisting in being hauled off.

The next day we started salvaging the *Miss Web*. On the low tide, we brought in a loader, backhoe, and bulldozer to the beach. First they cleared away rocks from the offshore side of the boat. Then the backhoe dug a trench in the sand about forty feet long, parallel to the boat and about thirty feet from it. In this trench we buried a weir stake—a "dead man"—with half a dozen strong ropes secured to it. With the stake buried and only the ropes out, we had ropes well secured to hold the boat from washing back ashore on the high tide.

⚓ "Hogging" is when a ship's bottom is so strained that it arches upwards in the middle, sagging at the bow and stern.

We then worked weir stakes under the keel of the boat, perpendicular to it, and out across the dead man. We fastened these stakes in position with the ropes from the dead man. These stakes would provide skids for the boat when it was hauled over on its offshore side.

But falling off from equilibrium onto the stakes would further damage its planking. So the loader first made up a large pile of sand on the offshore side of the boat. With heavy lines to the mast, the loader towed the *Web* onto an even keel, past it, and the boat dropped gently onto the pile of sand. With the inshore side now opened up, we put temporary patches over the holes in the hull.

As the tide rose, it washed away the sand, gently lowering the boat onto the skids. After the tide went down some, the bulldozer pushed the stem offshore, and then, with the front-end loader pulling and the bulldozer pushing, the stern skidded down the beach on the stakes. When suitably down the beach, we set it up with a wooden crab under each bilge, ran a line off to a mooring way down the beach, and waited for the next high tide.

That night Carman brought in our herring carrier *Bruce'n'Jacque* to tow the *Miss Web* on the high water. At five minutes past midnight, the *Web* floated clear enough to be towed off and taken to a boat shop in Grand Harbour.

> ❂ A "crab" is a portable framework that, when the tide is up, is worked with ropes under the hull, away from the keel, to keep the hull upright when the tide ebbs away

Over the next few months we had the damaged planking replaced in the hull. But we took advantage of this rebuilding to redesign our vessel to better suit our needs, providing some fish-carrying capacity too. When the work was completed, with engine and electronics all back aboard, we renamed our boat—the *Groundhog Gale!*

~

Having studied and written about shipwrecks for years, I never expected to have to deal with one on such a personal level. But it was a great experience and gave me an appreciation for the efforts of our

Back at work on the water, the Miss Web *sported a new name: the* Groundhog Gale.

forefathers who didn't have loaders and bulldozers and backhoes to use, but had to accomplish what they did with teams of oxen.

The vessel losses in the Groundhog Gale were exceptional, as this was the worst Fundy storm in the twentieth century, but the frequent losses we saw over the early years no longer occur. One of the factors reducing vessel loss and damage as we moved into the twentieth century and now through the twenty-first century is the use of engines to power vessels. Sails still provide propulsion for many vessels, but mariners turn more and more to engines, even if on an auxiliary basis. Engines help crafts seek shelter when storms approach and give mariners confidence in maintaining courses in fog, which has always been a concern in Fundy.

Incidentally, two major developments to deal with fog originated in Fundy creativity. Robert Foulis of Saint John invented the first automated steam-powered foghorn after he noticed that low notes travel farther through the fog than high notes, and a foghorn was built on Partridge Island, Saint John, in 1859. Decades later while pursuing his doctorate at McGill during the Second World War, Ernest Guptill, who was born and raised on Grand Manan Island (and a classmate of my mother), co-invented the slotted waveguide antenna, a device to allow radars to be installed in aircraft, ocean vessels, and fishing boats. The radar all but eliminated the hazards of fog.

In more recent years, we added global positioning systems (GPS), which provide the individual user with assurance on location. For added protection, shipping into the Bay of Fundy is monitored much like air traffic is monitored approaching airports. Entering the Bay of Fundy, ships normally track into the prescribed shipping lane, where they check in with Fundy Traffic and have their progress monitored on a radar located at Boars Head on the Nova Scotia shore. Farther into the bay, their progress is monitored by a radar located on Red Head, on the New Brunswick shore. This radar coverage monitors vessels in the shipping lanes from the radar limits about twenty-six miles below Grand Manan, right into Saint John.

With all the technical advances, it is easy to see why Bay of Fundy shipwrecks are now so rare. No longer does the sea win like it did in earlier years. But it still demands a deep respect.

ACKNOWLEDGMENTS

W hen I was a young diver interested in exploring the Murr Ledges for shipwrecks in the mid-1960s, an older, experienced lobster fisher offered to take me out to see what we could find. Deverne Green and I became informal partners to search the ledges for shipwrecks when he wasn't busy lobster fishing. I had a hundred percent confidence he would be right there in snowstorms or fog to pick me up when I was in the water. He knew the ledges well: where to anchor, how the tidal currents behave. I am very grateful to have had Deverne to work with.

Carman Cook, five years older than me, had been working in Nova Scotia and returned to Grand Manan to establish business on the island. He enjoyed diving and soon joined Deverne and me in the quest for shipwrecked brass and copper around the ledges through the late 1960s. Deverne liked to work close to home, so when Carman and I decided to explore wrecks around Saint John or in Nova Scotia, Carman lined up other boats as needed. I did the research and planning, and Carman looked after the business aspects. And, beyond shipwreck diving, we continued to work together in fishing and processing ventures throughout the 1970s.

Without doubt, the most influential person to put me on the path of historical research was L. Keith Ingersoll. Keith was the principal of the local high school and wrote regular columns for the county's weekly newspaper. But he had an unquenchable and infectious passion for history, penning a variety of books and scholarly volumes. He persuaded me to help as the new Grand Manan Museum was built, doing captions and illustrative work. This museum was a Centennial Project, opening in 1967 with Keith as curator. Not many years after that, Keith moved to Saint John to become the curator of Canadian history at the New Brunswick Museum, and I became the curator of the Grand Manan Museum (for the grand sum of one hundred dollars per year).

In his position, Keith persuaded me to broaden my research ambitions, providing me with a good reference to obtain a Ford Foundation Fellowship in marine history research for a year, from the fall of 1970 into the summer of 1971. He also persuaded me to write a junior high school social studies book, *Shipbuilding in the Maritimes*, published by Ginn & Co. A great deal of what is in *The Sea Wins* was started and expanded during those years, all made possible by the vision and passion of Keith Ingersoll.

For each summer of shipwreck diving for the museum, I needed a reliable and available boat and operator, paid for by the project. In 1973, Richard Green provided and operated a boat, and in 1974 and 1975, Ray Ingalls did the same. Their work made the project possible.

A lot of time has been spent in my office going through research materials, developing illustrations and paintings, writing and rewriting. I owe a debt of gratitude to my wife, Berneta, who has for so many years put up with my passion for this topic and the hours I spend on shipwreck stories.

GLOSSARY

BILGE: the curved part of a ship's hull that connects the keel to the sides

BOWSPRIT: a heavy spar projecting from the front of a ship forward to hold the base of triangular sails set from the foremast

CONCRETION: when corroding iron interacts with surrounding marine organisms and sediment, forming lump forms, encasing the iron

DEAD RECKONING: calculating a ship's current position—without the benefit of landmarks or star observations—through the course steered, the time taken, and the speed travelled

DEAL: a heavy, rough, squared log of lumber

EBB TIDE: the receding tide

FORESAIL: in a schooner, the sail set from the foremast; in a square-rig ship, the sail set from the foreyard (the spar mounted horizontally on the foremast)

FORESHEET: the rope that secures the sail on the foremast, the mast nearest the front

FLOOD TIDE: the rising tide

GUNWALES: the rails of a boat (pronounced "gunnels")

HAWSER: a thick rope used to tow a ship or secure it to a dock

HIGH WATER: the highest point the tide reaches

HIGH WATER SLACK: when the tide is at its highest, and the current stops moving in and has not yet started to flow back out

IN BALLAST: when a ship is not carrying any cargo, but requires ballast—that is, rocks, scrap iron, or whatever heavy objects can be stowed securely in the bottom of the hull—to give the ship stability

IRON KNEES: iron braces that secure the deck beams to the vertical timbers that frame the ship

JIB: a triangular sail from the front mast forward

JIB SHEET: a rope that secures the jib to the front mast or to the bowsprit

JURY-RIG: to improvise

KEEL: the bottom, centre beam on a ship; the "backbone" that strengthens the hull, reduces the ship's rolling motion, and helps maintain a forward direction

LEE SIDE: the side away from the wind

LOW WATER: the lowest level of the tide

LOW WATER SLACK: when the tide is at its lowest, and the current stops moving out and has not yet started to flow back in as the tide starts to rise again

MIZZEN-MAST: the mast nearest the stern on a vessel with three or more masts

NEAP TIDE: when the moon is farther away, and when the gravitational forces of the sun and moon are at right angles to the earth, the effect of the gravitational pull is weaker, and tidal rise and fall is less significant

PORT: the left side of the ship

SEINE: a net hung vertically that encircles fish; the bottom is gathered in with a rope to bring the fish to the surface to be harvested

SLACK TIDE: the period of time between the ebb and flow of the tide where the water is not moving, also known as slack water; a time of no tidal current

SOUNDING: a water depth measurement

SPRING TIDE: when the moon is closest to the earth, and the sun and moon and earth line up, the moon's gravitational pull is the strongest, and the tidal rise and fall is at its greatest

STARBOARD: the right side of the ship

TACK: setting the sails so that the ship can catch the wind at an angle (a sailing ship cannot make progress directly against the wind, but it can make progress at an angle, so sailors zigzag back and forth); when the wind is striking the left side of the ship it is a "port tack" and when it is striking the right side of the ship it is a "starboard tack"

WEAR SHIP: to turn the ship away from the wind, to follow a different tack.

WEIR: a heart-shaped enclosure made of a net and long poles driven into the sea floor, shaped to catch and hold fish that can then be removed using a seine

ENDNOTES

INTRODUCTION

1   N. T. Wright, *Evil and the Justice of God* (Downers Grove, IL: Inter Varsity Press, 2006), 14.

CHAPTER ONE

2   "Bay Of Fundy Tides: The Highest Tides In The World," *BayOfFundy.com*, accessed May 26, 2022, https://www.bayoffundy.com/about/highest-tides.

3   Walter B. McLaughlin Lighthouse Journals, March 16, 1899, Grand Manan Museum Collection.

CHAPTER TWO

4   Donna Marie Lee and Jean Marie Ivey, "Shipwreck of the 'Grand Design'" in *Facts and Fancy: Acadia, Mount Desert Island* (Facts and Fancy Universal Publishing Co., 1993).

5   Robert W. Tirrell, "The Wreck of the Martha and Eliza," The New England Historical and Genealogical Register 111, no. 1 (July 1957): 214–19.

6   Bill Caldwell, "The Survival of Sarah Porterfield: 1741" in *Rivers of Fortune: Where Maine Tides and Money Flowed* (Camden, ME: Down East Books, 1983), 71–76.

7   Caldwell, "Sarah Porterfield," 76–77.

8   Tirrell, "Martha and Eliza," 216.

9   Caldwell, "Sarah Porterfield," 75–76.

10   Caldwell, "Sarah Porterfield," 77–78.

11   Esther Clark Wright, *The Loyalists of New Brunswick* (Moncton: Moncton Publishing Company, 1972).

12   Howard Chapelle, memorandum to the Executive Committee of the New Brunswick Museum, September 22, 1964.

13   W. Stewart MacNutt, *New Brunswick: A History, 1784-1867* (Toronto: Macmillan, 1963), 146.

14   MacNutt, *New Brunswick*, 156.

15   *Eastport Sentinel*, February 5, 1820.

16   *Eastport Sentinel*, May 6, 1829.

17   *Saint Croix Courier*, January 3, 1935.

18   G. H. Russell, "Old Stuff," *Saint Croix Courier*, April 16, 1931.

19   *Yarmouth Herald*, November 1, 1833.

CHAPTER THREE

20   McLaughlin Lighthouse Journals, September 2, 1855.

21   McLaughlin Lighthouse Journals, September 4, 1855.

22   McLaughlin Lighthouse Journals, September 13, 1855.

23   McLaughlin Lighthouse Journals, May 13, 1863.

24 McLaughlin Lighthouse Journals, May 14, 1863.

25 McLaughlin Lighthouse Journals, May 15, 1863.

26 McLaughlin Lighthouse Journals, May 16, 1863.

27 Joshua N. Barnes, *Lights and Shadows of Eighty Years: An Autobiography* (Edwin N. C. Barnes & Co., 1911), 54–55.

28 McLaughlin Lighthouse Journals, May 17, 1863.

29 *New Brunswick Courier*, May 23, 1863.

30 *Lloyds List*, June 22, 1863.

31 *Lloyds List*, June 22, 1863.

CHAPTER FOUR

32 *Yarmouth Herald*, June 17, 1850.

33 *Yarmouth Herald*, June 27, 1850.

34 *Yarmouth Herald*, July 18, 1850.

35 J. Murray Lawson, "Yarmouth Reminiscences," *Yarmouth Herald*, 1902, 228.

36 *Yarmouth Herald*, March 29, 1860.

37 *Yarmouth Herald*, April 19, 1860.

38 *Yarmouth Herald*, August 2, 1860.

39 Lloyd Cheney to Keith Ingersoll, February 2, 1955, Grand Manan Museum collection.

40 *Saint John Globe*, January 12, 1897.

41 *Saint John Globe*, January 4, 1897.

42 *Shipping Gazette Weekly Summary*, January 15, 1897.

43 *Saint John Globe*, January 12, 1897.

44 *Saint Croix Courier*, April 15, 1897.

45 McLaughlin Lighthouse Journals, January 18, 1897.

46 *Saint John Daily Telegraph*, October 29, 1909.

47 *Saint John Daily Telegraph*, November 12, 1909.

48 *Digby Weekly Courier*, November 19, 1909.

49 *Saint Croix Courier*, December 2, 1909

50 *Saint Croix Courier*, December 17, 1891.

CHAPTER FIVE

51 *Shipping Gazette Weekly Summary*, November 13, 1891.

52 "Grand Menan [*sic*] news," *Eastport Sentinel*, March 27, 1872.

CHAPTER SIX

53 *Saint Croix Courier*, Sep 7, 1893, reprinted from the *Saint John Sun*.

54 Herbert A. McCabe to the *Saint Croix Courier*, February 22, 1936.

55 J. Murray Lawson, "Yarmouth Reminiscences," *Yarmouth Herald*, 1902, 196.

56 J. Murray Lawson, "Yarmouth Reminiscences," *Yarmouth Herald*, 1902, 194.

57 *Saint John Daily Telegraph*, April 25, 1901.

58 *Saint John Daily Telegraph*, October 31, 1901.

59 "Schooner Ground to Pieces on the Rocks near Saint John," *Daily Telegraph*, November 23, 1900.

60 Ibid.

61 *Telegraph-Journal*, August 17, 1999.

62 *Saint Croix Courier*, circa March 1930.

63 *The Daily News*, February 27, 1873.

64 *Yarmouth Herald*, March 6, 1873.

65 *Yarmouth Herald*, April 24, 1873.

66 *Lloyds List*, April 5, 1873.

67 *Lloyds List*, May 29, 1873.

68 *Lloyds List*, June 5, 1873.

69 *Saint Croix Courier*, August 3, 1916, 1.

CHAPTER EIGHT

70 McLaughlin Lighthouse Journals, August 6, 1885.

CHAPTER NINE

71 *Saint John Globe*, August 5, 1918, 1.

72 *Telegraph Journal*, December 8, 1941.

73 *Saint Croix Courier*, December 18, 1941.

74 *Lloyd's List*, October 9, 1869.

CHAPTER TEN

75 Sessional Papers of the Dominion of Canada, No. 11, A.1870, 270.

76 McLaughlin Lighthouse Journals, October 4, 1869.

77 *North Sydney Herald*, August 27, 1873.

78 *Halifax Morning Chronicle*, August 30, 1873.

79 *Halifax Morning Chronicle*, September 1, 1873.